THIS AUTOGRAPHED COPY OF

DOUG WILSON'S

REMARKABLE NEW BOOK

ABOUT AMHERST COLLEGE

IS BEING SENT TO YOU

COMPLIMENTS OF

FRED AND BLAIR SADLER,

CLASS OF '62.

PASSAGES OF TIME

PASSAGES OF TIME

Narratives in the History of Amherst College

∼

EDITED AND WITH SEVERAL SELECTIONS

BY

DOUGLAS C. WILSON

AMHERST COLLEGE PRESS

ISBN 10: 0-943184-11-8
ISBN 13: 978- 0-943184-11-1

Designed by Sally Nichols
Set in Granjon
Printed and bound by Thomson-Shore, Inc.

"Hopeful Piety," an excerpt from "Piety and Play in Amherst's History"
by Theodore P. Greene, originally published in
Five Colleges: Five Histories, © 1992, edited by Ronald Story,
reprinted with permission of Five Colleges, Inc.,
and Historic Deerfield, Inc.

"Magnetic Visitors," excerpts from "The Annals of the Evergreens"
by Susan Huntington Dickinson, reprinted
with permission of the Houghton Library, Harvard University,
call number bMS Am 1118.95 (9).

"The Mischief of Robert Frost," excerpts from *Robert Frost:
A Literary Life Reconsidered*, © 1984 by William H. Pritchard,
reprinted with permission of the author and
University of Massachusetts Press.

"Truly A Great American," from "In Tribute: Charles Hamilton Houston"
by Judge Robert L. Carter, *Harvard Law Review*, 1998,
reprinted with permission of the publisher.

"At Work as a Teacher" by Walker Gibson,
from *Traditions of Inquiry,* © 1985, edited by John Brereton,
reprinted with permission of Oxford University Press.

"Reflections of a Black Son" by Horace Porter,
published © 1977 in *Change* magazine, reprinted in *Amherst* magazine
(Fall 1977) and here with permission of Heldref Publications.

"An Englishman at Amherst" by Julian Symons,
published in *The Times* of London, © Times Newspapers Ltd. 1977,
reprinted in *Amherst* magazine (Summer 1977).

"The World According to Darp" © 1985 by Eugene Carlson,
published in the *Wall Street Journal*, reprinted
with permission of Dow Jones & Company.

To Sherry

CONTENTS

INTRODUCTION

xi

HOPEFUL PIETY

By Theodore P. Greene '43

With prayer, revivals and missionary zeal, the earliest students and
faculty set out to save their own souls and the world at large.

3

WOOD FIRES AND MUD

By Edward "Doc" Hitchcock 1849

Selections from Hitchcock's memoirs describing the rustic campus in the early days.

11

ANTISLAVERY ACTIVITY

With a Link to the *Amistad* Story

An account of early antislavery attitudes at Amherst and a student
who tutored African captives of the slave ship *Amistad*. (DCW)

23

MAGNETIC VISITORS

By Susan H. Dickinson

Excerpts from reminiscences by Emily Dickinson's sister-in-law, telling
of golden days in the nineteenth century when Emerson, Beecher, Stowe,
and other illustrious visitors came to Amherst.

31

LOOKING AT EMILY DICKINSON

By Daria D'Arienzo

Two unexpected treasures given to the College Library
let us "see" the reclusive poet here and now.

45

BRAVE AMONG THE BRAVEST
By Polly Longsworth
Town and gown suffer casualties in the Civil War.

51

YANKEE SAMURAI
By John Whitney Hall '39
A distinguished historian tells the story of Joseph Neesima 1870, the
Japanese Amherst graduate who founded Doshisha University.

65

THE COEDUCATION DEBATE OF 1871
By Christopher Bohjalian '82
In the nineteenth century the college gave serious, if brief,
consideration to admitting women.

79

THE OLMSTEDS AT AMHERST
For half a century, college officials sought the advice of two renowned landscape
architects—first Frederick Law Olmsted and then his son. (DCW)

89

THE STORY IN THE MEIKLEJOHN FILES
Inside story of the controversy surrounding Amherst's
famous president, Alexander Meiklejohn. (DCW)

I. Early Trouble

101

II. Final Showdown

116

COOLIDGE RECONSIDERED
The reputation of President Calvin Coolidge 1895 is on the upswing. (DCW)

137

THE MISCHIEF OF ROBERT FROST
By William H. Pritchard '53
The Amherst literary biographer examines Frost's
unconventional teaching career at the college.

143

TRULY A GREAT AMERICAN
By Robert L. Carter
An appraisal of Charles Hamilton Houston '15, the black alumnus who is arguably the greatest of all Amherst graduates. Written by a U.S. District Court judge.

155

A GOOD DAY FOR STUFFY McINNIS
By John S. Lancaster '51
The story of the 1948 baseball season, when the Amherst team was memorably coached by John "Stuffy" McInnis of the Philadelphia A's.

163

UNFRATERNAL CONDUCT
In 1948 the "Phi Psi Affair" involving the first black fraternity pledge was an important moment not only at Amherst but nationwide. (DCW)

173

AT WORK AS A TEACHER
By Walker Gibson
An appreciation of Prof. Theodore Baird and his famous composition course, English 1.

187

REACQUAINTED WITH THE NIGHT
An evening with Robert Frost and other distinguished faculty in 1959 was more complex than a student observer realized. (DCW)

197

THE LONG AND HAPPY REIGN OF MAUDE MINER
A short profile of the imperturbable woman who was at the center of things as the college's switchboard operator for 33 years. (DCW)

203

WITH RESPECT TO JOHN MOORE
By Richard F. Teichgraeber III '71
An alumnus remembers the close attention that a beloved Amherst teacher gave to the work of his students.

207

REFLECTIONS OF A BLACK SON
By Horace Porter '72
A young man's account of adjustments he faced leaving home in Georgia and entering college.

213

THE CIVIL DISOBEDIENCE OF JOHN WILLIAM WARD
An Interview with the President
After his arrest at Westover Air Force Base for joining a demonstration against the war
in Vietnam, Ward discussed his action with a student editor, Peter E. Scheer '73.

225

AN ENGLISHMAN AT AMHERST
By Julian Symons
A memoir by the English author who spent 1975–76 at
Amherst as Visiting Writer in the English Department.

233

A NEW COURSE SURVIVES AMID DIFFICULTIES
By Hugh Hawkins
An inside view of how deliberations unfold in faculty meetings
and committees to shape part of the college curriculum.

243

THE WORLD ACCORDING TO DARP
By Eugene Carlson
When a *Wall Street Journal* reporter was assigned to write about the
Amherst-Williams football centennial, he found that Amherst's coach was
the best part of the story.

259

A HISTORY OF AMHERST WOMEN
By Terry Y. Allen
A telescopic history of women at the college—one that begins
almost before the founding and develops nearly to the present.

267

SABRINA DOESN'T LIVE HERE ANYMORE
By Eve Kosofsky Sedgwick
To a feminist scholar on the faculty, abuses suffered by Amherst's
Sabrina statue held a message for undergraduate women.

279

JOHN BELL AND HIS FRIENDS AT AMHERST
Observations made at a relaxed summer conference on quantum mechanics
where famous physicists shared ideas with Amherst faculty. (DCW)

293

INTRODUCTION

A privilege I enjoyed for many years as editor of *Amherst* magazine was the chance to write and publish articles about the college's history. I have thought for a long time that an anthology bringing a selection of those and other articles together, in roughly chronological order, could answer at least part of the need for a new, updated history of the college.

For more than 50 years there has not been a new single work covering a wide variety of topics from the college's past. An anthology, fragmentary in its nature, cannot meet all of that need. And, of course, a book of choices made by one editor is not only fragmentary but highly subjective. An editorial bias can be a strength—giving the collection perhaps more cohesion, a more uniform voice, than it might otherwise have. But the personal touch has liabilities, too. As a journalist more than a scholar I may be guilty, for example, of favoring the "news stories" of history (Amherst in the Civil War; the Westover protest; the *Amistad*, Meiklejohn, and Phi Psi affairs) over more analytical accounts of past trends in student admissions, say, or the development of the faculty tenure system.

Other topics are conspicuous in their absence. The reader will quickly find what is missing: administrators and presidents (with the exceptions of Alexander Meiklejohn and John William Ward), prominent subjects and college figures—the playwright Clyde Fitch (1886), Admission Dean Eugene S. Wilson (1929), President Kennedy's 1963 visit, Professors

Charles Garman (1872) and Laurence Packard, Charles and Vincent Morgan, and other favorites. The list would be long.

I wish more women were represented. Amherst has been coeducational for 32 years—at this point, less than a sixth of the college's lifetime. I have tried to offset this gender imbalance with an extra effort to include essays by and about women, and on coeducation.

At best, then, the writings here are passages—excerpts from a larger story that remains to be told. Amherst still needs a true institutional history written by a professional historian. Such a book is long overdue. Yet, in spite of its gaps, this book portrays Amherst and Amherst people from the college's earliest days to the recent past. It describes both the unsightly college grounds of the Hitchcock era and, more than a century later, the pastoral setting Julian Symons called "a lotusland [that] nobody but an incorrigible city-dweller like myself would ever want to leave." It takes the reader from the very first days, when students had to know "Vulgar Arithmetic," to a 1990 faculty conference on quantum mechanics.

There are pieces about Amherst's dealings with the landscape architect Frederick Law Olmsted, baseball glories, faculty deliberations, a black student's sensitive view of his college experience in the 1970s. Included, too, are portraits of prominent teachers and alumni: Robert Frost, Theodore Baird, Joseph Hardy Neesima (1870), Calvin Coolidge (1895), Charles Hamilton Houston (1915). And there are several references of course to Emily Dickinson, who seems to hover forever near the center of almost any story about the town and the college.

Colleagues and friends provided me with many degrees of help in preparing this volume. Just as the Amherst faculty at commencement awards diplomas to seniors ranked in simple alphabetical order, I follow that practice here, finding it sometimes difficult to make clear distinctions between one level of contribution and another. In this case, however, happy coincidence lets me recognize Patricia M. Allen of the college's Public Affairs Office both at the top of the alphabetical list and in the forefront of those who helped with this project. In preparing a hydra-headed manuscript she's been preternaturally able, unflinching and calm.

Thanks also to Terry Y. Allen, Chris Bogan, Daria D'Arienzo, Katherine Duke, Carol Frenier, Frederick Greene, Allen Guttmann, Hugh Hawkins, Kannan Jagannathan, Chris Jerome, Barbara and Peter Joy, Michael Kiefer,

Anthony Marx, Sam Masinter, Sally Nichols, Susan Pikor, William H. Pritchard, Holly Saltrelli, Stacey Schmeidel, Susan Snively, Norman Spencer, Helen von Schmidt, David Wills, and Maryann Wood. Acceptance and support of the project by President Marx and his administration have been indispensable. I am grateful to them for letting me prepare this collection.

Four people especially—Lecturer von Schmidt, Professors Jagannathan and Wills, and Stacey Schmeidel of Amherst College Press—took generous time from crowded schedules to read the manuscript and offer suggestions and corrections. Improvements were made by them, by Chris Jerome, the most sympathetic and discerning of copy editors, and by several others, while the chief merit of the collection must be credited, of course, to the authors themselves. The shortcomings that remain are the fault of the author who is the editor.

For friendly, unfailing help over many years, I am indebted to those working at the Archives & Special Collections, and in the Reference department, at the college's Robert Frost Library. They respond to never-ending requests with good humor and the utmost professionalism. Further acknowledgments go to the Houghton Library at Harvard University, the Sterling Library at Yale University, the Library of Congress, and the Olmsted National Historic Site in Brookline, Massachusetts.

I have held one name aside for heartfelt personal mention—Cheryl B. (Sherry) Wilson, to whom I dedicate this work. As always, she has been the most patient and astute editor and critic I know.

Let me also acknowledge a particular debt to my Amherst thesis advisor of long ago, the late Professor Theodore Greene (1943). A rigorous scholar, he knew that history is a "nonconductor" unless it is made appealing, and that one of the best ways to make it so is through narrative storytelling. Above everything else, Ted Greene was a consummate storyteller who especially loved writing and speaking about yesterday's Amherst. I hope that this anthology, had he lived to see it, would have won his approval.

Douglas C. Wilson '62
Amherst, Massachusetts
October 2007

PASSAGES OF TIME

It is especially fitting that the first selection for this volume is written by Theodore P. Greene. Through nearly 40 years of service to Amherst as professor of history and American Studies, Ted Greene was a conscientious teacher, scholar, and faculty leader. Perhaps the work he enjoyed most was writing and lecturing about the history of Amherst, both college and town. He enlightened and delighted students and colleagues with many lectures and essays on the college's past. For Greene it was family history, too: he was a 1943 Amherst graduate and a third-generation alumnus whose father was in the Class of 1913 and grandfathers were both in the Class of 1882. Historian of town as well as gown, Greene was called upon over the years to speak at nearly every public commemoration. The narrative here is an excerpt from "Piety and Play in Amherst's History," which appears in *Five Colleges, Five Histories* (1992). It is included with the kind permission of Five Colleges, Inc., and Historic Deerfield. In it, we see Greene's ready eye not only for apt quotations and colorful detail, but also for history's relevance to our present day.

HOPEFUL PIETY

By Theodore P. Greene

On the third Wednesday of September in the year 1821, over 170 years ago, a small group of young men assembled for the first time on Moot Hill near the town center of Amherst. With them began the history of Amherst College. What had been at first an idea, then an outpouring of support from the surrounding communities, and then one empty building on a hill, became with their arrival that mysterious blending of ideas, aspirations, architecture, and human relationships which is a college.

The total number of students enrolling on that day was 47—31 of them freshmen, 3 seniors, and among the group 15 upperclass transfers from Williams College. These 15 had faithfully followed the former president of Williams, Zephaniah Swift Moore, down from those western hills when—in a desire to move somewhat closer to civilization—he decided to accept the presidency of this new institution.

If the first 47 Amherst men were, like Amherst's present students, a select group, the principles of selection were somewhat different. No one had tried to place any statistical measure upon their verbal and mathematical aptitudes. Academically, the requirements for admission as stated in the first catalog (a catalog, incidentally, consisting of a single sheet printed on one side like a handbill) were simple indeed. Candidates were expected to be able to read Virgil, Cicero's orations, Sallust, and the Greek

Testament as well as to display a knowledge of Latin and Greek grammar and of something described as "Vulgar Arithmetic."

In the minds of the founders of the college, of the new president, and of all *three* faculty members, however, these academic requirements were of secondary importance. The whole enterprise had begun some three years earlier not with raising an endowment fund for a learned faculty nor a capital fund for buildings, but by soliciting pledges for a charity fund which could pay all the expenses of tuition and rooming for, as the Constitution of the Charity Fund put it, "the Classical Education of indigent young men of piety and talents, for the Christian Ministry." Despite a very severe depression which struck in 1819, the farmers, crafts-men, ministers, and merchants of several Connecticut Valley towns contributed $50,000 to the Charity Fund and then scraped their barrels for $30,000 more in a subsequent appeal. Amherst began as a community enterprise supported by the gifts of more than 1,300 men, women, and children whose contributions ranged from 50 cents to $3,000. Though their resources were modest, their aspirations embraced the whole world. Again as the Constitution of the Charity Fund expressed it, these gifts were made "under the conviction that the education of pious young men of the finest talents in the community is the most sure method of relieving our brethren by civilizing and evangelizing the world."

What the community and the college authorities looked for among these first 47 students, therefore, was not so much their academic prepa-ration as what was called a state of "hopeful piety" and a serious interest in civilizing and evangelizing the world. Looking back some 40 years later at the careers of Amherst graduates, a subsequent president of the college found the statistics, as he put it, "certainly gratifying." Of Amherst graduates from those first four classes, nearly 60 percent had gone into the ministry. Of all graduates up to 1860, over 50 percent had become ministers. And during the same period, one out of every 20 Amherst graduates had gone out to mission fields throughout the world, to Africa, Greece, the Near East, India, China, and to the islands of the Pacific (where one was eaten by cannibals).

Obviously, by modern standards, such statistics imply a rank discrimi-nation on the basis of creed in the selection process. If this was so, it was what we now call de facto discrimination, since the charter of the college forbade any religious tests for students or faculty. From the beginning, there was no discrimination on racial grounds. In 1822, the second year of the college's existence, Edward Jones, a black student from Charleston, South Carolina, entered Amherst on a career that would take him as an Episcopal missionary to Liberia and eventually to become the principal of the Fourah Bay Christian Institution in Sierra Leone.

One other possible discrimination stemming from the charity fund's initial concern for "indigent young men of piety and talents" disturbed President Moore. Before accepting the offer of his new post from the trustees, he wrote them desiring to be "assured that you will make the provision for the admission of those who are *not* indigent, and who may wish to obtain a classical education in the Institution." This request caused the trustees to issue a public announcement that—providing they met the academic requirements customary at all New England colleges— Amherst would also accept for admission those who could actually afford to pay the full expenses for tuition and room rent, a sum amounting in total to $10 each term. The college would not discriminate against the wealthy.

In 1821, of course, it never occurred to anyone that limiting enrollment to young *men* (rich *or* poor) with no provision for young *women* was in any way discriminatory. That exclusion seemed simply a natural part of the order of things as God had created them. Only at the fiftieth anniversary of the college in 1871 did a movement first arise for the admission of women to Amherst. On that occasion this innovative step was urged by a number of alumni, including the very prominent Reverend Henry Ward Beecher—whose sister Harriet had been credited by Abraham Lincoln with starting the Civil War through the publication of her novel *Uncle Tom's Cabin*. At this 50th-anniversary celebration it was announced that one of the trustees, Governor Bullock, had donated funds to endow a scholarship on condition that it should be awarded to a young woman who proved her equal fitness on the entrance examinations. The proposal, however, aroused immediate fears and objections. Professor Seelye, the professor of English literature, expressed the apprehensions of many about coeducation when he explained: "Any one who has any true conceptions of the early struggles, and temptations of life, must feel great solicitude for young people, when the restraints of expediency are weak and the appetites most inflammable." Four years later, Professor Seelye himself found what seemed to him the ideal solution when he became the first president of Smith College—safely located seven miles away. One of Amherst's trustees had strongly urged Seelye to accept this post, writing him: "If you should take the presidency of this institution, you would, I think, be an important agent settling the present dispute with regard to female education and would be a means of *preventing* well-established colleges from introducing women into their existing course of study and *would thus save the community from a great amount of evil.*" After 1871, in any case, the subject did not arise seriously at Amherst for another 100 years. [A detailed account of the college's first coeducation discussion is given in "The Coeducation Debate of 1871," on page 79.]

Let us turn back again to the situation of those 47 mostly pious, frequently indigent young males who assembled on that hilltop in 1821. What kind of men were these first Amherst students, what kind of place did they come to, what kind of life did they lead? We have the firsthand recollections of one member of that initial group, Charles W. Shepard, who later wrote: "I remember that I was the youngest of my class. Most of my fellows were mature youths who did not appear to me youths at all, seniors in character and manlike in purpose, with an air which seemed to tell of years of yearning for the ministry, and of a brave struggle with the poverty which had kept them from this goal. They seized their late opportunity with eagerness, they were in general patient, painstaking and earnest students." (This is the kind of comment one makes on a recommendation when the student has not done very well.)

He goes on to describe the scene. Amherst then, he suggests, might well be described as "a village in the woods. Something more than a score of houses, widely separated from each other by prosperous farms, constituted Amherst center. Along two roads running north and south, were scattered small farmhouses with here and there a cross-road, blacksmith's shop or schoolhouse by way of a suburb.

"But," he continues, "the fine dwellings, public or private, of that early time had their features, whether tasteful or the reverse, greatly concealed by the wide prevalence of trees. Primal forests touched the rear of the College building; they filled up with a sea of waving branches, the great interval between the village and Hadley; towards the south, they prevailed gloriously, sending their green waves around the base and up the sides of Mt. Holyoke; to the east, they overspread the Pelham slope, and they fairly inundated vast tracts northward clear away to the lofty hills of Sunderland and Deerfield."

On Moot Hill, overlooking the village and the forests, rose the one college building (now known as South College). During the summer of 1820, this edifice had been reared in a mere 90 days of Herculean labor. It had been a true community enterprise. Men had left their farms and their shops in nearby towns to assemble on this site with contributions of bricks, granite, beams, mortar, and labor. Some slept here on the hill beside large bonfires in order to start work again with the first rays of dawn. Amherst housewives rallied to cook meals for the workers. Noah Webster and the town ministers came to lay the cornerstone, to offer prayers, speeches, and sermons. In the most eloquent of these, entitled "A Plea for a Miserable World," the Reverend David Clark proclaimed his belief that "this Institution . . . will yet become a fountain pouring forth its stream to fertilize the boundless wastes of a miserable world." He assured his audience that "any man who shall bring a beam or a rock, who shall lay a stone or drive a nail . . . shall not fail of his reward."

As a symbol of the community's dedication and zeal, the new building left nothing to be desired. As the sole facility for a college of some 50 members, however, it was a tight squeeze. By night the students studied or slept in its rooms. By day some of those rooms became classrooms or primitive laboratories. One six-foot-wide bookcase contained the college library.

Plain living and high thinking were clearly the Amherst style in those early decades. Students rose at 4:45 a.m. for morning prayers and two recitations before breakfast. The darkness of winter forced them to postpone the hour until 5:45—but the added burdens of splitting and carrying wood for the fires in their rooms as well as breaking the ice on the college well before washing their faces prevented any undue sense of luxury from the later hour.

Nor did the curriculum afford any luxury of intellectual choice— either to students or faculty. Every course was required of every student— and in a sense almost for every faculty member. The president, for example, taught every course in senior year plus a good share of the sophomore courses. Not only the courses but even the particular book for a course was rigidly set. The catalog did not list courses. It simply specified those books which would be read each year. Classes consisted for the most part of recitations upon the assigned portions of the standard texts. Everyone knew what a classical education meant. Everyone at Amherst knew what the saving truth was. The purpose of education was to discipline the faculties of the mind, to inculcate the great truth already revealed, and, if possible, to awaken in the student a sense of Christian grace and of Christian vocation.

The latter aims, of course, though ever present, were pursued most regularly on Sunday. Students were discouraged from doing any assigned study on the Sabbath. They were, however, expected to attend two services in the college church, where the president, occasionally assisted by the professors, did the bulk of the preaching. At intervals the college would be swept by a revival—the first occurring in 1823. Again one of those original students, Justin Marsh, has left an account of this revival:

"They held early morning prayer-meetings," he recounts, "and would sometimes even in study hours, go into each others' rooms and spend a few moments in prayer, often for an unconverted roommate. At no time in the day perhaps could a person go into an entry and pass up to the fourth story without hearing the voice of prayer from some room. Prayer meetings were held at nine o'clock in the evening in each entry, also at other times and in other places. The work of God's grace seemed to go right through the college. . . . The results have appeared in churches and the missionary fields, foreign and domestic, ever since."

From our present viewpoint, of course, the noble aspirations of the founders of Amherst College shrink to very provincial and parochial proportions. They aimed to civilize and evangelize a miserable world by extending to that world the particular notions of civilization and of orthodox Congregationalism then current in these towns of the Connecticut River Valley. They presumed that they could and should convert all the other races and religions of the world to New England Congregationalism. The Reverend Clark's cornerstone-laying sermon had gone on to predict that because of the influence of Amherst graduates, "The heathen will be tamed to civility, and will burn their temple idols, Ethiopia will stretch out her hands unto God, the posterity of Abraham will own their intelligence to their Savior, and be again engrafted into their own olive tree, the Turk and the Arab will exchange the mosque and the Koran for the sanctuary and the Bible, the Tartar will pitch permanently his tent about the house of the missionary."

Closer to home a good part of the founders' zeal, in fact, stemmed from the partisan desire to combat those Unitarian heresies which Harvard College had begun to foster. Noah Webster wrote: "We do hope that this infant institution will grow up to . . . check the progress of errors which are propagated from Cambridge."

What, then, do those partisan, pious, provincial predecessors have to do with us? From our present historical perspective, from our sense of the relativity in all notions of saving truth, can we not simply dismiss these Amherst ancestors as quaint irrelevancies? I do not think so.

Do we still have anything to match the sense of *community* which in 1821 raised the funds, erected the building, and defined the purposes for this infant college? Do we have anything like the sense of *vocation* which brought those first 47 students to this hilltop and sent them forth throughout the world? Do we have anything to compare with the sense of *salvation* which broke forth here in periodic revivals, which led to concern for the sake of one's roommate, which persuaded the founders to take as the college motto that grand and presumptuous phrase *Terras Irradient*— "That they may illumine the earth"?

Today's alumni know it as "The Fairest College," but in its early years Amherst was a primitive, backwoods campus, something of an eyesore. Here the college of the 1840s is described in reminiscences that Edward "Doc" Hitchcock—a venerated professor of hygiene and physical education—wrote in 1902. Hitchcock was an 1849 graduate of the college and son of the Edward Hitchcock who was Amherst's president from 1845 to 1854. "Doc's" memoirs, handwritten in separate notebooks, are a hodgepodge covering many topics, including social events, student pranks, and campus hygiene. To produce a more orderly narrative, originally for the Fall 1991 issue of *Amherst* magazine, we reorganized some textual sequences. But every word and sentence is Hitchcock's. The notebooks are preserved in the College Archives. For readers seeking more information about President Hitchcock, the author's eccentric and illustrious father, we recommend *Curious Footprints: Professor Hitchcock's Dinosaur Tracks and Other Natural History Treasures at Amherst College* (Amherst 2006), by Nancy Pick and Frank Ward.

WOOD FIRES AND MUD

By Edward "Doc" Hitchcock

THE CARRIAGE ENTRANCE to the grounds in these days and up to the '60s was by the road going east from the front of the President's House about as it does now, only there was a lumbering gate for team traffic and posts for the foot path. Looking at it from the present standpoint, I cannot now see of what early use a gate was there, except the traditional custom of fencing your property and locking the gate. For there was nothing which could tempt stray cattle to get away from boys who were driving them to pasture. . . . The road into the grounds ran east and west very near Williston Hall [not built until 1857] and then curved to the south sharply to reach chapel and the dormitories, for then there was no building east [of them] which needed a road.

The present knoll where now stands Woods Cabinet [part of the Octagon, built in 1847] . . . after 1828, when the First Church became the present College Hall, was just an unsightly place, there being the relics of the holes from which the stones were taken from the foundation of the old church to put in to the creation of the new one, College Hall. Not only these ruins of the old church were there, but the whole hill [where the Octagon now stands] was common property for anybody to come there and cart away the gravel for highways, filling, or for any purpose where gravel was wanted. It was prodigiously unsightly, since it was not only a series of holes, but there wasn't a shade of a tree on high, or of scarcely any vegetation.

Oh the walks . . . the walks! In 1840 there was no prepared walk in front of buildings, or even to the President's House, merely the gravel was occasionally turnpiked a little. And from the President's down to the post office, mud, mud, mud, was all there was to it. . . .

The next walks built were from North College a little ways towards College Hall, and these so rough and poor that the students finally tore them up. One of the early works of my father's administration was the securing and laying of the stone walks in front of dormitories and chapel. They are there today, those shining smooth slabs of Berlin talcose slate. These walks, with blinds on the dormitories, were about as valuable improvements as anything which my father did. And yet the whirligig of time! Now the blinds are made into kindling wood.

The buildings in the '40s were shabby. Even in carpenters' repairs there was sad neglect, and as for paper on the walls, it was very rarely seen, and generally if a dormitory room was painted it was done by the student himself. Each dormitory residence consisted of the main room about 15 x 20 feet, and on the dark side two so-called bedrooms about 8 x 10 feet, and a wood closet 4 x 10. In the upper part of each bedroom door there were two openings near the top, about 8 x 12 inches, for air and light. Why didn't the inmates suffocate? The entries were awfully bare and neglected, save that a pretty liberal supply of whitewash was administered inside all the buildings in summer vacation. The rooms of the buildings were simply the walls, a fireplace, and a lock and key to the door. . . . The windows were very loose [and] let in any amount of cold air, and the entry doors were left to swing all day and all night. How the students were comfortable, I cannot now understand. But remember, there was a long six-weeks vacation after Thanksgiving and everything about College was shut and locked up. Even College clock usually was run down.

There was some aid in the shape of furniture and bedding. College was in possession of a small quantity which was loaned without fee to poor students who might apply. This was done through the janitor, each recipient giving a receipt for what he borrowed to be returned when he was through.

Each student lighted his own room as he chose, but there were only whale oil and candles then, for such use.

Each student procured his own wood. Some Pelham wood dealer was around almost every day and with him the best of wood, hickory, could be bought all the way from $1.25 to $2 per cord. Each man had his pile near the rear of North and South College, and he could saw a little every day or get it all sawed and carried up at once. College owned one or two "hods" of a skeleton pattern, which were generously borrowed when the janitors were not using them for the public rooms.

There was a good deal of cheer around those open fires when there was a good bed of green hickory coals. However, before '50 the airtight stove was growing common. But why the college did not burn up, the Lord only knows. The fact is that Old North College did burn up, because a lounge was left too near the open fire in Dick Mathews's room, 28 Old North [in] 1857, and it is a marvel that it did not sweep the hill.

We had a "bath house." This was a wooden building, perhaps 20 feet long, 6 broad, and 8 to 10 feet high, with five or six compartments in it, say 2 to 3 feet wide, 5 or 6 feet deep, and 7 feet high. Overhead was a tank which could be supplied from the well by a trough reaching from the spout to the tank. When a man wanted to take a bath he had to go to the well and draw water of as many buckets full as he was able and willing to draw, empty it into the trough, then go and strip, and pull the string, and get a cold shower bath. This was an establishment previous to my day, but I remember it.

In this line came the privy and the urinal. The former were a series of brick stalls with a door, and a plank perforated with an oval opening, say 12 by 8 inches, [pitched] at a steep angle so that a subject must place himself on the orifice not by sitting but by a bracing of himself by his feet in a crouching posture. There was also a projecting plank made to reach the back of the occupant so that he could not mount the seat and defile it. Oh, the freezing of the defecating students for the first 40 years of Amherst College life.

The urinals were a disgrace. They were unsightly nondescript structures of whitewashed rough boards with no roof, perhaps 10 feet high with five or six compartments, and the waste allowed to gather below and be soaked up by the soil. There were two, one behind each dormitory, about 100 feet in the rear, and they usually got afire and burned up once or twice a year. And not the least nuisance about them was that when we were going around College with our lady friends we were generally asked what those buildings were for. . . .

While I was in College the chapel got a renovation. Till then, the desk was an old-fashioned pulpit with steps going up on either side, and a little platform slightly raised for speakers and on which the extemporized communion table was placed. And till that time the front of the gallery was of plain cheap paneling, and the supporting posts to the gallery were simply big logs of wood smoothed off with a little O.S. [?] on the top. Also on the floor there were pews with regular doors. . . . There were none in the gallery. Except on special occasions, no one sat in the gallery but the choir with the big double bass and the four monitors.

Chapel and recitation rooms were all warmed by box stoves, about 18 to 20 inches high and wide, and 36 inches long, with a very large door, and a huge wood box nearby. These were intense and rapid heaters. In the chapel there were two of these, each side the center door, with a long pipe going east over the present aisle, and making a turn and entering the chimneys just at the front end of the present sophomore and junior seats.

The wood used was dry chestnut, of which a big lot was gathered and piled away in the cellar at the west end of chapel. When the janitor was not otherwise occupied, he was down there sawing the four-foot sticks in two lengths.

The chapel was not heated in my day for prayers, but in later years I think the fires started before chapel time. For the recitation rooms, a hired student went half an hour before the time it was to be used and started the fires. In 20 minutes the room was hot, and by the close of the hour the fire was almost out. If it did get low, or the teacher made the hour long, we could put in more wood.

One thing I ought to mention here about the hardships of the early president's life of my father, and this was the care and furnishing of [the President's House]. . . . It was a great strain on my father's purse to furnish [it]. He had to get nearly complete furniture for the two parlors, his study, and two chambers, for that big house. And another kind of strain was that the house had not been painted or papered for 10 years, and College could not give him a dollar towards it. The consequence was that my mother, [my sister] Mary and the hired girl had an immense deal of backbreaking scrubbing to do in trying to make that yellowed white paint (for the whole house was white inside) look passably. And my back and knees can ache now, when I think how I put down and took up those big parlor carpets.

And the coldness of that house. For though we had 20 cords of wood, the halls were never warmed, there was no means of doing it, and the parlors had nothing but open fireplaces, which wouldn't both draw at the same time. So we practically never used the parlors in winter. In fact, we used the back one for storage of food and various other things. I had a fire in my room with an airtight stove, and part of the time the girls had one in their rooms. The dining room was the study. Mother's bedroom had to be supplied with wood, and the woodshed was down one story, so that bringing in the wood was no trifle. Pa, however, generally took care of his wood box, he doing it for physical exercise. The whole third story, when we lived in this house, was one great garret, with no light or ventilation save two windows in the west end. In the northeast corner there was a kind of board fence in which were a lot of Dr. Humphrey's effects [President Heman Humphrey was Hitchcock's immediate predecessor], among them lots of old papers and pamphlets. Those I plundered and got my first start in statistics and memorabilia. Oh! If only I could dig in among them now. . . .

As to the entertaining of relatives, friends of the family, and specially those interested in the church and College work, there was no end, and the amount of [it] now seems to me a marvel. It was continual, for nobody ever was allowed to go to the hotel. From a man from Deerfield with a load of grain, the men in the hay field, up to Mary Lyon and every stray minister, there was always a place at table and a bed for them. We children had to squeeze and be turned out of table and bed, but we always got round somehow.

At commencement and public occasions we were over full always. Sometimes some of us went and slept on cushions in the church, and half-made beds in the garret. We were uncomfortable but we expected it as a matter of education and above all, for our interest in College. My mother was never rattled, impatient, or fretful at any of these calls, or apologized because she hadn't anything better, but always had enough of something on the table and did not sit up nights to make delicacies, although I often had more running to do at times of company. Another way my mother helped to eke out a living, at and about commencement time, was to exchange salt pork with the women from Pelham for huckleberries as a dessert for the trustees and other guests.

But what a contrast now! Why, my mother entertained 10 times more then than my wife does now. It was nature to her and she had to do it for the good and life of College. Besides this, my mother took boarders, frequently two or three at a time, often a tutor or professor and not infrequently a student. H. W. [Henry Ward] Beecher, for instance.

Parties and entertainments were occasional. When my father was president he had what we now call receptions. One, a freshmen party at which a large part of the town, all the faculty and the freshmen were invited in the early Fall, and another the Senior Levee in July, when the seniors were invited with the same other people. . . .

The Society of Religious Inquiry was rather feeble in my time, but more owing to the small numbers in College than a decline in religious interest. It was really a missionary organization, and had a room filled with idols and bric a brac sent by missionaries. The room was, I think, No. 5 in Old North, the second story southwest corner, very nearly the same place as is now occupied by Professor Cowles's quarters. This was adjoining the room of the Natural History Society in Old North, northwest corner. . . .

Above [the chapel] was the Library occupying the whole west end. It was lined with shelves which had doors of wire netting so that the books could be seen but not touched. They were arranged in two stacks, with a gallery so that there was no climbing for the books. They were kept carefully locked up for fear of thefts, and yet, so far as I can remember, more books were stolen then than there are now. . . . One hour a week the library was open when we could go and draw books. [It] was not very well patronized, for in cold weather there was no fire. There was nothing like a table to consult books, or a reading room. . . .

As far as literary and historical training was concerned, the men must have dug it out themselves by thoroughly reading from the [Alexandrian and Athenian student literary societies'] Society libraries. As far as I remem-

ber, the Society libraries were open once each weekday, from one to two
o'clock, and were generally pretty well attended by the students. In Alpha
Delta Phi there was a tremendously strong pressure for high scholarship
and literary culture. . . . Up to 1840 or thereabouts, the room of Alpha
Delta Phi was 32 South, the southeast corner fourth story. Then they
moved to [North]. . . . They left South College because Psi Upsilon Society located themselves directly in front of them in the southwest corner
upper story.

Just about 1845, I suppose, the feeling between Alpha Delta Phi and Psi
Upsilon ran at its highest point. March and Henshaw [Francis Andrew
March '45 and Marshall Henshaw '45] were the exponents of this feeling,
both determined to get the valedictory, and the parties were intent on its
being so. These two men would only just recognize each other as they
met on the street. There were no demonstrations at all, but a tremendous
undercurrent running through College and downtown among the ladies,
particularly the girls of the faculty.

We had three Exhibitions in my day, and two of these came from way
back. Spring in April and May, Summer a little later, and then in the Fall
an Eclectic on Academia Exhibition. The appointments to these were
eagerly sought and labored for, and hearts broken to those who were not
successful. These were held in College Chapel, and the appointment in
them of usher and schedule distributor was a high honor. Mock schedules
here had their showing. They were most clandestinely and surreptitiously
got in, and were vile, profane or nasty, or all together.

Skating, sliding down hill, chestnutting and, for a few, hiring horses,
were all the chances for fun in my day. There was occasionally a fair of
some sort to raise money by, perhaps two a year, and a Fourth of July
celebration. . . . There were precious few lectures and shows or concerts.
Our class had the first of the commencement week concerts.

[Hitchcock's memoir includes several descriptions of early athletic
equipment, from which the following selections are taken.] . . . there was
a circular swing. This consisted of a very heavy oak timber 18 inches
in diameter and about 15 feet high, set 6 feet into the ground. On top
of this was an iron pivot [an] inch in diameter, upon which was placed,
with a bottom socket, a cap with four hooks at right angles to each other,
on which was hung four ropes reaching to the ground. Upon each of

these ropes a man could hang and then run around and swing as much
as possible. Sometimes three men working hard would carry around a
light fellow with no exertion on his part swinging 5 or 6 feet from the
ground. . . .

There was also a running track around the grove, just within the
shade of the trees, less than a quarter of a mile in length. Besides this, we
had a log of soft pine, say 10 inches in diameter, set up in the ground, and
at that we cast javelins, pine or ash poles 1½ inches in diameter with an
iron point. When the log wore out, we put in a new one. . . .

The social life of the college was mainly calls by the students on the faculty, and an occasional invitation to tea by faculty and rarely some citizen of the town. South Hadley was a terribly tabooed place, for, except
to [visit] our sisters, all that we could [do to] see the girls was to . . . send
our names in to Miss Lyon, and then, if she thought best, we could see
the girl, but it must be only in the parlor, and in the presence of a teacher
who must be a watch over us both in deed and word for a limited call.
Occasionally a "buss" load came over to go through the buildings, but only
under the strict watch of a teacher. . . .

Student deviltry and depravity were as great then as now. I have in
my pocket at this moment a paper apparently voluntarily drawn up and
signed by a large part of a class not far from '50, in which they deplore
the troubling of freshmen and pledge themselves as sophomores not to
disturb or maltreat freshmen. Yet there was a small party composed of
some of these very men, and one of them is now a shining light, who went
out on a tear one night and broke freshmen windows to the tune of more
than $50. At that time, all such breakages were charged upon every man
in College as "public damages."

Our class got together and by a bare majority voted, that while we
would not "tattle," volunteer information about class abuse, we would if
questioned by the faculty tell all we knew about such malfeasance. It
did check the business, but it made those of us who took the stand the
most unpopular men there ever were in College. We were called Faculty
Dogs, and had to watch when going in to the hall doors or we should get
a bucket of water on our heads.

College laws in our day expressly forbid eating and drinking in our rooms. And as there was no saloon or place in town where we could go and have a little something, occasionally there was something "sneaked in." For instance, at the annual initiations of Alpha Delta Phi we always had a little something to eat. But it was a military campaign to get the "fodder" in. Old Mrs. Ferry, who kept boarders, always helped us to the "provisions" and held her tongue. The way we got it in was in the late evening for two of us to load the basket and then get it up as far as the east side of Woods Cabinet, and then lie down in the grass with it till we got a signal that the way was clear and we could rush it across and get it into North College.

The Antivenenean Society was in full vigor from '40 to '50, a pledge against the use of liquor and tobacco. It was presented to the freshmen, and the college president was its president. The Freshies were invited to meet the president and secretary, and after the claims of the society were presented, the long roll was exhibited and a chance for each man to sign was given. It really was an undue pressure, for there was hardly a man who would dare decline or neglect to sign under the circumstances. Up to somewhere in the '60s, I think, a signature meant a pledge against liquor and tobacco. . . .

Only once in my course did I go to a convivial occasion where there was any liquor, and that was only malmsey wine. Jim Richards invited us up to his room in the northeast corner of "old" North to do it, and there I remember Dr. J. M. Manning and Jim Harris besides myself were present. We only drank a little wine and kept very still, for the partitions in that building were very thin and would tell tales.

As the "laws" were very strenuous against convivialism, of course there were provocations to break them. Stories are rife of roasting turkeys and chickens, and the large open fireplaces conduced to that end. I have reason to believe that it was often done, though I never participated.

There was only one fellow in my day who threw a stone at a flock of Moses Dickinson's turkeys which often wandered into College territory and killed one. Then he took an old cloak and threw it over his head, picked up the dead turkey, and brought him to his room and afterwards cooked him and had a feast.

Hazing was very much in the line of "ducking," watching when a man came into the lower door and throwing a pail of water on him. Also sometimes a bed was wet, and it was considered the thing not to notice it. But in '44 [?] one Torrance [possibly Dwight Jonathan Torrance '51, who died in 1848] got wet in his bed and he slept in it. This gave him a cold and he died as a result. This was rather the end of this style of hazing.

Another way was to squirt water in through the keyhole. Another was for a lot of smokers to go in and smoke the room full, and make the occupant sick. Sometimes a bomb was placed at the door and fired by a fuse. One historic prayer meeting was broken up in this way. A kind of disturbance was to put some gum asafetida on the recitation room stove, and so "stink out" a recitation. . . .

A good deal of my father's help to College came from the fact of his being one of the very early state geologists, and the discoverer of the science of ichnology. The securing of the state collection of rocks and minerals and the missionary collection gave much zest to his department, and prestige to the college in those early days. The gifts of Woods and Appleton Cabinets were very much due to his exertion and friendships directly and indirectly with the men who gave them. His class instructions were fertile not by the hard work which he made students do, but by the many illustrations and specimens which he could show, and the fact that he had discovered many of these things himself.

His discoveries of the [dinosaur] tracks set him up well outside of College with scientific men. His books and lectures on the religion of geology established a wide reputation for him on both the continents. But he did not like the discipline of college students, nor the discussions and scrimmages with his faculty when he was president. Faculty meetings shortened his life, and would have killed him had he not got out of the presidential chair.

One peculiarity of my father ought to be remembered by his College friends, for to much of his success that feature was a leading power. He inherited a despondent, humiliating temperament from his mother. They depreciated their abilities and power and worthiness to a very great and wrong degree. . . . He was timid and self-distrustful, and then was not sure that the Lord was on his side. He would often say, I don't think we shall succeed, or, it is hardly worthwhile to try. And yet he would go to work exactly as if he knew he would succeed. He was timid but hopeful.

There is an incident. When a boy 8 or 10 years old, I went with him in the old green wagon to Springfield. He attended to the business, and was just starting on the sidewalk of Main Street when he slipped and struck the back of his head on the sidewalk. He supposed very naturally that he was seriously hurt. We started along, and he remarked that he didn't think he should survive the accident for he had probably broken his skull. So we rode mournfully along up to Chicopee when we reached a quarry where he had once found some footprints. It was up a lane perhaps 25 rods from the main street.

He stopped the horse and said to me, "You may sit here while I just run up and look for those tracks I once saw here." I waited I should think 20 minutes when I followed him up and found him getting out some specimens. I remember it was long after dark when we got home, but I never heard another word about the broken head. . . .

In begging for money—and he did a lot of it—he generally told the approachee that he didn't really suppose he would help him, but the need was great, and he need not fear to refuse the request. During his administration my father saw gathered in the college money and educational appliances to the amount of $100,000, and in those times it was a big sum. He got it because everybody saw he was honest, self-sacrificing, and zealous in a very modest and diffident way.

The college's president and faculty in the early 1830s were alarmed when Amherst students formed an Antislavery Society. President Heman Humphrey said such an organization did not exist at any other "respectable" college. Despite protests, the group was disbanded. But one member, William Raymond, continued to act on his beliefs, which led to a scandal. He was expelled for a year, transferred to Oberlin College, and soon was chosen to teach a famous group of Africans who had come ashore in America and remained for two years in Connecticut after they mutinied aboard the slave ship *Amistad*. Raymond joined them as a missionary when they returned to their homeland in Sierra Leone. (Ironically, a man who settled there a short time earlier was Edward Jones from the Amherst Class of 1826. Jones was one of the first African-Americans to graduate from an American college. The open racism of the day had not been so virulent as to bar him from enrolling at Amherst.) This account is based largely on Raymond's letters in the American Missionary Association Archives, 1839–1882: Sierra Leone Correspondence, at the Amistad Research Center, Tulane University.

ANTISLAVERY ACTIVITY
With a Link to the *Amistad* Story

$\frown$

Millions of Americans came to know the story of the slave ship *Amistad* thanks to the dramatic movie about it produced by Steven Spielberg. But Spielberg's account did not include a story-within-the-story: the strange account of William Raymond and Amherst College. It's a tale of prejudice, indiscretion, and redemption.

Raymond was born on a farm in Ashburnham, 45 miles from Amherst. As a youth he worked for a while as a mechanic but then moved to Cambridge, where he waited on tables at a boardinghouse. He hoped to further his studies and eventually go into the ministry. He later recalled in a letter that in the evening after waiting on tables he "would crawl away into the garret lit by a skylight & there pore over my Latin Grammar." Before entering Amherst in 1833, Raymond attended school in Woburn, north of Cambridge. He lived in poverty. "My feet were covered with the remains of what was once a pair of boots," he wrote. "As for socks, I had none."

The Amherst that Raymond entered in 1833 was embroiled in controversy. Students the year before had formed a new organization, the Amherst Antislavery Society. Soon after the newcomer arrived there were 77 members—a third of all the students. Raymond was among those who joined. The society elected as its president an Amherst senior,

Samuel Tappan, nephew of Lewis Tappan, the prominent New York abolitionist. The group's constitution pledged members "to effect the abolition of slavery in the United States; to improve the character and condition of the free people of colour . . . and obtain for them equal civil and political rights, and privileges with whites."

Those were early days of the antislavery movement, and abolitionists almost everywhere were seen as troublemakers or worse. Amherst's president Heman Humphrey was alarmed to have this new radical element on campus and told the group, "We are not aware that any such society as yours exists in any respectable College but our own, in the land." He took prompt action against the organization, informing its members that—although he and the faculty did not wish "to interfere in the slightest degree with your private opinions on the subject of slavery, nor with your avowal of them as individuals"—the college had "to guard against those evils internal and external, which we are fully persuaded would result from frequent meetings, earnest discussions, and newspaper notoriety." (Little could Humphrey know at the time that one of his near-relatives would become the most notorious abolitionist of his era. The relative was then an obscure tanner living in Pennsylvania named John Brown.) At first the college tried to restrict the group's activities, saying it should meet no more than once a month and then "chiefly for prayer," and that it could not sponsor discussions or speaking programs, could not actively recruit new members, and could not seek newspaper publicity. In February 1835 the society refused to accept these conditions, and it was forced to disband. In a "Memorial" to Humphrey the young abolitionists wrote: "Many of us are expecting to be Missionaries, and our hearts throb with emotions of the deepest sorrow, at the thought of relinquishing our exertions as a Fraternity for the bleeding and degraded African."

Raymond decided to continue some of these exertions on his own. Amherst's population at the time included about 50 blacks who were employed throughout town as domestic servants, mill workers, and field hands. He began tutoring several of them in reading, spelling, writing, and geography on weekdays; on Sundays he conducted a Bible study class. Perhaps he wished to get an early taste of the missionary life; no doubt he also hoped to carry out part of the Antislavery Society's original goal of improving "the character and condition of the free people of colour." In scarcely more than a year, however, Raymond's notoriety so upset the Amherst faculty that it charged him with *"glaring and disgraceful improprieties"* and dismissed him from the college on a year's probation.

What had happened?

Raymond related the story candidly in a long, unpublished letter he sent to William Lloyd Garrison, the great abolitionist editor of the *Liberator* in Boston. Garrison had asked for the explanation; in a reply dated November 13, 1836, Raymond said he made "mistakes" but insisted that his intentions were "perfectly pure." As he pressed ahead with his tutoring, he said, he had become the subject of local gossip, and "suspicions arose in the minds of some that all was not right.

"It could not be, thought they, that I visited the colored people so often with good motives. Therefore I was watched with the keenest scrutiny." As time passed, "Every possible opportunity for misconstruing my conduct was improved. If I visited in the evening it was because I was ashamed to go in the day time & if I visited in the day time it was because 'I was as bold as a devil,' as one man told me. . . . Among other things, it was reported that I was paying my address to a colored young lady"— eventually, even "that I had become the father of a child by this young lady." Nowhere does Raymond mention her name or indicate that she was expecting a child. But the distraught young woman talked about leaving town, and in the spring of 1836 Raymond arranged for her to live with friends of his in Ashburnham. They took the stagecoach together from Amherst. That, Raymond acknowledged, became the last straw. "It caused excitement not only in Amherst but in the neighboring towns." Worst of all, the gossip appeared in a Boston newspaper, under the caustic title "A Whole Hog Abolitionist." Raymond told Garrison that while the paper's "insinuations were not only false but scandalous in the extreme," he considered it "the belching of a foul stomach which was not worth noticing."

The president and the faculty took notice, however. "Newspaper notoriety" appalled them. They asked Raymond to account for himself, which he did; and while they concluded, ultimately, that he was innocent "of any immorality whatever & did not doubt but what I was actuated by the purest motives," they found him guilty of *"disgraceful improprieties"* all the same, and expelled him for a year. "If they were satisfied that my motives were good," Raymond said, "they ought to have possessed a spirit of mercy. But College laws know *no mercy*."

Six months later Raymond wrote to President Humphrey from Springfield, Ohio, asking him to vouch for his character so that he could transfer to Oberlin College. He hoped Humphrey would recommend him, because "public opinion, which then seemed to demand my punishment to preserve the character of your institution," he said, "is now entirely satisfied, & the excitement which existed is now allayed, & my being admitted to another institution in a distant part of the union would have no tendency to dissatisfy the former or renew the latter." Humphrey probably agreed, for Raymond enrolled at Oberlin later that year and studied theology.

After college he was ordained as a minister and worked in Canada among former slaves who had fled the United States. In the course of his work—or perhaps through his former acquaintance with Samuel Tappan at Amherst—Raymond came to know Samuel's uncle, Lewis Tappan, the merchant, philanthropist, and founder of the New York Antislavery Society. By the fall of 1839 Tappan belonged to a three-man committee organizing the defense of the 40 *Amistad* prisoners whose fate would be decided in a series of celebrated court cases. These culminated in the Supreme Court's rulings in 1841 that the Africans were not the property of the Spaniards who claimed them, and that they could all go free. The abolitionists immediately made arrangements to settle the group—mostly Mendians from Sierra Leone—in rural Farmington, Connecticut, until further plans could be made. The group's leader was a charismatic, commanding figure named Cinque.

With missionary zeal, Americans had been teaching English—and Christianity—to the Mendians. Now Tappan and the others planned to continue this tutoring and ultimately to establish a mission in the Africans' homeland. Raymond visited Farmington and afterward urged Tappan to let him become one of the tutors and missionaries. "Since I visited Farmington," he declared, "I have felt my soul drawn out towards Cinque and his companions." Furthermore, he wrote, "That God has called me to go to Africa has long been a settled point with me—even before I ever heard there was such a race as the Mendians or that any of them had been cast upon our shores."

The young minister won the tutoring job just as his wife, Eliza, was expecting their first child. The couple arrived in Farmington near the end of August 1841. A prominent abolitionist in town, John Norton, wrote to Tappan that "Mr. Raymond arrived on Saturday & will commence teaching today. I like his appearance & hope he will do well." A baby girl, Jane, was born to the Raymonds three weeks later. The father wrote to Tappan: "The Mendians think the world of the little thing. . . . They take it and hold it—kiss it and sing to it in their native tongue."

Raymond quickly made friends with the Africans. "The longer I am with this dear people," he wrote Tappan, "the more I feel knit to them, & the more I am convinced that they are my people." Raymond's teaching went well: around mid-October he wrote, "I think I never had scholars learn so fast. I do not attribute this however to the excellency of my teaching but to their power of acquiring knowledge."

But word that Raymond might be sent to Africa as a missionary among the Mendians soon raised concern. People began hearing about his earlier troubles at Amherst. A Boston abolitionist, Amos Phelps, wrote a note cautioning Tappan: "I don't think Raymond is the man," he said. "We should not tempt God. . . . Perhaps I am wrong in my impressions, not knowing all the facts in the case. But I have felt greatly tried in regard to the matter—lest the mission should fail from our haste, or our sending unsuitable men." Whether Raymond specifically knew of Phelps's objection or not, he wrote to Tappan that he had nothing to hide. Again, as he had told Garrison three years earlier, he said the Amherst faculty had "acknowledged that they did not consider me guilty of any immorality whatsoever and that they believed me actuated by purest of motives in doing what I did."

Winter approached. The Mendians were eager to return to Africa, and Raymond told Tappan, "the quicker they go, the better. I believe that should you decide to keep them another year you would lose their confidence entirely. Cinque said to Dr. Booth [another tutor] the other day, 'I hold up my hand in court & God hear all I say. Merica people hold up their hands & say they send Mendi people home & God hear all they say.'" Another of Raymond's letters reported to Tappan: "They dread the cold weather . . . the fact that they are expecting to go home naturally

brings vividly before their minds the objects of their love. Their fathers &
their mothers—their brothers & sisters—their wives & their children—
their homes—their native palm trees and everything that is dear."

Tappan and his committee devised a scheme to raise money for a
voyage. He and Raymond would take 10 or so of the Mendians, including
Cinque, on a fund-raising tour through parts of New England. The
young teacher asked Tappan "what will be the exercises they had better
go through [on] those occasions. By knowing beforehand I may be able
to train them so they will appear to better advantage. . . . I have thought
of learning them a part of the Multiplication table to repeat all *together* in
the Mendi language. There will doubtless be great curiosity to hear them
talk, sing, or do something in their native language."

His advice was followed, and the tour was a rousing success. For two
weeks in November the Africans made 16 appearances in southern New
England, including a stop at Northampton, not far from Amherst. According to an abolitionist paper, *Philanthropist,* "Besides paying the heavy
expense incurred on the tour, upwards of a thousand dollars were col-
lected" to pay for the voyage—along with further pledges and contributions raised in Farmington. Undoubtedly the road tour also gave Tappan
a chance to evaluate his assistant's character and effectiveness. Raymond
passed the test. On November 27, accompanied by his wife and their
infant Jane, he was one of two white missionaries who set sail with the
Mendians for Sierra Leone (the other was a Reverend James Steele).

With Cinque's help, Raymond established a mission and school at
Kaw-Mendi, a river town 30 miles from the sea and about 100 miles south
of Freetown. At least a few members of the *Amistad* group stayed with
him. All four children who had been aboard the slave ship—the boy
Kale, and the three girls, Teme, Kaguem, and Margru—became part of
the Raymond household.

Mrs. Raymond was frequently ill, and before many months had passed
Jane died. The family was abysmally poor, which stirred sympathy and
anger in Thomas Raston, an English missionary in Freetown. To Tappan,
who had become treasurer of the Union Missionary Society in New York,
Raston wrote: "When their sweet little Jane was dead in the house—
they had 6 cents. When Mrs. Raymond was thought to be breathing her
last they had 1 cent!!! In both cases I supplied them. O ye Americans

how can you send forth devoted men and let them starve and die in this treacherous climate!" Raston urged the society to pay Raymond a fixed salary of at least $800 a year. Eventually it did.

There was frequent tribal warfare and slave trading around Kaw-Mendi. Along with the British Colonial Government at Freetown, Raymond did his best to condemn slavery and broker peace in the region. Late in 1845 the Union Missionary Society heard allegations that Raymond was too involved in African politics and had even become a British agent. In an echo of the Amherst affair, a committee voted censure. "He thinks he acted as a Mediator, but that he erred in several respects for which he feels regret," the society found. Raymond himself sounded more defiant than regretful: "It was by my intercession that the country was saved," he protested to Tappan. Around Kaw-Mendi, he said, the Africans themselves "look upon me as the savior of the Country."

Despite the rebuke from his employers, Raymond moved ahead in his work. He told Tappan proudly the following year: "God has blessed this mission beyond my anticipations. I never have had the least shadow of a doubt as to [its] ultimate success . . . but I must confess that I did not expect the Mission would gain the universal favor of the people so soon."

His work would soon end. Raymond came down with a fever on November 19, 1847, and died a week later. He was 32.

The missionary's youthful indiscretions were all but forgotten. In a tribute to the short, remarkable life of William Raymond, the American Missionary Association adopted a minute that said, in closing: "He had the deepest sympathy for the colored man, bond or free, and a peculiar adaptation to be their teacher."—DCW

In the nineteenth century Susan Dickinson and her husband, Austin, entertained many of the college's notable visitors at The Evergreens, their elegant house in Amherst next door to the Dickinson Homestead (where Austin's sister, poet Emily Dickinson, lived until her death in 1886). Austin Dickinson was an 1850 Amherst graduate who succeeded his father as treasurer of the college, serving from 1873 to 1895. Susan Dickinson composed this memoir in 1893 and called it "The Annals of The Evergreens," writing it for her children, Edward ("Ned") and Martha ("Mattie"). Here she describes golden days when Emerson, Henry Ward Beecher, Harriet Beecher Stowe, and other "high-minded, earnest men and women" came to visit and "the best viand" at the Dickinsons' table was the talk and the laughter. The original manuscript is in the Houghton Library at Harvard University. With that library's permission it was published in the Spring 1981 issue of *Amherst* magazine. The work was condensed and, in the interest of clarity, certain spellings, punctuation, and paragraphing were revised.

MAGNETIC VISITORS

By Susan H. Dickinson

As I HAVE BEEN looking back in meditative fashion upon my life of late, I am gratefully impressed by the personal influences which have stimulated and delighted me, my relations with rare people who have given me their best wealth and sympathy, sometimes a life of devoted friendship. This has been increasingly true in my married life—partly, it seems, as a happy accident, but more as the result of a hero-worship in the genuine nature of your Father, inherited from his own Puritan Father, who was born loyal to the Gods.

I realize, too, most keenly, how far better than money, or material good in a home, is the constant association with high-minded, earnest men and women and the refreshment of their informal talk about literature, affairs, religion, the supernatural, and of course other men and women. Children too young to fathom the depth or follow the philosophy of such talk listen and are fascinated as they are lifted into new, enraptured heights by the Spirit touch upon their opening eyes, as the Divine Spirit whispers in their ears, although their elders little heed or suspect the transmission.

I can see you both as youngsters listening with wide eyes to much of the home talk with magnetic visitors—perhaps feeling the charm a little more keenly as the bed hour drew on, in fear of the chilling summons to say good night, inducing a shrinking into the protecting shadow of a

large easy chair, knowing very well the parents, in an abandon of enjoy-
ment, would easily forget, for the time, the home rules. You remember
much of the people who have been in our home from time to time, but I
am sure your memories can be freshened by a few details written out in
some order. . . .

I think we never entertained a more unique guest in all our lives than
Colonel Benton, in the people's parlance "Old Tom Benton."[1] In the winter
of '57 your Father secured a rare lecture course for the Village, which was
the means of bringing this notable man to our home, during his day and
night in town. He had been most flourishingly advertised, and public
expectation was keen to hear the famous hero of thirty honorable years in
the U.S. Senate. A heavy snowstorm of the old New England type set in
the day before he was to arrive, blocking our roads and drifting into
formidable waves by a bitterly cold wind that rose in the morning.

Our at-that-time puny and helpless New London Northern Rail Road
was to bring him in at three in the afternoon. The morning train failed
to appear, the track was buried deeper than Herculaneum, and the whole
outlook was "unbroken Parian," as Aunt Emily says, from East to West.

Of course the lecture was given up by everybody in deep disappointment, but with much wondering as to the whereabouts of our southern
orator. College Hall, the Village church of those days, was nevertheless
warmed and lighted, with a stage built—as even the most hopeful persons
pronounced—for a Barmecide feast, as any arrival in the village seemed
impossible for such a night except by wings.

But in the early dusk, above the roar of the North wind, we detected
the faint whistling of an exhausted engine. In half an hour, covered with
snow, resolute as a gamecock, with nose as red as a tippler's, Colonel
Benton arrived and was unwrapped before a blazing fire in the Library.

How full of glee was the brave old man that he had come twenty miles
by special engine through the drifts from Palmer, assured by the engineer
that it was one of the coldest days known in New England. The hero of
the War of 1812 tingled with a fresh sense of victory in having met the
mercury at its lowest and won. Every half hour of his stay he would beg

1. Missourian Thomas Hart Benton was a leading Jacksonian Democrat and Unionist in the U.S.
Senate from 1820 to 1850.

us to give him just the degree the thermometer registered, very much as a general counts up his enemy slain and routed after great conflict. It was delightful to see him so cheery—so undaunted by obstacles, with seventy-four years upon his head. The picture in his book *Thirty Years in the U.S. Senate* must have been a truthful portrait, for at this long distance of years it brings him distinctly before me. Of course, when we saw him, the firm muscles about the mouth had relaxed, but the nose was the same bridge of strength and the brow as indicative of brain power.

The audience which gathered to hear him was large and enthusiastic, in spite of the weather obstacles and the sleigh loads which were stalled in the drifts (from Northampton and Greenfield, and the smaller towns near us). I remember his manner well, as he walked up and down the stage, built for this occasion with no thought of irreverence over the pews where the firm believers so often prayed, with a sort of martial tread, drawing a large silk bandanna handkerchief through his hands in a nervous fashion as he reviewed the striking points in his career under Jackson, in the Senate, and his defeat at last for the governorship of his own state. His self-confidence would have seemed like silly conceit in a charlatan, but only a pardonable weakness for so truly a strong man.

As he recounted crises in the Senate, he would step quickly to the front of the stage, exclaiming with an emphasis of his right foot, "Where was Benton then!!" If he was an egoist, a lifetime on the right side was ample palliation for it all.

He lingered over the fire after the lecture, until the hours were small, talking of his public life, dwelling with pride and devotion on the fascinating traits of his daughter Jessie, the wife of Gen'l. Fremont, who has ever held a romantic interest in the hearts of the American people. Our last reading of the thermometer, as we bade him good night, was twenty degrees below, and in spite of our best efforts to make a tropical atmosphere in his room, we trembled lest we find a dead hero in the morning. But he was rosy and rollicking when called to breakfast, where we seated him as close to the airtight stove, with which we aided a faint-going wood furnace after winter fairly set in, as we deemed safe for his clothes and epidermis.

Thirty below was the record at nine in the morning, and he fairly clapped his hands when assured that it was never colder—his "Veni, Vidi, Vici" mood was delightful to see.

We urged his remaining 'till the weather softened, but he insisted that he must make a train which would get him to New York for an engagement that evening, although we found upon inquiry that the road north of us to South Deerfield was the only one that could be broken open for twenty-four hours. We prepared to speed the parting guest by collecting all the coats, furs, tippets, and soapstones the house afforded, spreading them around the fire in hopes by wrapping him as tightly as his circulation would permit, that he would endure the bitter cold 'till turned out by the drifts into the shelter of some farmhouse near us on the north, for any farther progress seemed impossible.

I shall never forget his comical outline as, after adding layer upon layer of wraps, more furs, more mittens, a long red muffler of Papa's was twisted into almost a hangman's knot, about where his neck should be. We had cordial adieus, hoping to meet again, the smoking stones were tucked about him, the driver cracked his whip, and dear old Tom Benton was gone.

Whoever met this wintry craft would not have fancied anything more alive was being trans-freighted through the snow than a gingerbread man, or an Egyptian mummy.

The next year he died, and we went about saying, with softened breath and real affection, if with a bit of reverent humor, "Where was Benton then!!"

The same winter of '57 brought Emerson and Wendell Phillips[2] as lecturers to Amherst, and both were our royal guests—the latter, I think on the whole the most brilliant fireside talker I ever met. As I look back upon him as he was then in full efflorescence of life, I involuntarily exclaim with Curtis, who pronounced his eulogy in Boston at his death: "He was an illuminated vase of odors." He fell into our household ways during his short visit with us, as if ours were his home, showing everywhere the simplicity of greatness, too preoccupied to feign. At supper he became so interested in some exciting topic of the day that he forgot to touch what was on his plate, but at last partook in a most absent fashion, as if eating was quite out of his realm.

---

2. Phillips was one of the country's leading abolitionist orators and, later, an advocate of women's suffrage. "The Lost Arts," a lecture he gave at Amherst, was so popular that he delivered it to more than 2,000 audiences.

The lecture was his "Lost Arts." I sat and listened as children to a fairy tale, and came home feeling that to be a dead Egyptian was better than a live Anglo Saxon. The old church was crowded with students who hung upon his lips in complete fascination, a few taking notes, many watching him closely, thinking doubtless in crude apprehension of his power that if they stood quietly, as he did, upon the platform, gestured precisely as he did, imitated his musical cadences, they should all in four years become just like him.

After the lecture he overflowed with fun and stories, telling us in his magical fashion the story of the Lyceum committee man out West who, sitting behind him in the pulpit, in which they obliged him to stand as he lectured, grew restless under the even flow of his quiet oratory, tugged at his coat tails now and then, crying in sotto voce "Roar, roar, roar louder!"— telling Phillips, at the end, he feared the people would feel cheated of their money's worth if he did not make more noise.

I think it was in the same winter a little poem of Emerson's, entitled "Brahma," appeared in the *Atlantic Monthly*—it seemed subtle to the thoughtful, absurd to the dull and uncultured, and soon became the butt of newspaper jokes and caricatures and a frequent topic in general society. Those who received it were almost afraid to utter their translation of the puzzle, lest their insight excite only the jeers of their duller friends. I ventured to question the "Rosetta stone" after the lecture, as we sat about the fire (for he was our guest at the time). He smiled in his grave, wise way when I spoke of it as a sort of sphinx, and replied, "Oh there was nothing to understand! How could they make so much fuss over it!"

Before he came, I grew almost nervous in my anticipation of the vision of our New England Seer—for years I had read him, in a measure understood him, revered him, cherished him as a hero in my girl's heart, 'till there grew into my feeling for him almost a supernatural element, so that when I found that he was to eat and sleep beneath our roof, there was a suggestion of meeting a God face-to-face, or one of the Patriarchs of Hebrew setting, as Aunt Emily says, "as if he had come from where dreams were born."

I remember very little of the lecture except a fine glow of enthusiasm on my own part, and an almost unconscious contempt for anything but Emerson and his table-lands. I felt strangely elated to take his transcendental arm afterward, and walk leisurely home. I remember with how much warmth he spoke of Julia Ward Howe, indeed he talked of her nearly all the way home, begging me to read her "Passion Flowers." He seemed greatly pleased to find Coventry Patmore's *Angel in the House* on the library table, which we were just reading, and praised it with great warmth.

His manner in talking was so very quiet that it quite put me out. He turned his gentle, philosophic face toward me, waiting upon my common-places with such expectant, quiet gravity, I became painfully conscious that I was I, and he was he, the great Emerson, and I shut up like a spent flower. It suited your Father, whose own way of giving and taking in conversation is so deliberate, quite relieving me of any part but a listener's.

He was our guest at several other times. Once, when I was away, your Father invited him to tea with a little company of young people. Professor Neill, then in college, was one of the number who longed to meet him. They said he was wonderfully sweet, and simple with them, and seemed greatly to enjoy their fresh enthusiasm. His last coming to Amherst was after his memory became enfeebled, which made it necessary for his daughter to travel with him, and the Hotel seemed a more suitable place for him. The matter which he read at this time was, as ever, unique and original; he was Emerson still, meandering through prose and poetry, Heathen and Oriental proverbs, "old saws, and modern instances," in illustration of his old and yet fresh, if reiterated thought.

"But the golden bowl was broken," one felt the shadow of the "cold gradations of decay," something had gone—flesh and spirit rebelled—we could have wept.

> Nature who lost, cannot remake him
> Fate let him fall
> Fate can't retake him.

We saw Bishop Huntington[3] several times that winter: once, I believe, he came to lecture. He was chaplain and professor of Moral Philosophy at Harvard, not having as yet reached his decided Episcopal views, although, from a lecture on St. Augustine which he gave many times the

3. Frederic Dan Huntington became a Unitarian clergyman after his graduation from Amherst in 1839; he ended his career as Protestant Episcopal Bishop of Central New York.

winters following, one could see whither he was trending. You know him so well, you hardly need any reminder of him. His transition from Unitarianism to Orthodoxy was a topic of general interest—his oldest friends disappointed at last that he found refuge in so inelastic a church as that of the Apostolic succession. The poetical side of his nature never appeared more charmingly than about our dinner table, I think in the year '75, with Uncle Sam, Dr. Storrs, and Beecher for a stimulus.[4]

Beecher, as he came in the parlor shortly before dinner, made for a large vase of red lilies in the fireplace, stooping over them as if to caress them in his admiration. Their beauty seemed to charm all the company, quite making the subject matter of conversation for the first part of the dinner. Someone spoke of the Syrian lilies in the illustration of our Lord, then of Julia Ward Howe's "Battle Hymn," "Christ was born among the lilies," then of the rare beauty and picturesqueness of this whole family of plants. The talk was very informal, but brilliant.

As we strolled back to the parlor afterward, the gentlemen began to smoke, and Beecher grew very sober and tender in his mood, and fell to talking of our emotional natures, their responsiveness to slight external causes, and associations quite indefinable. For instance, he said, "When I was a boy in Litchfield I used to sit in the door of my home, listening to the wind in the branches over my head, looking up at the sky. I could hear the faint hum of the spinning wheel in the garret, and a tender sadness seemed to gather about me and melt my nature 'till I cried like a grieved child. What was it?"

As we all sat hushed and softened by this revelation of the great man, Bishop Huntington in a reverent tone said, "It was doubtless, Beecher, a sense of the Infinite pressing down upon your young soul."

Uncle Sam [the Dickinsons' close friend, Samuel Bowles], always iconoclastic, quickly added with a fascinating shrug of his shoulders, "You had probably been eating green apples, Beecher!!" A shout of laughter broke the spell, and talk ran upon affairs, until the company dispersed.

These Commencement days brought many rare men about our dinner

---

4. Richard Salter Storrs, like Huntington, graduated from Amherst in 1839, later serving the college as a trustee. At his church in Brooklyn he was almost as popular as his fellow trustee Henry Ward Beecher, the 1834 graduate and antislavery preacher and lecturer who drew 2,500 people a week to his Plymouth Church, also in Brooklyn.

table, and it is needless to add, that the best viand offered there was the rare talk.

Judge Lord,[5] a perfect figurehead for the Supreme Court, from his stiff stock to his toes, never seem[ed] to coalesce with these men, though he was often here with them, as the guest of your Grandfather. But his individuality was so bristling, his conviction that he alone was the embodiment of the law, as given on Sinai, so entire, his suspicion of all but himself so deeply founded in the rock bed of old conservative Whig tenacities, not to say obstinacies, that he was an anxious element to his hostess in a group of progressive and mellow although staunch men and women.

At an informal dinner with us once, we saw him at his best. Your Father was ill, and he kindly took the head of the table. Your Aunt Vinnie[6] sat at his right; the other guests I do not seem to remember. Perhaps because it was Sunday we naturally got on the subject of hymnology in New England. The Judge, remarking that he was brought up on "Watts and Select," unabridged, asked if any of us were familiar with the hymn beginning:

> My thoughts on awful subjects roll
> Damnation, and the dead.

In astonishment we answered, "No!"—whereupon he laid down his fork, made himself a little more stiff and erect behind his old-fashioned silk stock than usual, if that were possible, and recited with an energy worthy of himself and the subject, the whole hymn. There was really a horrible grandeur about it, although our nervous laughter must have misled one in the next room as to our real emotions.

Your Aunt was inspired by this to give us one of her famous representations of one early choir, with bass viol accompaniment, as familiar to us in the Village church a generation ago, when they worshipped in what is now College Hall. She sang stoutly and with real minor threat and pathos the first two lines of "Broad is the road which leads to death,"—but in the third line, where "Wisdom shows a narrow path," the melody running too high for the superannuated Village soprano, she dropped off in a cracked subsi-

---

5. Otis Phillips Lord, an associate judge on the Massachusetts Supreme Court, was an 1832 Amherst graduate.

6. Lavinia Dickinson, the sister of Austin and Emily Dickinson.

dence from the key, leaving the bass viol to moan in harrowing discord, rejoining it again after an interval in the fourth line, where they each, somewhat spent, strove to deepen the gloom of "Here and there a traveler"— the viol quite outstripping its rival and prolonging the last few notes in such grating woe that I remember, in the old days, the little boys used to look 'round furtively after sitting down to the prayer to see if anything was the matter with the good old man who bullied this kindly, misplaced instrument.

The imitation was a most remarkable artistic performance on your Aunt's part, arousing such applause that your Father's bell rang, requesting us to remember that it was Sunday.

I think [Governor Alexander H. Bullock of Massachusetts, an 1836 graduate and later trustee of Amherst, and George W. Curtis] never met but once in our home as guests, although so many times with us separately. They were much alike in graceful courtesy, although Curtis surpassed all in his flow of fascinating conversation, for it was conversation, never a Coleridgian monologue, the shyest talker being drawn into his subtle net almost unconsciously by his kindly and adroit grace, presupposing by his "you remember Seneca says," or Molière or Chateaubriand, that you were his peer everywhere in literature.

At the time of his last visit I remember suffering from an interregnum of a slow, stupid housemaid, but during a long dinner I soared quite away from the blunders and delays, enchanted by his mellifluous talk. It just occurs to me that he took in the situation, and hastened to cover the maid's awkwardness with his own grace.

I wonder if you remember the night raid of Governor Bullock and Mr. Gillett[7] for a bit of wine and bread. It was at Commencement time, and the night of the ball. Amid the confusion of the time, regularity and routine were lost sight of; the servants had gone to bed, leaving the house at midnight not only unlocked but with doors and windows wide open. Governor Bullock with Mr. Gillett were the first of the night revelers to come in, and quite to their surprise found no one about. They were both tired and hungry and felt it no breach of good form to go to the dining room for something refreshing; but nothing, not even a cracker, could be found. After a little conference they

---

7. Edward B. Gillett, a Springfield lawyer who graduated from Amherst in 1839 and served as a trustee for 35 years.

decided there must have been claret left from dinner, and were satisfied, if they could find it, they would fall asleep most peacefully.

I wish I could give you Governor Bullock's verbatim report of it, as he with every possible contrition and confession of guilt made a clean breast of their prying search at breakfast next morning. In relating the escapade to me, he said they looked about for a candle for a long time and finally found one in the large candelabra in the parlor, which they lighted and bore about in their fingers, in a man's dull fashion, quite overlooking the filled candlesticks in every corner of the house. Bearing the dripping thing in their fingers, they shyly ventured into the kitchen, peering into an empty pantry, with a trembling sense of shame at their audacity, as he told me; but growing bolder with defeat, they peered into every cupboard and dish they could find, with no effect, their thwarted purpose driving them to the ice chest which they were sure must yield the longed-for bits. They found it and were rewarded—all, saving the claret. Mr. Gillett bore the chicken and bread to the dining room; Gov. B. being the candlestick could do little else.

As they were sitting down to their well-earned lunch, but deeply disappointed as to the claret, the candlebearer spied a door partly opened into your Father's dressing-room. Silencing his one last polite qualm, with candle in hand, resisting a feeble remonstrance of his comrade, he gently pushed the door a little farther open, and lo, two broken bottles of life-saving St. Julien were theirs, which they quickly bore to the dining room with fingers hopelessly stiff with sperm[aceti], although their hearts were light.

I shall never forget dear Governor Bullock's honest fear lest he had overstepped the delicate boundary of our hospitality, asserting that he had never done such a thing in his life before, and never would again, while Mr. Gillett insisted that he was an innocent man who would never have thought of making such a midnight assault upon a friend's larder unless urged on by the Governor. The latter's gift of a box of choice claret, coming to us soon after, possessed an exceptionally fine bouquet. We were greatly pleased that our home seemed so much theirs that they did not hesitate to look for what they wanted, although I confess my housewifely pride shrank from even their brief inspection of my ménage after a week crowded with company and dining at all hours.

I have enjoyed greatly in years past the architects whom circumstances and your Father's taste and affairs brought about us. The first botanic superintendent of Central Park, when with us for a visit of few days, proved a most interesting companion of our drives. We drew out of him much delightful information about the flora of all countries, with which he was entirely familiar. On one of our excursions with him, as we were climbing Mt. Warner, he pulled up the fern which I have since called the "Austrian fern," asking me if I had ever noticed the root. With his knife he cut an oblique section of it, disclosing a rude but real figure of an eagle, the state emblem of Austria.

Vaux and Olmsted[8] were frequently with us, while both were busy developing Central Park years ago. We had the most fascinating talk with them of shrubs and plants, the habits of trees, and the possibilities of landscape gardening. We seemed, as it were, to forget that these were all impersonal objects, so individual did they become to us by a study of their specific habits and inclinations. . . .

Lest you forget a little of our pleasant day with Mrs. Burnett in the May of '80, I will recall it to your minds. Indeed, Mattie was a little girl then, too young to appreciate the opportunity of spending a few hours with a woman who had made herself famous as the author of "The Lass of Lowries." Ned was a freshman in College, but not especially interested in her stories, although he came to lunch and enjoyed it very much.[9]

Sam Bowles, "young Sam" as we call him, wrote me saying that he was making a little carriage trip through the valley, with the already famous woman, also Kate Foote, of Springfield, a woman of some literary note, and Mr. Griffin, senior editor of the *Republican*, and would like to bring them all to lunch with us on a certain day as they returned to Springfield via Amherst, adding with his usual gentle thoughtfulness, not to trouble about the lunch in the least, as bread and butter with a plate of soup would be quite enough.

They arrived about noon, in the fresh glory of a perfect May day. I invited Arthur Gillett [son of Edward Gillett], then a senior, to come down and take Mrs. Burnett out to lunch, your Father being in Boston. Fresh asparagus and salad from our own garden and hotbed made an appetizing garnish for the

---

8. Calvert Vaux and Frederick Law Olmsted, the landscape architects who designed Central Park, came to Amherst to design a plan for the campus. Olmsted is the Central Park superintendent mentioned in the previous paragraph.

9. Frances Hodgson Burnett is best known for her later work, *Little Lord Fauntleroy*, for which one of her precious little sons—Lionel?—is said to have been the model.

luncheon. Arbutus filled the center of the table, bright sunshine looked in at all the windows, as if eager to rival the sparkle of the talk within.

Mrs. Foote was a keen, ready woman, the gentlemen as alert as men could well be, so that "mots" flew back and forth and repartee flashed in meteoric fashion. Mrs. Burnett was dressed in a plain suit of black velvet; her manner was velvety, too, and a little shy; her hair was soft, abundant and wavy, quite the kind Browning talks about so much. Her eyes were poet's eyes, large, and soft, and so dreamy that their impression upon me quite made me forget her nose, mouth, complexion, and the expression of her hands. Her manner was quiet, but a little intense, revealing an undercurrent of appreciation, quite beyond, as everyone knows, a more verbose manner.

After luncheon we strolled over the grounds in the sunshine, without hats or wraps, stopping constantly to pick the wildflowers in the grass and wonder at the day. I remember Mrs. Burnett was quite buried under the knots of wild violets and houstonias gathered for her. When we were by ourselves, she spoke to me fondly and freely of her boys. I can speak here without indelicacy of her story of one of them, I think of Lionel, who was leaning on her dressing table as she put on a décolleté gown to attend an evening reception in Washington. After seeing her robed, he exclaimed "Dear Mamma, aren't you going to put something over the skin of your stomach!!" Blessed little reformer, how much better he preached than he knew.

They drove away in the fading afternoon, leaving a very agreeable impression, which has grown into a cherished memory. This little visit, of course, heightened our interest in her literary success, as well as added to the sincerity of our sympathy for the irreparable loss in the death of her son.

As I went out the next day I found the news of the visit had reached the ears of our friends, who upbraided me sharply for my selfishness in keeping so famous a woman to myself; Admiral [Theodore Phinney] Greene, our neighbor, loudest of all in his reproaches. It was a bit of thoughtlessness on my part, which I regretted extremely as an informal reception would have given great pleasure to her many admiring friends in town.

It was about that time that I met Mrs. Stowe [Harriet Beecher Stowe] very pleasantly at the house of her daughter, Mrs. Allen, the wife of our Episcopal rector. She was in a fascinating and talkative mood, and fell into some talk of her prolonged stay in Paris, and dwelt with great enthusiasm over the simple but artistic French plays she constantly heard there,

relating the plots of several, describing the stage accessories and the audiences, with much other interesting detail. Later on in the evening she
seemed a little more on her native heath, as she told stories of old New
England deacons, and their slips into impulsive profanity, and—truth
compels me to say—hinting of her own family in fine caricature.

I remember her distinctly as the light from the chandelier fell upon
her mobile face, her eyes twinkling with fun and merriment, her forehead
covered with soft brown curls, confined with a band of black velvet, as
seen in her pictures.

I invited her to drive a day or two afterward, and as I knew she was
taciturn at times, I took no pains to draw her out, allowing her the freedom of her larger nature undisturbed. The glory of the October morning
was too much for her—she clapped her hands in her joy over the yellow
maples, begging me to stop now and then that we might sit longer in the
golden glory. I never pass the little cemetery at South Amherst without
recalling her interest in the clean, cared-for look of it, quite insisting that
the dove finishing one of the marble slabs at the top was a real feather
bird; and she would only be convinced to the contrary when I strolled
through the grass and put my hand upon it.

I realize more and more as I have met persons who knew her much better than I, who described her silent way, for the most part, in society, that I
was most fortunate in her mood, for she talked constantly until we reached
home. I can but count it a choice memory and a real honor to have been so
long with an ideal New England woman, who under the stress of heavy
burdens wrote a book[10] which tells its story in twenty different languages.

Cousin Maria, Lucy [Mrs. Edward] Gillett, and scores more of elect
women and men pass before me as dear, strong factors in all our lives. But
this little journal has been written simply to remind you of what I feared
you might have been too young to remember distinctly. Today we hear that
Curtis is dying—I do not wish to oppress you with sad thoughts, but I see
plainly how my ranks are thinning, and if I am not left solitary, I must turn
back and outward, as the dependent vine, to the fresher life of yourselves
and your friends, for new points of contact. Your own natures promise you
as high comrades as your parents have enjoyed in our home—May you ever
find them, and as Shakespeare says, "May your worth prove your welcome."

---

10. *Uncle Tom's Cabin*. (Henry Ward Beecher was Mrs. Stowe's brother.)

The collecting instinct is seen early in the college's history. Edward "Doc" Hitchcock, President Hitchcock's son, wrote that when he lived with his parents in the President's House in the 1840s he discovered and "plundered" a cache of old documents to get his "start in statistics and memorabilia." In 1851 the faculty approved a more orderly practice, calling for the collection and preservation of "all documents pertaining to the history of the College." No doubt they hoped the collection would become what it is today: an important resource for the students of the college's history, and for other scholars and alumni. But neither Hitchcock nor the faculty could foresee that items added to the collection in the twentieth century would make it a destination for many hundreds who admire the life and work of a non-alumna. Today the reputation of Emily Dickinson, the college treasurer's daughter, draws visitors to Amherst from all over the world. The repository with her manuscripts and mementos is directed by Daria D'Arienzo, head of Archives and Special Collections, who tells here the story of two particular treasures.

LOOKING AT EMILY DICKINSON

By Daria D'Arienzo

Even today, after decades of scholars studying her poetry, her letters and her life, Emily Dickinson still haunts us. We want to know her, to follow her every move. She remains a very real part of our lives. We would like to see her when we walk along Main Street in Amherst—to stop at her window at the Homestead—though she's been gone for all these many years.

While we all have an image of Emily Dickinson in our minds, we want to know what she really looked like. She painted a picture of herself with words—"small, like the Wren, and my Hair is bold, like the Chestnut Bur—and my eyes, like the Sherry in the Glass, that the Guest leaves — ."[1] But can we take her at her word?

The earliest image of Dickinson is in Otis A. Bullard's 1840s portrait (now at Harvard University's Houghton Library) of the Dickinson children—Emily at 9, Austin at 10, and Lavinia at 6, almost 7. The painting tells us little—the siblings look almost interchangeable—though it is interesting that the painter has picked up on Emily's interest in nature (as well as Lavinia's in cats).[2]

---

1. Thomas H. Johnson, ed., *The Letters of Emily Dickinson* (Cambridge, Mass.: The Belknap Press of Harvard University Press, 1958), p. 268.

2. Lavinia is holding a piece of paper on which is depicted a cat. In some reproductions of the image, the bottom of the portrait is cropped so the cat is not visible.

We glimpse a maturing young woman through a silhouette image that arrived at Amherst College in 1956, together with many of Dickinson's manuscript poems, notes and letters, a gift from Millicent Todd Bingham, who had inherited the collection from her mother, Mabel Loomis Todd. The silhouette was cut by an Amherst student, Charles Temple, in 1845, the year he graduated, when Emily was 14. "A native of Smyrna" (now Turkey), Temple was Dickinson's French instructor at Amherst Academy in the early 1840s. Temple's silhouette gives us an impression of the young girl she was—bobbed hair, upturned nose, distinctive chin and mouth. It's a tantalizing image in its way—suggesting the plant slip before it grows to flower—and its darkness underscores the mystery that attends her.

Yet, even with these two youthful images, many of us will "see" Dickinson through another lens: that iconographic image captured forever in black and white, the single documented photographic likeness of the poet as a young woman—a sixth-plate daguerreotype (see page 263), showing a three-quarter view of her seated with her arm resting on a cloth-covered table, holding a small bouquet of flowers and looking directly at us.

The story of this daguerreotype and how it came to Amherst College is, like Dickinson's own story, full of twists and turns and mystery. There are more questions than answers. Is this the real Emily? Who took the daguerreotype? When was it taken? Why was it taken? Where did she sit for it? Why did it go astray? When, and by whom, was it found? And why is it now in the Archives and Special Collections at the college? Though the image was known to exist during Dickinson's life and to have survived her, it was presumed lost for more than 50 years. Today we have Amherst resident Mary Elizabeth Bernhard to thank for her scrupulous work tracking down the name of the photographer who captured Dickinson's likeness. Bernhard tells us that the photographer was William C. North, "Daguerrian Artist," and that Dickinson and her mother, Emily Norcross Dickinson, sat for him in his rooms in the hotel known as the Amherst House sometime between December 10, 1846, and late March 1847.[3]

---

3. Mary Elizabeth Kromer Bernhard, "Lost and Found: Emily Dickinson's Unknown Daguerreotypist," *The New England Quarterly* 72:4 (December 1999), pp. 594–601.

The daguerreotype then passed from one person to another. Lavinia Dickinson, the poet's sister, said in the 1890s that it belonged to Maggie Maher, the family's Irish servant. But did it really? It was photographed at least once, and those photographed images were retouched several times before the original daguerreotype apparently vanished, leaving only the derivative versions. The story picks up much later, on May 28, 1932, with the publication of Mabel Loomis Todd's new edition of *The Letters of Emily Dickinson*. This edition used the derivative cabinet photograph of the daguerreotype for the frontispiece. It was then that Todd heard from Austin Baxter Keep (Class of 1897), a distant relative of the Dickinsons and one of three brothers who graduated from Amherst. Keep wrote to Todd about a treasured image that he had of the poet. He enclosed two prints of the image with his letter. But it was only in 1945, after Mabel Loomis Todd's daughter, Millicent Todd Bingham, published *Ancestors' Brocades*, that Austin Keep's brother Wallace (Class of 1894) sent the daguerreotype to Bingham. According to Wallace Keep's later recollections, Lavinia had given him the daguerreotype that he had seen in Emily's room "as an expression of her affectionate regard"[4] in the early 1890s, when he visited Lavinia at the Homestead after the poet's death.

So when, in 1956, Millicent Todd Bingham gave Amherst College her Dickinson collection of poems, letters, and fragments, the resurfaced daguerreotype came too, after being essentially "lost" within the family for many years.

The daguerreotype's next journey began on May 23, 1978, when it traveled for conservation work to Rochester, New York, to the International Museum of Photography at the George Eastman House. There the conservator, Alice Swan, discovered some vestiges of previous coloring on Dickinson's forehead, on the pin, and on the flowers.

But there is a bit more to this story. Despite the evidence of some pigment on the daguerreotype, it is only in the last 20 years that we have been able to see Dickinson in true color. In April 1983 William R. Bailey, of Middletown, Ohio, learned that Amherst College had some connection to Dickinson. He wasn't sure what it was, so he called the college to see if

---

4. Millicent Todd Bingham, *Emily Dickinson's Home* (New York: Harper & Brothers, 1955), p. 521.

someone could tell him something about the poet and to ask whether the college would be interested in some Dickinson-related items he had. After his call was passed around a bit, Bailey ended up with John Lancaster, who worked as special collections librarian and archivist in the Robert Frost Library. After talking with Lancaster, Bailey clearly understood the nature of the library's connection with Dickinson. So, on April 18, 1983, William Bailey gave Amherst a letter, personal and affectionate, from Dickinson to her lifelong friend Emily Fowler (later Ford), who was away from Amherst.[5] Bailey also gave Amherst a shiny ringlet of Dickinson's striking auburn hair, which the poet had sent to Emily Fowler in 1853. The letter made the biggest splash at the time, but today it is this lock of hair that has the greatest impact on how we "see" the poet.

The undisputed provenance of the hair makes the gift particularly significant. Emily Fowler Ford was William R. Bailey's great-grand-mother, and was herself the daughter of William Chauncey Fowler, who taught rhetoric, oratory, and English at Amherst from 1838 until 1843. She was also the granddaughter of Noah Webster, one of the founders of the college.

The New York Public Library's Berg Collection has Emily Fowler Ford's collection of her many friends' hair—and Emily Dickinson's is noticeably absent from it. Instead, thanks to William R. Bailey, Amherst College has the hair, though the Berg Collection has the letter Dickinson sent with it. In that letter Dickinson writes, "I shall never give you anything again that will be half so full of sunshine as this wee lock of hair. . . ."[6] Bailey inherited the hair from an uncle in 1940 and made the gift to Amherst College in memory of his mother, Gillian Barr Bailey (Emily Fowler's granddaughter), in the name of all her children. So, for 130 years this important clue to seeing Dickinson in color was in the possession of Emily Fowler Ford's descendants.

William Bailey's call to the college was serendipitous; that he ended up talking with John Lancaster was luck, and that Amherst ended up with

---

5. The letter, in an altered form (*Letters,* no. 161), had been dated 1854 by Johnson. The actual date was spring 1852; see Alfred Habegger, *My Wars Are Laid Away in Books* (New York: Random House, 2001), p. 259, n.

6. *Letters,* p. 99.

a lock of beautiful auburn hair was fate. Bailey's gift of the lock of hair to the college cemented the nineteenth-century relationship between the Dickinson and Fowler families. It is also the single piece of physical evidence of Dickinson herself that has survived 175 years. Something of the mystery is solved, and Dickinson's ringlet and the daguerreotype are reunited safely in the Amherst College Library. When the two are held next to each other, the lock truly "colors" how we see the poet, and its intensely personal nature helps bring her to life.

While the hilltop memorial to Amherst men who died in World Wars I and II is a prominent landmark with a breathtaking view of the countryside, the college's other war memorial—a cluster of chimes honoring the dead of the Civil War—is all but invisible. People once in a while may hear the bells ring, but they're unlikely to climb high inside Stearns Steeple to read the only inscription. There it says the bells were "made to chime on all suitable occasions in commemoration of the brave patriots, connected with Amherst College, who lost their lives in the war against the great rebellion of 1861." It is estimated that 384 Amherst College men served in the conflict and 31 lost their lives. As we see in this account by the Dickinson scholar Polly Longsworth, the hometown soldier most celebrated by town and gown was a popular young adjutant, Frazar Stearns, son of President and Mrs. William A. Stearns. He was killed at New Bern, North Carolina, in 1862. The brass cannon that was captured at New Bern and later given to the college in Stearns's memory can be seen today inside the entrance to Morgan Hall.

BRAVE AMONG THE BRAVEST

⁓

By Polly Longsworth

For Amherst, with no telegraph, the Civil War began on April 17, 1861, when news of the attack on Fort Sumter reached town four days later. Shock and disbelief ran through the village that nestled with its college in a Massachusetts pocket formed by the Connecticut River, the Holyoke Range, and the Pelham Hills.

Once those hills had warded off winds of Unitarian heresy blowing from Boston.

Now they protected the pious Calvinist community from radical strains of abolitionism emanating from the same source. Voters of the region— hardworking farmers, artisans, and small-businessmen—were mostly Whigs, diehard Daniel Webster men, which meant they were Unionists through and through. Not for them William Lloyd Garrison's exhortations on emancipation. Although they were staunchly opposed to the spread of slavery into new western territories, loyalty to the Union held priority in their minds and hearts.

"By the help of Almighty God, not another inch of our soil, *heretofore consecrated* to freedom, shall *hereafter* be polluted by the advancing tread of slavery," growled the Honorable Edward Dickinson of Main Street, father of poet Emily Dickinson, while he served his home district in Congress in 1855. Woven into the Whigs' conservative philosophy was an expectation that if slavery could be contained, it would die a natural death. Few in western Massachusetts were prepared to believe the South would secede over the issue. Fewer still were ready for the crippling sacrifices of war.

In response to President Abraham Lincoln's initial call for three-month troops, four regiments of state militia (the Third, Fourth, Sixth, and Eighth) quickly mobilized at the eastern end of the state in April 1861. Days later, the Sixth Regiment headed south and was attacked by a mob while passing through Baltimore, resulting in the deaths of three men. This galvanized Amherst. If people hadn't believed their ears about secession, now they called public meetings, aired the Declaration of Independence, sang patriotic hymns, ran up flags, and made speeches. Young women employees of Amherst's palm leaf hat factory paraded through the village with small flags. A company of volunteers was raised.

At Amherst College, students assembled in Johnson Chapel to hear their Greek professor, the Reverend William Seymour Tyler, preach a rousing Sabbath sermon. Moving words, with references to a powerful, personal, somewhat militant God, were delivered in the evangelical strain familiar to young men in the pews. As they filed out, stirred by thoughts of courage and self-sacrifice, they found their chemistry professor, William S. Clark, an 1848 Amherst graduate, calling for a hundred students to go with him to war. Within a half hour the popular teacher had his company. The first name on the list was that of sophomore Frazar Stearns, son of the college's president, William A. Stearns. Professor Clark hustled to Boston the next day to learn how to equip his company, but he found Governor John A. Andrew swamped by recruits. Students' services would be required later, the governor decided. He urged Amherst College youths to pursue their studies. Nevertheless, four southern students— Elipha Fenn '61, Edward Maynard '62, Edward Robbins '63, and James Rhea '63—packed their bags and went home, three to enlist in the Confederate army.

The North was scarcely ready for war. Its standing army was scattered from Maine to California with over 90 percent of it stationed west of the Alleghenies. Few stockpiles of guns or equipment existed, and there was little money in the state and national treasuries to pay for mobilization.

As Mason Tyler '62, Professor Tyler's son (who would become a major in the Thirty-seventh Regiment), later pointed out, "The military establishment and the financial establishment to pay for [the war] both had to be created anew. It was a large school without teachers."

Lincoln's second call for volunteers in early May 1861 demanded of Massachusetts six regiments of three-year infantry troops. The town of Amherst supplied 15 men for four of these, most recruits going into the Tenth Volunteers, the first regiment to be formed in the western part of the state. In mid-June came Lincoln's third call, for which Massachusetts raised 18 more regiments during the summer and fall. Like other communities, Amherst had no difficulty at first in finding volunteers to fill the quotas. Later the town paid bounties to encourage enlistment, while some citizens, like Emily Dickinson's brother Austin, paid anywhere from $300 to $500 for substitutes. But in the beginning enthusiasm was high, for everyone thought the insurrection would end quickly.

The first townsman to be killed, in October 1861, was Francis H. Dickinson of the Fifteenth Regiment, whose legs were shot away in the Battle of Ball's Bluff. Dickinson was not related to the poet (in Amherst there were more Dickinsons than Smiths), but in a community of 3,000 every person was known, and the soldier's death moved Emily Dickinson. Thirty years old, living quietly in the family homestead, she was privately writing poetry.

When I was small, a Woman died—
Today—her Only Boy
Went up from the Potomac
His face all Victory

To look at her—How slowly
The Seasons must have turned
Till bullets clipt an Able
And He passed quickly round—

If pride shall be in Paradise—
Ourself cannot decide—

Of their imperial conduct—
No person testified—

But, proud in Apparition—
That Woman and her Boy
Pass back and forth, before my Brain
As even in the sky—
I'm confident, that Bravoes—
Perpetual break abroad
For Braveries, remote as this
In Yonder Maryland—

Until recently the poet's remoteness from the Civil War was a pet theme with scholars, who thought her too bound up in private sufferings and her art to concern herself in any vital way with the national turbulence. But the poem attests to Dickinson's psychic involvement with the young men of her region who went off to fight—and with those they left behind. Emily's father, Edward—the lawyer, treasurer of the college, and prominent civic leader with whom she lived—and her brother Austin, a lawyer next door, were both active recruiters and outfitters of Amherst soldiers, raising funds for bounties and boosting levels of local support and patriotism.

Like them Emily pored over the *Springfield Republican* and Boston papers, reading battle accounts and casualty lists. She, too, read the letters from soldiers published in the local papers. If she had no one immediately dear to her in the army, she carried a burden for friends and neighbors who did. She or her sister-in-law, Susan Dickinson, also sent several of her poems to publications that aided the war effort, the poems among the few published anonymously during her lifetime.

After Amherst College's August 1861 commencement, 21 students enlisted. Five had just graduated; another 16 interrupted college. "I am willing that students who are qualified for officers should go in the capacity, with their parents' consent," said President Stearns, "but I can not see my way clear yet to send them as privates." His concern focused on the high price paid by enlisted men for the mistakes of inexperienced officers, most of whom achieved their rank simply by raising companies at the request of somebody more prominent.

Two regiments had formed in the Amherst vicinity at Lincoln's third call. Frazar Stearns followed Professor William Clark into the Twenty-first Regiment, along with 12 area men, all as part of Amherst's quota. Clark was commissioned major of Company I, and Frazar Stearns became its first lieutenant. Frazar's good friend, newly graduated Frederick M. Sanderson, joined the Twenty-first Volunteers as well. Forty-seven other area men, including two Amherst College undergraduates and a graduate, joined the Twenty-seventh Volunteers as part of the town quota; also, six other new graduates and undergraduates joined the Twenty-seventh. Both regiments would participate in the fateful coastal expedition led into southern waters by General Ambrose E. Burnside six months later.

Twenty-one-year-old Frazar Stearns prepared himself for officership and for combat by bayonet, revolver, and sword exercises, and by boning up on medical practices. An impulsive youth of strong convictions, he was the most enthusiastic of the students who rushed to serve the Union. Stearns had been born in Cambridge, Massachusetts, the second son of six children of a Congregational minister, and came to Amherst at age 14 when his father became president of the college. He was an engaging youngster, quite generally loved, for many in the village had suffered with him sympathetically through a turbulent adolescence.

According to family accounts an uncommonly conscientious child, Frazar had professed Christ early and had been permitted to join the church by public confession of faith at the age of 12. But the death of his mother the year after moving to Amherst precipitated a series of depressions that centered on loss of faith. He was only an average scholar; his academic record grew spotty, his health poor. "His religious life was like a harp . . . unstrung and discordant," his father said of Frazar's spiritual struggles during a revival his freshman year at Amherst. "His skeptical questionings . . . took the form of fear approaching desperation."

During his sophomore year Frazar fell dangerously ill with typhoid fever and was so weak and unsettled afterward that his father sent him on a sea voyage to India, where the elder Stearns son, William, had become a successful Bombay merchant. The 11-month trip restored his health, mind, and spirit. Amherst people were amazed at the robust, assured young man who returned in the fall of 1860, ready to start his sophomore year over. He began again at the Classics, and by the academic year's end had earned commendable class standing.

By then, the war had started. Despite all his father and friends could say, Frazar was set on accompanying his admired chemistry professor, Clark, into the army. The Reverend William Stearns had called this war a means of grace, his son reminded him, and his own state of urgency might be a call from God. As family and friends acknowledged the portent, Frazar became the second Amherst student to enlist for the Union, departing with ardent backing from fellow students. For a young man who yearned to make his father proud, it was a happy moment when he received his commission in the Twenty-first Regiment in late August 1861.

The regiment spent the entire fall at Annapolis guarding the railroad line and a hospital of prisoners who had smallpox. During four months of inaction, while the impressionable, straitlaced Frazar made new friends and discovered the hardships and responsibilities of soldiering, he and his father engaged in a remarkable exchange of letters. In the South for the first time, Frazar was amazed at the complexity of the slavery discussion. He had come to fight for unity, but encountered among Annapolis denizens a great fear of emancipation. Conditioned to detest the fanaticism of abolitionists, Frazar still had to conclude, he wrote home, that "the North *now* as a nation will *never* succeed until they say Slavery shall die." A few days later, after talking with some Maryland slaveholders, his sympathies swung to a new view. Slavery should end, he now thought, but not till God pointed the way, and then through African colonization rather than simply emancipation.

President Stearns, a man of thoughtful, fair, and balanced mind, who by now had had considerable experience guiding his excitable son, sensed Frazar's confusion. "One question, I see, labors in your mind," he responded. "It is whether the President ought to proclaim universal emancipation? . . . I think *not*—certainly not *yet*. For 1st we have now a united North and a divided South—& here is one strength—but the moment such an act was passed we should have a divided North and a united South, & here would be one weakness. Besides 2nd, we have professed to be fighting for the Constitution,—by such an act we violate the Constitution . . . & thus the war becomes the war of the abolitionists instead of the nation. 3rd. An act of emancipation would do no good unless we want to excite slave insurrections, & arm the slaves, or take them under an immediate protection. What horrors would follow this untried experiment, God only can tell. . . . 4th, I cannot yet hear God's voice bidding us to go any further, in the matter of freedom, than the government had gone, but when God by his providence says the word, I am ready. . . . I am confident . . . this war will give slavery its death blow. Meanwhile . . . we must not go faster than God goes—Let him lead—& we follow."

But Frazar needed no convincing that the war was holy, or that he was part of God's inscrutable plan. His resignation to God's will was uttered almost casually more than once: "how can you terrify one who can look *death* in the face and has made up his mind that his life is his country's and *expects* it at any time? If I can serve my country better by *dying* now than living I am ready to do it."

By late December, General Burnside was ready to head south. The Twenty-first Massachusetts Regiment, eager for action, had been joined at Baltimore by the Twenty-seventh, with its large complement of Amherst men in Company D. "Why can't you come & see me before I go—" Frazar wrote his father. "You have only one son fighting for his country—you know the chance—perhaps I may never see you again—" Thus it was that Emily Dickinson, reporting to cousins on December 31 the death of a young soldier in a neighbor's family, added, "Frazar Stearns is just leaving Annapolis. His father has gone to see him again. I hope that ruddy face wont be brought home frozen."

General Burnside's first objective, the taking of Roanoke Island in North Carolina, was accomplished in early February 1862 after his fleet of 28 vessels, six transports with 15,000 troops, and a battery of six guns survived violent storms off Cape Hatteras. One of the first Northern victories in 11 gloomy months of rout and defeat, the Roanoke Island fight raised the spirits of the Union army. A young Amherst College graduate in the Twenty-seventh Regiment, Henry Hubbard '61, was killed in the battle, and among those wounded in Major William Clark's regiment was Frazar Stearns, grazed by bullets along the right temple and the back of his neck. He had been in the thick of fighting, participated in a successful charge on the principal battery of the Confederate right flank, and his regiment won praise from General Jesse L. Reno for its commendable performance. By now Amherst had acquired a telegraph, but casualty lists, published in newspapers, lagged behind the wired news of wins and losses. So word of Frazar's condition didn't reach home until February 20, when bells in Amherst were clanging over the fall of Fort Donelson in Kentucky. Within two days Frazar's letters assured his family the wounds were not serious and announced that for valorous services Major Clark had been promoted to lieutenant colonel, and he himself to acting adjutant.

Burnside next prepared to move against New Bern, North Carolina, a strategic target in his campaign to gain access to the interior of the state. He sailed from Hatteras Inlet on March 12 with 11,000 men: parts of three brigades under Generals Reno, John G. Foster, and John G. Parke, accompanied by several gunboats under the command of Commodore Stephen C. Rowan. With him were five Massachusetts regiments, three from Connecticut, two from Rhode Island, and one each from New Jersey, New York, and Pennsylvania.

"We are now moving in a magnificent column of more than fifty large vessels up the Neuse river on our way to Newberne," Colonel Clark wrote to his mother the afternoon of March 12. "*The Northerner* with all my regiment on board leads the way for the transports, following close behind the gun boats and the flagships of our Generals. It is now 5 and we expect to land tomorrow morning. We are all in excellent spirits and eager for the fight which is just at hand and may commence at any moment."

Frazar had written a shipboard letter three days earlier, his words striking a more somber note. "Always remember," he warned his family, "that *any hour* or *any moment* may bring you news that I am killed or dangerously wounded. If either, then God's will be done, and I hope I may always be prepared for any issue."

Knowing Frazar wasn't recovered from the fatigue and excitement of Roanoke Island, Colonel Clark advised him to stay on board *The Northerner*, but he would not. Five classmates—Ami Dennison, George Fuller, Parker McManus, Ransom Pratt, and Charles Storrs (graduated 1867)— were among the advancing troops, and some two dozen fellow townsmen. He would not sit idle while they fought.

Next morning, the troops landed early at Slocum Creek, 18 miles below New Bern, and began a three-pronged advance upriver toward the heavily fortified city. The Twenty-first Massachusetts Volunteers, with Frazar's company in front, led the left flank advance along a railroad track. It took all day, trudging in mud, mire, and heavy rain, and hauling eight howitzers, to arrive within three miles of New Bern. There the approach to the city was protected by extensive fieldworks with heavy mounted guns, three batteries, and entrenchments manned by some 5,000 Confederates from four North Carolina regiments under General Lawrence Branch.

The battle began early next morning in dense fog. General Foster's brigade, which included the Twenty-seventh Massachusetts Regiment, attacked the enemy's left flank nearest the river, while the Twenty-first formed part of General Reno's effort against the Confederates' right flank. General Parke brought his brigade up the middle behind the other two forces. Fighting was fierce for several hours along the entire line. Late in the morning, to create enemy disorder, General Reno ordered the right wing of the Twenty-first Massachusetts Regiment under Colonel Clark to charge a Confederate battery from which 300 rebel riflemen were keeping his flank pinned in a gorge. Clark led the way, rushing with four companies through a hail of gunfire over the enemy's right flank battlement, and routed the men within. Jumping atop the cannon that had been shelling his men, he waved the company colors.

It was a short-lived victory. Clark was unsupported by other troops and had to retire from the exposed position. Soon the battery was retaken by Federal troops, and the Confederates were overcome by noon. The Union army swarmed across the railroad bridge over the Trent River into a city in flames.

But back on the battlefield Colonel Clark was inconsolable. In the charge that he led, Frazar Stearns had been killed.

Bells rang for joy when news of the New Bern victory reached Amherst. Not until three days later, on March 18, 1862, came the telegram from Frazar's college friend and fellow officer, Lieutenant Fred Sanderson—he was bringing Frazar's body home. Only the evening before, the Stearns family had received Frazar's last letters, and they were unready for the devastating blow.

Professor Tyler broke the crushing news to students, while shock and grief spread rapidly through town. It wasn't Amherst's only loss at New Bern. Two other townsmen had been mortally wounded and died in the days that followed. Five more were also wounded, one losing his arm. An 1853 Amherst College man, Henry Reuben Pierce, was killed among the Fifth Rhode Island Volunteers. But Frazar Stearns was an emblem; his death touched nearly everyone in town. His story was picked up by newspapers all over the Northeast, including papers in Boston and New York, and he was quickly martyred for his valor, cited in General Reno's report, and for his selflessness.

"He has fallen in the morning of life," read a resolution offered in the state senate. "His sun goes down in splendor," added the *Boston Congregationalist*.

The funeral on March 22 brought to town as great a crowd as an Amherst Commencement. There was general bereavement, fed by stories of how Frazar had been struck in the chest by a minie ball (the large exit wound below his right collarbone was mistaken for the point of entry); how he had died from loss of blood after two hours, asking only once or twice for water; how Colonel Clark had cried like a baby, and others had prepared the body, made the coffin; how Fred Sanderson rowed it six miles downriver to a boat bound for home. Several fellow soldiers, including the heartbroken Clark, wrote President Stearns about Frazar's premonitions that he would die. The outpouring of affection from those who were touched by the simplicity and goodness of this earnest young man eventually led William Stearns to write a widely circulated book, *Adjutant Stearns*, about his son's short life.

"I can never forget the impression produced by the sight of the body as it lay in a rude box in the Library," wrote one of Frazar's classmates. "The cheeks were bloody and the forehead wrinkled under the matted hair but there was the old firm look about the thin lips and under the right shoulder was the gaping blue bullet hole—the ball went quite through the body from right to left. It was only a mass of clay but there seemed to come a voice from the blue lips: 'Be a man! Be a man!—don't shrink when your trial comes and you may find the hero's heaven also—'"

Amherst's noted 1834 graduate Henry Ward Beecher eulogized Frazar from the pulpit of his Plymouth Church in Brooklyn: "Of the hundreds of generous young men who will surround his bier will there be one whose heart will be unsusceptible to the lesson taught by the self-sacrifice of this young patriot?"

Many spoke of sacrifice, but one voice called it murder. "Austin is chilled by Frazar's murder," wrote Emily Dickinson in one of two oft-quoted letters about the soldier's death. "He says his Brain keeps saying over 'Frazar is killed' 'Frazar is killed,' just as Father told it—to Him. Two or three words of lead—that dropped so deep, they keep weighing—"

"Murder," she said again in a poem that struggles with the same themes:

> It dont sound so terrible—quite—
> as it did
> I run it over—"Dead", Brain—"Dead".
> Put it in Latin—Left of my school—
> Seems it dont shriek so—under rule.
>
> Turn it, a little—full in the face
> A Trouble looks bitterest—
> Shift it—just—
> Say "When Tomorrow comes this way—
> I shall have waded down one Day"

I suppose it will interrupt me some
Till I get accustomed—but then the Tomb
Like other new Things—shows largest—then—
And smaller, by Habit—

It's shrewder then
Put the Thought in advance—a Year—
How like "a fit"—then—
Murder-wear!

A week after the battle of New Bern, General Burnside ordered
that the captured Confederate six-pounder brass cannon Colonel Clark
had charged so heroically be presented to the Twenty-first Massachusetts
Regiment, and the regiment voted to give it to Amherst College in
Frazar Stearns's memory. The piece was returned to its manufacturer
(ironically, in nearby Chicopee, Massachusetts) for an elaborate inscription describing the gallant capture and listing the 19 men of the Twenty-
first Regiment killed at New Bern. Heading the list was Frazar's name,
together with the message "he was an honest man, a true Christian and
model Soldier, faithful, active, intelligent and brave among the bravest."

The ceremony of presenting the cannon, presided over by the Honorable Edward Dickinson in Amherst on April 14, 1862, seemed a second
commemoration of Frazar's death. Extra cars were put on the local train
to carry crowds from Boston. After the speeches, the scramble to see the
cannon was so uncontrolled that few saw it at all that day, and most had
to return later to visit the object, which has been on display at the college
ever since that day.

"So our part in Frazar is done," Emily Dickinson wrote after his burial
in West Cemetery. "Just as he fell, in his soldier's cap, with his sword at his
side, Frazar rode through Amherst, classmates to the right of him, and
classmates to the left of him, to guard his narrow face!"

There were far more significant battles to follow, far bloodier ones;
but New Bern became for this New England town the emblem of the
glory and the terribleness of war. To the Irish private of the Twenty-first
Regiment who had carried Frazar Stearns off the battlefield, he was "the
noblest soldier that the world ever afforded; I fear too brave for his own

good." Yet Amherst accepted the young man's loss as the sacrifice he somehow needed to be.

Deep in the text of a tribute, one small New York state newspaper, the *Binghamton Democrat*, struck the fitting epitaph for all concerned: "His spirit shows the worth of liberty and his silent corpse its price."

In 1903 the Class of 1870 presented the college with the portrait of a favorite classmate, Joseph Hardy Neesima, the famous Japanese educator and founder of Doshisha University in Kyoto. Through peace and war, the Neesima portrait has always been displayed—first in the College Church, and then in Johnson Chapel, where it has long held a place of honor. Thanks to their relationship through Neesima, Amherst and Doshisha are connected more than symbolically; they have enjoyed the benefits of educational collaboration for nearly a century. Neesima was the first Japanese to graduate from a Western college. As a student he wrote to an older friend, "O! What a charming place Amherst is! I am just as busy as bees, and cannot spend much time for doing else but study." A fellow student, Anson Morse, once said: "Of all the human beings I have ever known, Neesima seemed to me most perfectly to embody my ideal of a saint." Certainly no American was more ideal for writing Neesima's story than the author of this article, John Whitney Hall '39. Hall was born in Kyoto, the son of missionaries; after graduating from Amherst he became a pioneer of Japanese studies in the United States, teaching at the University of Michigan and later at Yale.

YANKEE SAMURAI

By John Whitney Hall

On October 9, 1874, a nervous, fragile young Japanese mounted the stage at the annual meeting of the American Board of Commissioners for Foreign Missions at Rutland, Vermont, to make the customary farewell address of one who was about to leave for a foreign missionary station. He had intended to raise the "samurai issue," namely to plead that special attention be given to the conversion of the samurai class in Japan, a class which, no longer a recognized privileged class, still provided leadership to Japanese government and society. Once on the stage, he put aside his prepared speech and instead made an impassioned plea for funds to start a Christian school in Japan. The man was Neesima Jo.

Neesima's later record of his spur-of-the-moment plea for funds was characteristically modest. After a minute, he wrote, "my trembling knees became firm and strong; a new thought flashed into my mind. . . . While I was speaking I was moved with the most intense feeling over my fellow countrymen, and I shed much tears. . . . But before I closed my poor speech about five thousand dollars were subscribed on the spot to found a Christian college in Japan." Others who witnessed the memorable event put it more dramatically. According to one report, Neesima had indeed shed tears: "Swept away by his feelings, refusing to resume his seat until his appeal was answered, declaring that he would not return to Japan without the money he asked for and he should stand on that platform until he got it, the young Japanese carried his audience with him. Honorable Peter Parker of Washington rose and subscribed one thousand dollars; Ex-Governor Page of Vermont and Hon. William E. Dodge of New York followed with like sums, and before Mr. Neesima had finished, his daydream had become a reality."

Neesima went on from Rutland to Japan as the first ordained Japanese minister and one of the first Protestant missionaries to evangelize Japan. Overcoming great obstacles and frustrations, he succeeded in founding the Christian school he had in mind in November of 1875. Before his death at the age of 47 in 1890, the Doshisha had become a full-fledged university, and Neesima had become a legend as a pioneering force in the Japan of his day—a great man, a mover of people, and a builder of institutions. Accounting for his capacity to influence his world is an easy matter. His diaries and letters are filled with the answer. He was a man of tremendous energy and conviction. He burned intensely and brightly; his mind and spirit constantly overran his body's capacity to keep up. His dedication and singleness of purpose were irresistible. And this was especially so in his last years when his health was so precarious that every public appearance had the look of being his last and every request he made of his listeners carried the weight of being a dying wish.

But like so many historical greats, Neesima was helped by history and circumstance. Neesima was first of all the product of a particular moment in Japanese history. He was not alone among Japanese pioneering greats of the 1850s to the 1890s. He was, first of all, a samurai, a member of the class that brought on the Meiji revolution and led to the creation of the modern Japanese state. He was part of the set of historical circumstances that produced the *shishi*, samurai of dedicated purpose, who became the founding fathers of new Japan, the entrepreneurs of Japan's economic development, the creators of newspapers and educational institutions. It was the mark of the samurai to cultivate sincerity of purpose. And in the years after Commodore Perry had opened Japan that sincerity was manifest in acts of frantic self-sacrifice on behalf of country and society. For this class, dedication took on religious fervor. Neesima's conversion to Christianity simply gave a particular focus and direction to that fervor. And in fact, throughout his life, Christianity was linked to a sense of patriotism (if not nationalism). At Rutland he had proposed to speak to the need of converting the samurai class so as to save Japan. Ten years later, in 1884, on a tour of Europe, when he collapsed at the St. Gotthard Pass and thought himself to be dying, he wrote, "Whoever reads this writing, pray for Japan, my dear native land. . . . Please cut a little portion of my hair and send to my dear wife in Kyoto, Japan, as a token of the inseparable bond of union in Christ. My plan for Japan will be defeated; but thanks to the Lord that he has already done so much for us! . . . May the Lord raise up many true Christians and noble patriots for my dear fatherland! Amen and amen."

As a samurai Neesima was brought up to accept the serious responsibilities of being a leader, of making his life count. He was born in 1843 into a middle-rank samurai household serving the house of Itakura, lords of a small domain based in the provincial castle town of Annaka. His father served as house steward and calligraphy instructor for the domain bureaucracy. Neesima began quite young to learn the Chinese classics and to engage in martial training of swordsmanship and riding. This latter activity was urged upon him in response to the alarm created by the Perry expedition of 1853. But while the young Neesima was concerned with the need to defend Japan militarily against foreign encroachment, his deepest interest was in book learning, and he found himself assigned to an utterly routine job of scribe in the domain office in Edo. Frustrated in his aim to expand his own knowledge and to use his intellectual talents on behalf of his country, he began to study at home at night, an exercise that led to the deterioration of his eyes and a permanent weakening of his physical stamina.

With the opening of Japan's ports to foreign ships in 1854 and to foreign trade in 1858, knowledge of the West was gaining currency in Japan. Neesima's first experience of doubt in his own country came when he picked up a book written in Chinese on the history of the United States. Learning of the democratic political and educational systems in America, he exclaimed, "O Governor of Japan! Why do you keep down us as a dog or a pig? We are people of Japan. If you govern us you must love us as your children." From this time he knew he must learn English. But lacking an instructor, he began to study Dutch on his own time, again at night. His persistence in this finally led his lord to assign him officially to study Dutch and also navigation at the Shogunal Naval Academy. But he was now more discontented than ever. Each new experience of foreign contact convinced him of Japan's technological backwardness and the inadequacy and moral corruption of the men in power. Step by step he became determined to escape from Japan and study the secret of Western power at first hand.

Not until after the 1868 revolution were Japanese freely permitted to travel abroad. The death penalty awaited any who were caught in the attempt to leave Japan or who sought to return after having left illegally. Nonetheless, Neesima made a secret escape from Hakodate, then an open port, on July 18, 1864. Reaching Shanghai, he transferred to a ship, the *Wild Rover*, whose ultimate destination was Boston. He served as the captain's personal servant in exchange for passage and lessons in English and navigation. After nearly a year on board the *Wild Rover*, Neesima reached Boston. Then, after some delay, he was taken in by Alpheus Hardy, owner of the *Wild Rover*, and Mrs. Hardy. The couple agreed to give Neesima a Christian education.

On board the *Wild Rover*, Neesima pursued three activities: he ceaselessly sought to improve his English; he kept a diary in English in which he recorded minute scientific observations, sketching mechanical contraptions that came to his attention; and he sought to learn about Christianity. By the time he had arrived in Boston he was sufficiently versed in Christian beliefs and vocabulary that he could be accepted as an eager convert, a person worthy of support. Neesima's sincerity was deeply felt by all who came into his presence. But it was his Christian belief that opened New England to him. A young, bright, dedicated Japanese eager to become a savior to his own people on behalf of the Christian cause was an irresistible combination at that time. New England in the mid-nineteenth century was strongly motivated to spread the gospel. Although direct attention to Japan was to await the end of the Civil War in America and the change of anti-Christian policy by the Japanese government, Japan had been added to the list of heathen countries awaiting salvation ever since Perry had dramatically "opened" Japan to the rest of the world. In 1869 the American Board made the official decision to start a mission in Japan.

An almost miraculous coincidence brought Neesima to America on the ship owned by the wealthy Mr. Hardy, who turned out to be a frustrated minister. In a talk given at the Amherst Psi Upsilon Society in 1893, Hardy spoke as follows:

> I am not a college man, and it was the bitter disappointment of my life that I could not be one. I wanted to go to college and become a minister; went to Phillips Academy to fit. My health broke down, and in spite of my determined hope of being able to go on, at last the truth was forced on me that I could not. . . . It seemed as if all my hope and purpose and interest in life were defeated. . . . [O]ne evening alone in my room, my distress was so great that I threw myself flat on the floor. The voiceless cry of my soul was, "O God, I cannot be thy minister." Then there came to me as I lay a vision, a new hope, a perception that I could serve God in business with the same devotion as in preaching, and that to make money for God might be my sacred calling. The vision of this service, and its nature as a sacred ministry, were so clear and joyous that I rose to my feet and with new hope in my heart exclaimed aloud, "O God, I can be thy minister! I will go back to Boston. I will make money for God, and that shall be my ministry."

If we can take Hardy at his word, Neesima obviously presented him with a heaven-sent opportunity to work for his beliefs through others. And Neesima was astute enough to accept this role. How irresistible is the following letter sent to Mrs. Hardy during his early days at Andover:

> Andover, July 24, 1866
> So you (like the Samaritan) relieve me from the misery, and help me to get a good education, therefore I will call you my neighbor. Nay, I will call you my mother whom God gives me. I pray to Him for you day and night that He may bless your family bountifully. . . . O, be cheerful to help me (a poor boy, like a wingless bird). Our Father which art in Heaven will rejoice your charitable deed; and will reward to you with the best thing. . . . I am very glad I got through arithmetic in this term. . . . My eyes are not very well, but I expect they shall be strong if I stop my study little while and take much exercise in this vacation.

Neesima went on from Andover to Amherst College, graduating in 1870, then to Andover Theological Seminary, where he prepared for the ministry and his eventual return to Japan as a Congregational minister.

Neesima saw spiritual and moral reform as the absolute need for Japan. Christian belief gave him an absolute, unquestioned authority to justify his goal—a justification that could not be challenged by reason or reference to his cultural inheritance. Thus Christian belief provided Neesima with yet another weapon. It protected him from the need to acknowledge Japanese law and the pressure of the Japanese government. Belief in a God which existed outside the Japanese pantheon made him free of social and political constraints and obligations as a Japanese. (At one time before his return to Japan, it was debated whether, as the first Japanese missionary, he should become an American citizen. He did not do so.) Having left Japan with the realization that his life could be taken were he captured by Japanese authorities, he felt himself above national commitments.

In 1872, when the Japanese Diplomatic Mission led by Prince Iwakura traveled through the United States on its way to Europe, Neesima was sought after as an interpreter and an advisor to Tanaka, the Commissioner of Education. The story of his negotiation with the mission members before he undertook the job is informative. Neesima was particularly worried that if he became beholden to the Japanese government he would lose his freedom of action and become a "slave of the Japanese government."

It was agreed that Neesima would retain his personal identity, separate from other employees of the Mission. To symbolize this Neesima refrained from bowing to the Commissioner in humble Japanese style but shook hands and bowed only to the 60-degree point. Writing later, he said, "I am glad to say I kept my right and my right was granted to me . . . for I am a free man, a free man in Christ!"

Neesima for the next two years traveled through the United States and Europe assisting Commissioner Tanaka in his study of Western education. It was an experience invaluable to his future plans to found a Christian school in Japan. Throughout this trip he steadfastly refused to join Tanaka's team. "If I become useful to him," he wrote back to America, "he may possibly lay a snare to catch me and take me back to Japan. . . . I believe the Commissioner is a perfect gentleman and would not treat me treacherously. Yet what I have said above is my Yankee speculation." Neesima had added Yankee shrewdness to his own stubbornness.

Thus Neesima returned to Andover from Europe to continue his training for the ministry. He was ordained on September 24, 1874, spoke at Rutland two weeks later, and landed in Yokohama December 6, 1874. His first act was to speed to Annaka by express rickshaw for a tearful reunion with his parents and friends, whom he tried to convert to Christianity with some success. "My father," he wrote, "has discontinued to worship the Japanese gods and his ancestors. By his consent I took down all the paper, wooden, earthen, and brass Gods from the shelves where they were kept, and burned them up." But Neesima soon left Annaka to pursue his central purpose, the starting up of a Christian school.

He ran into unexpected difficulties. Having decided on Kyoto as the best location, he was confronted by his countrymen with the official ban against Christian teaching outside of treaty ports. Moreover the American Mission Board authorities gave him less than full support, being more interested in using Neesima for evangelism than for educational purposes. His American fellow missionaries, however, went along reluctantly, with the expectation that the school would be a training school for Christian workers.

Neesima argued for something else. "I fully believe we shall not prosper in our work unless we have a collegiate institution in addition to a training school. . . . If we simply teach theology and the Bible I fear the best Japanese youth will not stay with us. They want modern science also." Furthermore, the local authorities would agree to the establishment of the school only on condition that it refrain from religious training.

At this time Neesima and his American missionary colleagues faced the fundamental problem of the priority of religion over science. Neesima insisted upon emphasizing both science (or Western education) and Christian study. In Protestant New England, in Andover and Amherst, he had not found the two incompatible. He himself had been led to respect Christianity by the awesome power of Western technology manifest in the ships he saw off the coast of Edo. And from the first he had had a practical, patriotic purpose in establishing a Christian school. It was to train Japanese who could serve their country as morally upright leaders.

To Neesima the saving of souls was never detached from the saving of Japan. Later, as he sought to expand his school into a college, he wrote:

> I am strongly convinced that we can't keep up our reputation in future unless we provide a few professional studies besides theology. . . . To sum up my view, let me briefly state as follows: 1. Give our students a thorough English course. 2. Make the theological course more attractive to our ambitious students. Let the foreign professors devote their time and strength for instructing this important class. 3. Provide for other professional studies to keep those boys who will not become preachers within the sacred walls of our school. 4. If I secure a few scholarships I should like to use them exclusively for the best students, intellectually and spiritually, among the theological graduates. This provision will certainly make the theological class honorable and attractive in our school. . . . Why should we seriously object to raise up Christian statesmen, Christian lawyers, Christian editors, and Christian merchants, as well as Christian preachers and teachers, within the walls of our Christian institutions? It is our humble purpose to save Japan through Christianity.

This wish was not to be fulfilled. It is ironic that for Neesima the cloak of Christianity in which he wrapped himself served different and contrary purposes in America and Japan. In America his adherence to Christianity legitimized the support given him to pursue an education at the best of institutions, an essentially scientific education. In Japan the situation was reversed. Western (scientific) education legitimized the possibility of Christian training. While the Doshisha in its early stages was a small band of students most of whom were Christian converts, it did seem that the main purpose of the school was to train Christian leaders to save Japan. As the Doshisha grew, the Christian element was increasingly diluted. By the time of Neesima's death, the Doshisha had become an institution of higher education containing five divisions: Preparatory, Collegiate, Scientific, Theological, and Women's. The theological element was prominent but relatively small in terms of faculty and students.

Before Neesima's death, also, the country which he sought to save through Christianity had undergone a basic change. It had survived the early years of political uncertainty and defense against foreign pressure. It had entered upon a program of social reform and economic development. It had adopted basic Western legal code as a way of gaining recognition by the Western powers for having a "civilized" legal system. It had adopted what for its age was a progressive Constitution in 1889. By diplomacy, political reform, and scientific education, Japan had won its place in a world dominated by Western civilization. Christianity had not functioned as a major requirement in the process, demanded neither by the Western powers nor the pragmatic men of action in Japan who brought off Japan's success.

Thus from the start, the relationship between Christianity and science, Christianity and patriotism, took on a different meaning from what it had in New England. And while Neesima worked ceaselessly to extend his school into a college and his college into a university, the effort to sustain the relevance of theology to the accepted necessity of scientific education remained unsolved. Among later arrivals from the West, neither the conviction nor the pioneering spirit could be sustained. The early missionaries, pioneers placed in roles larger than themselves, became—like Neesima—bigger-than-life heroes. But the charisma was personal and non-heritable.

While Neesima clung to his faith in the absolute necessity for Japan to be Christianized, his country and many of his close associates did not sustain the conviction. During the 1880s an important intellectual and political debate took place in Japan over the issue of Christianity in particular and the nature of Western civilization in general. When in 1872 an important educator wrote that if Japan adopted the material aspects of Western culture without adopting Christianity, the country would be like a puppet without a soul, he expressed the suspicions of many of the most enlightened Japanese leaders. When the American Board missionaries began their mission in Japan, the assumption was that they were the bearers of that missing soul. Yet before the Christian movement could spread uninhibited throughout Japan, counterforces were at work. Opposition of Confucianists, Shintoists, and Buddhists was not the main problem. The force that defeated the effort to Christianize Japan came from within the Protestant church itself and from the proponents of Western science. In the first instance there was the work of Unitarian missionaries, in the second the work of the social Darwinians and especially the followers of Herbert Spencer. Just as the Dutch in the seventeenth century offered Japan trade without religion, the foreign scientific and academic community in Japan of the 1880s offered Japan "civilization and progress" without Christianity.

By the time of Neesima's death, the prospect of continuing conversion of Japanese to Christianity had begun to fade. And this was clearly a result of the failure of the idea that Christianity was the absolute essential of Western civilization. Inevitably also it was due to the increased difficulty that both foreign and Japanese Christians had in maintaining the degree of earnestness and selflessness possessed by the first-generation pioneers. A number of Japanese Christian activists in fact had begun to have second thoughts, and the issue of patriotism had raised its head.

Among the speakers at Neesima's memorial service, the most interesting and prophetic was Kato Hiroyuki, President of Tokyo University:

> I do not praise Neesima because he was a Christian. I praise him for
> that steadfast spirit, so essential in every sphere, of religion, learning,
> politics, or trade. I believe this spirit a great necessity in this country.
> For the young Mr. Neesima is in this respect a great example. Not only
> those who follow him in his religious faith, but all,—merchants,
> statesmen, scholars,—should strive to acquire his spirit. It is well to
> understand in this age of the survival of the fittest the necessity for this
> capacity to endure, and I earnestly desire that more men of his temper
> may be raised up among us. . . . In this audience there are Confucian-
> ists and Buddhists as well as Christians; but I think the latter are in
> the majority, and I would therefore take this opportunity to make an-
> other suggestion in respect to which also Mr. Neesima is an example.
> . . . A belief in Christianity seems to weaken patriotism and loyalty to
> the emperor. This is the opinion of some, and I think it is confirmed
> by the conduct of some Christians. . . . I hear a great many "Noes," and
> I am glad if this charge is not true. There is no reason why belief in
> Christianity should decrease loyalty to country, but as Christianity is
> of foreign origin men of other faiths naturally bring this charge even
> if it be only in defense of their own creeds.

In the years after Neesima's death, Doshisha grew in size. An American-endowed School of Science was added in 1890, and in 1892 a School of Law and Politics. In 1912 Doshisha gained the status of private university, and finally in 1920 it obtained official government recognition as a university capable of granting degrees equal to those of the state-supported Imperial Universities. At that time the student population numbered about 2,500. After World War II, Doshisha continued to receive official recognition and support. In 1948 the School of Engineering and Commerce was added, and in 1950 a graduate school. Current enrollment is close to 30,000. The percentage of Christians within the faculty and student body is quite small.

But Doshisha University does have a special quality among Japanese institutions of higher learning, and this is due to the continuing connection with the Congregational Church and Amherst College. Before World War I, Doshisha's connection with the United States was chiefly through the Congregational mission group. Amherst was brought into the picture in 1919. It was in that year that Ebina Danjo, president designate of Doshisha, spoke at Amherst and urged that closer relations be developed between Amherst and Doshisha. Answering this call, Alden Clark, Amherst 1900 and an officer of the American Board, stimulated the Amherst Christian Association to raise money to send a graduating senior from Amherst to serve at Doshisha for a two-year term as Amherst Representative.

The motives behind this move were mixed. There was a residue of missionary spirit behind the plan, though there was no intent that the Representative be a professional Christian. There was a belief, among the Amherst student body in particular, that an Amherst graduate had something to offer the Japanese. There was as well a sense of the need for American youth to serve humanity. This feeling was well expressed by President Alexander Meiklejohn as he inaugurated the program: "Our American experience in the war left us with hopes aroused and enthusiasms awakened but with no power to bring those hopes and enthusiasms into definite, well-directed action. . . . I think it essential for this college and for the men in it that they define definite purposes to which they can give themselves with hope and enthusiasm. In such a field the Doshisha plan makes a peculiar appeal to us."

The first Amherst Representative, Stewart Nichols, sent out in 1922, was, like Neesima, an unusual person who in his way was a charismatic pioneer made larger than life by the circumstances into which he was projected. Nichols was not a trained Christian, but he was to return from Japan to enter Union Theological Seminary. He was in all but fact a missionary whose impact upon the Doshisha students he befriended was most powerful. He was tall, handsome, talented, a good athlete, a good speaker, and above all sincerely giving of himself. His impact was made doubly strong by his tragic, premature death in 1925, just a year after his return from Japan. He had contracted tuberculosis, presumably while in Japan.

Stewart's death added a depth of purpose and significance to the Amherst-Doshisha relationship, for it was as though he had given his life in service. And it was his memory that eventually led to the building of Amherst House at Doshisha. In 1929, at the instigation of his mother, a fund drive was started to raise money for a building to be erected on the Doshisha campus to serve as headquarters of Amherst-in-Japan. Completed in 1932, it served as home for five Amherst Representatives prior to the outbreak of war between Japan and the United States in 1941.

The symbolism of Amherst House is both intriguing and baffling. It was first a monument to the sincere desire of Americans to "do good" for others. Yet functionally it was planned with little concern for local needs. A superbly built brick colonial building modeled after Stewart's Delta Upsilon fraternity [now Porter House], by its very luxuriousness (it was the only building at Doshisha with central heating) it obscured the purpose of Amherst-in-Japan, which was personal and human. While cultural factors had always colored Japanese-American relations in the missionary movement, the strength of religious conviction had risen above such differences in actual practice. By the 1930s that religious factor was being questioned. Belief in the absolute superiority of Christian truth was no longer secure. In his idealistic way Nichols in 1922 had expressed his faith in the value of what he would do at Doshisha: "Never has there been in Doshisha a greater need for the purifying influence of Western ideals. Japan is a nation in transition, and the accepted principles of centuries are being discarded in favor of the new. In this temporary absence of standards and formulated ideas, more pronounced in the prosperity which has followed the great war, the younger generation is stumbling on in its search for truth."

But by the 1930s relations between educated Americans and Japanese had become less simple. Once the presumed superiority of the Christian message was questioned, American "representatives" to Japan, whether missionaries or Amherst men, were reduced to social and educational good works. Amherst House as a statement in brick reflected American good intentions as well as a hidden sense of institutional and cultural superiority. The effort of five Amherst Representatives to define their presence in Amherst House forms a fascinating story beyond the scope of this essay. By 1938, when the question of sending a Representative for the 1939–41 term was raised by the Amherst Christian Association, there was both campus apathy and political opposition. Japan's war in China and drift toward the totalitarian Axis powers brought into question whether the United States should continue to "do good" in Japan. But the student body was prevailed upon to send yet another Representative. Little did they know that [in sending Hall, author of this article] they were sending to Doshisha an American who was neither a proponent of Christian missions nor a believer in the superiority of the American way of life. In fact, he went to Doshisha with the desire to learn about Japan so as to become a missionary, in the reverse direction.

Looked at from a global, detached historical point of view, one can see that by the 1940s a new frontier was emerging in the relations between the United States and Japan. This was the frontier opened up by cultural anthropologists and behaviorists who saw human society not in terms of absolutes but relatively—who were prepared to say that Americans had as much to learn from Japanese as Japanese from Americans. It is significant that since the end of the Pacific War, Amherst House has been used both as a place of residence for American students to learn about Japan and for Japanese to befriend Americans. Today cultural and educational relations between the United States and Japan have become a two-way process. And Amherst directly or indirectly has had an important hand in bringing this about.

Reading this account of the college's earliest debate on coeducation, one may think of the saying from Ecclesiastes that there is "nothing new under the sun." But the coeducation discussions at Amherst in 1871 and again a century later had very different results. The trustees did not make the change until the second time around, in November 1974, and then only after four years of exhaustive study and controversy. On both occasions the proximity of the women's colleges, Smith and Mount Holyoke, figured in the debate; they were certainly a factor in Amherst's being one of the last of the men's colleges to "go coed." The undergraduate author of this piece, Christopher Bohjalian '82, received *summa* honors for his American Studies thesis on the coeducation issue of the 1870s. Today he's a best-selling novelist—author of *Midwives*, *The Law of Similars*, *Trans-Sister Radio*, and other critically acclaimed books. In this article we see him making early use of research and narrative skills that later become hallmarks of his best-selling fiction.

THE COEDUCATION DEBATE OF 1871

By Christopher Bohjalian

N EARLY 700 ALUMNI, almost half of all living graduates, poured into Amherst with their families in the second week of July 1871. Wearing white name tags with purple borders, they beleaguered the town for three days as they celebrated the college's semicentennial.

Older alumni, including the college's first graduate, Ebenezer Snell from the Class of 1822, were in the presence of a very different Amherst from the one built 50 years earlier by the farmers and local villagers. There were 15 buildings by the semicentennial, and over 260 undergraduates. By 1871, Dr. Edward Hitchcock could admit ruefully that as many as 76 students, or 29 percent of the school, smoked tobacco. The Antivenenean Society, a temperance organization founded in 1830, had modified its pledge so that signers did not have to abstain from tobacco, and wine was now an acceptable beverage so long as it was not drunk to intoxication.

On the other hand, a graduate from the 1830s would have found in 1871 that the school's ostensible purpose had changed little in its first half century. Boating was the rage in the early 1870s, and fraternities and literary societies may have taken up as much of a student's time as his class work, but revivals were as common in the years immediately following the Civil War as they had been earlier. While the school was producing fewer foreign missionaries in 1871 than it had during the 1830s, the percentage of its graduates who became ordained ministers had not fallen off significantly. The singleness of Amherst's purpose, what historian Thomas Le Duc defined as the training of eloquent "hilltop parsons," was only slightly diminished. The real break with the past, the institution of President Julius Seelye's "Amherst System"—in which students were suddenly considered adults, were alone responsible for their class attendance, and were expected to discipline themselves when attendance fell—was still a decade away.

The question on the minds of many returning alumni probably had less to do with the education of men than of women. When the cornerstone of North dormitory was laid in 1820, no one asked whether women should receive a higher education. By 1871, however, two questions debated by educators, students, and administrators were whether women should go to college and if so, whether a single-sex environment was more effective than a coeducational one. By the time the Amherst semicentennial rolled around, Oberlin had been coeducational for nearly 35 years; Mount Holyoke, though a seminary by name, functioned in most regards as a college; Vassar had graduated three full classes of women; and in nearby Northampton a woman named Sophia Smith recently had died, leaving over $300,000 in her will to endow a college for women. If any issue clearly marked the passage of time, it was the coeducation debate held near the Woods Cabinet at Amherst on July 12.

Among the principals in the drama were Henry Ward Beecher, the celebrated minister; L. Clark Seelye, a scholar of English literature who later would become president of the new Smith College; Samuel Bowles, editor of the *Springfield Republican*; and William Tyler, an aging classics professor.

Despite widely differing sensibilities, each of the four revealed similar attitudes toward women, attitudes that ran deeper than the issue of coeducation. Yet Bowles and Beecher favored coeducation, while Tyler, Seelye, and John M. Greene—a young Amherst graduate who had become Sophia Smith's minister and confidant—opposed it. Their thoughts may have reflected the more prevalent male conceptions of women in the Connecticut Valley in the 1870s.

Professor Tyler, an 1830 Amherst graduate, perhaps more than any other college figure represented the school during the nineteenth century.

On the faculty during the administrations of five presidents, Tyler was revered by his students and was viewed as the school's elder statesman by alumni and his faculty colleagues. He dedicated his 650-page history of the school to the "Alumni of Amherst College." Tyler understood better than most the changes that had occurred at Amherst during its first half century. "A noteworthy change has passed over Amherst," he wrote in his Amherst history, "in manners and customs, and especially in regard to recreations and amusements. Time was, when class-suppers and 'convivial entertainment' were 'strictly forbidden.' . . . Now the class-supper is the goal and garland of the College Curriculum." Although he admitted he was not "entirely converted either to the ethics or the aesthetics of this new regime," he also acknowledged as John Wesley had before him that "it is a pity the devil should have all the best music, or the best exercise, recreation and amusement."

In Tyler's eyes, a much greater threat to the old order than the new diversions of bowling or boating or fraternities was the prospect of coeducation. He firmly opposed it, and argued instead for the higher education of women in a single-sex environment. Along with L. Clark Seelye and John M. Greene, he was instrumental in making Smith College a reality.

Tyler's main arguments against coeducation were that male college students would be a dreadful influence on female students, and that women themselves would not, in the long run, desire coeducation. At the Mount Holyoke commencement ceremony in 1873, Tyler said the Amherst faculty feared coeducation "not because we do not believe there are many young women who are fully capable of competing with young men. . . . Facts prove the contrary"; but he had seen "how blindly young women, in some of our so-called Woman's Colleges, ape the follies of young men in theirs." He also compared the coeducation movement to the fight for women's suffrage, saying, "Women themselves, women generally—the truest, purest and best of the sex, for the most part, do not *wish* for the right of suffrage, and that because their unerring instincts and intuitions tell them they would lose more than they would gain by the change; because their good sense and right feeling teach them, there is a wiser and better way of exerting their influence and blessing mankind." Tyler also worried about the "obvious peculiarity of [a woman's] nature," fearing that because of her "slender, delicate and feeble constitution," a woman either would suffer physical collapse in a men's school, or the school would have to "lower the standard of college education"!

Speaking at Seelye's inauguration as president of Smith College in 1875, Tyler again managed to condemn coeducation as he presented his own interpretation of why Smith was developed: "The existing colleges of New England refuse to admit young women to their advantages. We may approve or disapprove this exclusion. Our approval or disapproval will not alter the facts. If the young women of this section are to enjoy the advantages of college education (and surely none can deny that they ought at least to have the opportunity), it must be for the present in institutions founded for that purpose."

Tyler concluded he would "be quite content if we can make [Smith] a real first-class college, like Williams or Amherst." He devoted the early part of the 1870s to raising funds for the women's college and organizing the curriculum. He also served as president of Smith's board of trustees. Perhaps Tyler's views on women were best demonstrated in his eulogy for the wife of former president Edward Hitchcock, Orra White Hitchcock—a eulogy he entitled "Our Wife and Mother." After commenting on the exceptional education she received as a child, he remarked that it was her cultivated intelligence that made her an exceptional wife and mother. "Like every true woman," he said, "her tastes and habits were eminently domestic. First of all . . . she lived at home—lived in, and lived for, her husband and children." According to Tyler, the purpose of education for women was to increase their talents in the women's sphere, the home, by providing them with refining culture and grace.

For Tyler, despite any pretensions about educating whole men or complete wives and mothers, learning was always secondary to religion. Education promoted religion and glorified God. To place men and women together in such a situation, an environment in which students needed to climb to a peak of holiness, could be a moral catastrophe. The sexes might distract each other.

Seelye, too, attacked coeducation on such grounds. "We find nothing which leads us to the conclusion that coeducation will benefit the sexes intellectually, but good grounds for apprehending serious intellectual injury." He feared immorality and bad manners in both sexes might result at a coeducational institution. On one occasion, Seelye warned: "Any one who has any true conceptions of the early struggles, and temptations of life, must feel great solicitude for young people, when the restraints of expediency are weak and the appetites most inflammable." He believed that the nine miles separating Amherst and Smith "would . . . save the community from a great amount of evil."

Seelye's most impassioned attack on coeducation occurred in his inaugural speech at Smith. He quoted the president of an unnamed coeducational school who had admitted that "most of the students are engaged to each other before leaving college"; and he quoted Horace Mann, who remarked that coeducation in colleges and universities demanded "a care and vigilance brought . . . near to omniscient supervision." Seelye scoffed at the idea that coeducation led to more mature graduates: "There is no evidence that co-education has eradicated or naturally changed the most deeply-rooted passions of human nature." He could not imagine why some people believed the presence of women would improve the morals of men. The experience of the theater, he said, proved the contrary: when women, instead of boys, began playing female characters on the stage, he said, "morals became more corrupt." Toward the end of his address he also took issue with the idea that coeducation was economically more feasible than separate education, an argument forwarded by Henry Ward Beecher, among others. "If coeducation is to give inferior types of manhood and womanhood," he concluded, "then it is not economy, but parsimony, which would force young ladies into male colleges for the sake of saving funds."

Like Tyler, the Reverend John M. Greene '53 served as a Smith trustee. In the biological sketch of Sophia Smith he presented at Smith's Quartercentennial, Greene may have described his view of the ideal woman: "She put a supreme value on education. . . . She also had an exalted idea of womanhood, and thanked God for her feminine birthright. She rather pitied men than envied them."

Greene also said it was important that men as well as women serve as professors, since "it is a misfortune for young women or young men to be educated wholly by their own kind." The irony of this last assertion, that of course there were no female professors or instructors at Amherst, and no women invited to speak in the coeducation debate, was probably lost on Greene. Perhaps because women served as teachers in every household, as wives and mothers, he saw no contradiction.

Tyler, Seelye, and Greene shared an idealized concept of women's intellectual capabilities and capacity for more leadership in the home, at the same time that they questioned the female temperament and discipline. Certainly, women could learn classics, and they should; but knowledge would facilitate their role as wives and mothers in the traditional female sphere, a sphere governed by feeling and intuition. Placing women in competition with men would damage the frail, female constitution; and to place women in Amherst, a school moving from a holistic faith in education to a more worldly orientation symbolized by courses in political science and economy and literature—would defeat the purpose of women's education. It would be unsexing.

Samuel Bowles and Henry Ward Beecher opposed Tyler, Seelye, and Greene. Beecher scoffed at fears that a coeducational Amherst would blur the distinction between men and women when he joked at the Semicentennial, "I was brought up in my sister's school at Hartford. That accounts for my womanish ways." But the concern persisted, as evidenced by his pressing assertion, "A woman would make a womanish use of this education. . . . Highly developed in culture her refining influences will be richer and more heavenly." Beecher placed women on the same pedestal as did Seelye and Greene and Tyler, but he was not afraid that coeducation would lead women to fall from that perch.

Editor Bowles made this point of view known in an 1870 editorial in the *Springfield Republican*. After announcing the terms of Sophia Smith's will, he observed that while her purpose was "a noble one . . . we almost wish she had bequeathed a smaller sum to some existing college, on condition that girls should be admitted thereto with equal privileges." Bowles believed that women needed an education equal to men's and that they needed to receive it in the same classrooms: "The qualities of the two sexes supplement each other in school." Bowles argued that "it would have been better boldly to confront the difficulties, such as they are, of educating the two sexes in college together, and to have added to the funds of Amherst College a sum sufficient to open a common course and on terms more liberal than now exist anywhere."

It is entirely possible, however, that Beecher and Bowles would never have squared off against the old guard of Seelye and Tyler had two young women not forced the issue. In that summer of the Semicentennial, a

Miss Frazier of Watertown and a Miss Lidd of Lynn applied for admission to Amherst. Under normal procedure, a prospective student could take the entrance exam either in July or September. The trustees first considered the applications of the women on Tuesday, July 12, the day before the Semicentennial celebration. Rather than decide the questions on the spot, the board appointed a committee of trustees—Beecher, President William A. Stearns, and the Reverend William Paine—to study the issue. Perhaps intentionally, the committee was asked to present its recommendations in October—a full month after the women would need to take the entrance exams!

That afternoon, the leading sons of Amherst debated coeducation before the returning alumni. Much of the debate centered on the question of whether or not coeducation would blur the distinction between the roles of the sexes. Certainly, the Amherst faculty—professors like L. Clark and Julius Seelye, and William Tyler—thought it would, as did alumni like Greene, who were closely affiliated with the college. Men like Massachusetts Governor Alexander Bullock, Beecher, and Bowles— alumni with a fair amount of distance from the isolated, pastoral school— disagreed.

Bullock, a trustee, offered a scholarship endowment for female students, telling the gathered alumni, "I am . . . in favor of making the experiment of admitting our friends heretofore excluded, to the privileges of the classes, if they shall . . . establish the usual qualifications." Beecher spoke next, asserting that the question "whether women shall have the right to the highest education which it is possible to gain in America, has been settled, and that long ago." He continued: "Why should we put two schools to do the work of one? Are women so much like men that they need but one church, one catechism, one minister; alike in almost everything, and yet so different that they need two sets of instructors, one for men, and one for women in ordinary matters of education? . . . Amherst is for universal education. If a man be black, and is fully prepared, or if a woman is fully qualified, its doors will open to them. Amherst should lead in this march of progress."

Finally, the 1871 debate ended rather abruptly. Professor Edwards Park of the Andover Theological Seminary, after promising that he would not speak about coeducation, could not resist telling an anecdote.

Admitting that he favored the higher education of women, and that he believed Smith College would "contribute much to the true honor of women," Park said he feared women would be a distracting influence to Amherst men if they shared in the same classrooms. He recounted the story of an Amherst student who was neglecting his studies. One professor concluded that the student either had headaches or a fever; another assumed that the boy was in financial trouble. Finally, President Heman Humphrey decided that the "remissness of the young man is owing to a shock which he has received from a *gal*-van-ic battery." L. Clark Seelye recalled later: "the uproarious laughter and prolonged applause which followed his address showed clearly enough that the audience made the obvious application of his illustration, and the attempt to make Amherst coeducational failed."

It failed in 1871 partly because most Amherst students themselves had little or no desire for coeducation. *The Amherst Student* concluded that the answer to the question "Shall we admit women?" was a decided "no." Wrote the editors, "the question is simply one of expedience . . . Amherst College was never intended for the education of females." The professors, courses, and even "the arrangement" of buildings and campus did not take into consideration "the peculiar wants and requirements of women." As women had a different sphere from men outside of college, so should "widely different educational means and methods . . . be employed" for them at college. "It is hardly conceivable that . . . the admission of women into men's colleges, the restraining, refining, and ennobling influences of home life, will ever be brought to bear, any more than at present, upon young men in process of education." More importantly, "No such intimacy or friendship, as now exists among classmates, could or would be encouraged or permitted between students of different sex. . . . Why delude ourselves with the notion that the presence of females whose approbation, should act as a stimulus and incentive to right action, would prevent a single student from becoming, or remaining, a spendthrift, a drunkard, or a debauchee, when the love for mother, sister or friends fails to restrain him."

One student who responded to the editorial systematically pulled apart the editors' logic, wondering exactly what privileges would be abridged by the admission of women, and whether what the editors called a privilege was not actually an abuse of privilege: "The privileges which would be taken from us are the very same which our parents, our friends, the Faculty, and the trustees have been trying for years to induce us to forego. The privilege of abusing innocent Freshmen, the privilege of destroying college property, the privilege of making night dreadful with hideous noises . . . and the privilege of being sent home in disgrace,—these, forsooth, are the *'privileges'* which would be 'materially abridged,' by the admission of women to our monastic community." The writer admitted that the opinion of the newspaper was that of the majority of the campus. He estimated that 20 students, and certainly no more than one tenth of the college, would welcome women "with unbounded joy." But, he said, "All reforms in government or society rise from very small beginnings," and he cited the antislavery and temperance movements as examples.

In the 1870s there were often petty—if enthusiastic—acts of violence resulting from class and fraternity rivalry. Upperclassmen caned lowerclassmen, and class-against-class tugs of war were little more than excuses for college brawls. For the students of Amherst College, perhaps, coeducation was unacceptable because the entrance of women might have prohibited the sort of camaraderie and class rivalry endemic to the environment. Only at college could males revolt against conventional mores and laugh at propriety. Women at Amherst might actually have interfered with the life of the fraternity, the literary society, and the unsubtle rites of passage.

Bowles continued pressing for coeducation that fall, but with less urgency. The *Republican* hinted it was unfair that two women who had applied to the college could not take the written and oral examinations with their male contemporaries, but instead had to "await at home the action of the trustees on their applications."

The women wound up waiting some time. The trustees did not seriously discuss coeducation again until November 23. The matter was not voted on because a quorum was lacking, but "it was found that all present were strongly opposed to the projected innovation." The following month, the board voted officially not to admit women, and the issue died. Amherst was changing by its Semicentennial, but few members of the college were prepared for coeducation. That change would have to wait for another century.

An air almost of infallibility surrounds the work and reputation of Frederick Law Olmsted, the American who did more than anyone else to establish the field of landscape architecture. Olmsted is still thought to be its greatest practitioner. So it is surprising, perhaps even refreshing, to discover that his judgment was not always the last word. In this account of his work for Amherst we see him declare, for instance, that the oldest campus buildings—landmarks like Johnson Chapel, the Octagon, and Barrett Hall—are "extremely uninteresting and of little value. The new buildings," Olmsted wrote, "including those to be erected in the next century or two, will certainly engage the eye and impress the mind a great deal more than the old ones." Tastes change, and those earliest buildings are now highly prized while some newer ones are disparaged. Still, those who visit the campus, or work and study there, may see—in the gentle curve of a path, the placement of a spire, an open vista—the faint but agreeable touch of the master's hand. Information for this article was drawn from Olmsted correspondence held in the Library of Congress and the College Archives, and from plans at the Olmsted National Historic Site in Brookline, Massachusetts.

THE OLMSTEDS AT AMHERST

A‌MHERST COLLEGE IN 1870 turned to America's great landscape architect, Frederick Law Olmsted, for advice on a small matter: finding the best site on campus for a new college church. William F. Stearns had given $30,000 to the college for such a building, and President William A. Stearns, his father, proudly took charge of the project.

The request came to Olmsted when the landscape architect, in partnership with Calbert Vaux, was in the midst of a flourishing and brilliant career. In 1870 he was busy with the further development of his masterpiece, New York City's Central Park; in the same year he also was designing parks for Brooklyn, Hartford, Chicago, and Buffalo. Somehow he found time for Amherst.

Olmsted's reply to President Stearns drew a large picture in response to a small question. More was at issue than the placement of one building, he argued; a bold new design for the campus was needed. The college, less than 50 years old, was still oriented toward the west and the town common, with most of its buildings ranged around South Pleasant Street (then known as Broadway). Regarding this as the focus of campus activity, college officials thought they might build the church in the center of things, near the Octagon. Olmsted was horrified. For one thing, the Octagon didn't impress him; it could "hardly be expected to remain permanently," he said, and when it was gone a church near the site "would seem to have been shouldered in to a corner where it would be completely detached from the College and be but awkwardly related to the village."

"In studying the structural plans of a college," he wrote, "not the use of years but of centuries should be considered." He then launched into an essay at the end of this article ("Disencumber your plans . . ."). He recommended that the college reorient itself inwardly, "around a common center"—a "quadrangle"—and that it begin the process by placing the church at the center of the new enclosure.

Over the next 55 years the college frequently sought first Olmsted's counsel and later that of his son and successor, Frederick Law Olmsted Jr. Eventually the son found the relationship with Amherst unrewarding; more often than not, it seemed, the professionals' advice wasn't followed. But the relationship began happily, for the college accepted the senior Olmsted's advice about the church, placed it where he suggested, and began in this way to build the campus around a projected quadrangle that would have been much larger than today's freshman quad.

Stearns Church, designed by William Appleton Potter, was completed in 1873. The church was razed in 1948, but its narrow steeple still rises above the center of the campus. President Stearns was delighted with the new building (though it was, he acknowledged, "a little *churchy* for us old puritans, Mr. Potter, the Architect, being the son of a Bishop . . ."). College officials were also interested in Olmsted's broader scheme, so he followed his letter to Stearns with a grand, rectangular plan—the "Preliminary Sketch" that is illustrated on page 98. It was not an exact drawing, he emphasized, but "it may be intelligently discussed and the general policy involved be approved or discountenanced." The plan looked like a miniature of Olmsted's prizewinning design for Central Park—including little Columbus Circles at two of the corners.

No official college response to this sketch has been found, but it's clear that while the idea of a quadrangle was adopted in part, the college over time "discountenanced" other basic features of the plan, such as the proposal for avenues along the northern, eastern, and southern sides of the campus, the removal of the Octagon, and the addition of wings to Johnson Chapel.

If Amherst did not rush to carry out Olmsted's entire design, it continued to value and seek his advice. Stearns's successor, President Seelye, told the trustees in 1884 that the college a year earlier had asked Olmsted for "a complete plan for the grading & roads & walks of the whole college grounds. This has been done, much to our acceptance, and work according to it has begun," he said. "To complete it will yet take some time and much expense, but in the present condition of the college I know of no expenditure likely to give us better returns." The designs for campus walks and roadways bore the distinctive Olmsted look: a Tiffany-like quality that seemed to anticipate Art Nouveau. An art historian has described one of the main characteristics of Art Nouveau as "a long, sensitive, sinuous line that reminds us of seaweed or creeping plants."

Meticulous in all his concerns, Olmsted personally drafted instructions for the landscaping, even directing that "before the surface soil is returned a dressing of coarse barnyard manure is to be spread upon the subsoil and plowed in." In one aside he wrote, "I will venture to advise the Trustees also that the trees of the College Ground should be carefully surveyed with a view to the removal of some that are failing and greatly injuring the development and vitality of their juniors and also with a view to additional plantings." Olmsted at this time also advised the college about a site for the new Pratt gymnasium—today's Charles Pratt dormitory—which was centered on the south side of the larger quadrangle that Olmsted had proposed.

A question arose in the 1890s regarding plans for a proposed new science laboratory (later Fayerweather Hall). William Austin Dickinson, the college treasurer, had chosen a site he preferred over one recommended by Olmsted. President Merrill Gates, who was Seelye's successor, urged the Olmsted firm to attend a meeting on the subject as soon as possible. "The fact that there may possibly be some difference of opinion as to the site chosen makes it particularly desirable that the opinion of Mr. Frederick Olmsted be obtained at this interview," Gates wrote, "since his opinion on similar occasions in the history of the College has been received as substantially decisive."

By this time, however, most of the Olmsted business had been passed to Olmsted's two sons, John and Frederick Jr. The brothers replied that their father, now in his 70s, was "withdrawing from all but a few of the larger works of the firm and feels confidence in the judgment of his partners." They said the senior Olmsted "regretted that Mr. Dickinson insisted upon pushing the physical and chemical laboratory away from the position first recommended [probably a site closer to the present

Morrow Dormitory], but [Olmsted Sr.] hopes that a still more imposing and handsome building may eventually occupy this site."

In line with his 1870 concept, which would place new buildings with "a double frontage outwardly upon a public street, the other around a common center," Olmsted had expected that the laboratory would face north and south. But Gates now called the sons' attention to another problem— a difficulty seen by physics professor Arthur L. Kimball. "Prof. Kimball has serious doubts (upon mature reflection and the effort to rearrange his working-rooms) as to the feasibility of the present plan for the building, if it faces toward the south," Gates wrote, "since this will give him no western or late afternoon light for any purpose or in any room in his part of the building. He also dreads laboratory gases and odors which would be swept directly toward him by the prevailing westerly winds."

Gates finally decided that "the working uses of the laboratory should predominate over architectural and landscape effect (if there is a clash between them)," with the result that Fayerweather was placed according to Kimball's wishes rather than Olmsted's. This thwarted whatever prospect there was for building the grand quadrangle the senior Olmsted had proposed. So the scheme of 1870 began coming apart. The brothers accepted the decision and served as consultants for landscaping and the design of approaches around Fayerweather and north of Walker Hall in the years that followed.

Then, in 1903, alumni from the Class of 1893 spearheaded a dramatic beautification scheme. They enlisted the 1867 graduate William R. Mead of the prestigious architectural firm of McKim, Mead, & White, along with Frederick Law Olmsted Jr. and other nationally known figures, to serve on a new commission that would make a comprehensive plan for the campus. The *Boston Transcript* said the appointment of such eminent people gave Amherst "a foremost position in the movement for beautiful exteriors."

Mead and Olmsted did most of the work of the commission, shaping plans and directing surveys. Before one of their campus visits, the trustee Charles Pratt wrote to President George Harris, urging that no one interrupt the two men's creative genius: "I telephoned to Mr. Mead," Pratt told him, "and find that both he and Mr. Olmsted prefer to be absolutely alone. As this is their wish I think they should be left alone 'to discuss matters and blackguard each other's ideas,' as Mr. Mead expresses it."

After one of these sessions, Olmsted wrote in a memorandum that he and Mead "agreed that the three old buildings at the summit of the hill, consisting of the chapel and the dormitory on either side of it, should be regarded as permanent and as the culminating feature; that the space to the east of these buildings should be treated as much as possible as a plateau surrounded by buildings and promenade from which there would be a sweeping outlook over the surrounding country."

The idea of a hilltop quadrangle surrounded by buildings was more modest than the scheme Olmsted's father had initiated 35 years earlier. Also, architectural tastes were changing by the early 1900s. While the senior Olmsted in 1870 had dismissed Johnson Chapel and other buildings of College Row as "extremely uninteresting and of little value," and said the newer buildings—like the neo-Gothic Walker Hall—were much finer, the son now found that the first buildings were "charming," and he recommended that they "be accepted and preserved as the central features of any project." The *Transcript* quoted an Amherst faculty member's opinion that buildings of the classical Greek form, like Johnson Chapel, were the best of the lot: "That's the only model for a college anyway," the professor sniffed. "We are founded on the classics, and Gothic's only a barbarian idea." The paper noted that Amherst had a mixture of both, "But considering the architectural 'reign of terror' of two or three decades ago, Amherst has reason for congratulation on what it escaped— as compared with Harvard, for instance, where you find debased Gothic, Richardson, Romanesque and classical colonialism within swearing distance of one another."

The commission's work culminated in a printed report and two large plaster models of the college, one depicting the campus buildings and grounds as they existed at the time, and the other showing how the college would look if the recommendations were carried out. The models have disappeared, but the recommendations are in the report written by Olmsted. These were:

1. To preserve College Row. (Done.)
2. To remove Williston Hall and the Appleton Cabinet, described as "crude, ill designed and poorly built structures of an unfortunate period [the 1850s] in American architecture." (The two buildings were modified but remain to this day.)

3. To improve the east end of Johnson Chapel, giving it a "second front." (Done.)

4. To remove the Octagon and its knoll "so as to open up a good view of the Johnson Chapel across the Common from the highway in front of the Library [now Morgan Hall] and the President's house." (Never done.)

5. To preserve the open fields on the slopes to the south and east, leaving the views. (The fields to the south, now the athletic fields, are preserved, but buildings have risen on the eastern slope.)

6. To develop, in time, an "orderly group" of new buildings along the northern edge of the campus. (Done, but not exactly in the order recommended.)

7. To build a central heating plant near the railroad tracks. (Done.)

There should be flexibility in college planning, Olmsted concluded, "yet unless there be some plan, the essential points of which are unflinchingly adhered to, the ultimate result of meeting each temporary problem as it arises must in the long run lead to a confused, inconvenient and extravagant result."

The trustees voted in 1906 to accept the plan with vague qualifications, adopting it "as a guide to be followed . . . so far as shall be possible with due regard to the pecuniary and other interests of the College in the view of the Board for the time being." Scarcely more than half of the recommendations have been followed in the years since that time. These plans, like many others, apparently became victim of practical considerations, contrary opinions, changes in taste, and changes in the college administration.

By 1914, when older members of the commission had died, there was an effort to reconstitute the 1903 group with Olmsted, Mead, and new members. Charles D. Norton, one of the 1893 graduates who had advanced the earlier plan, complained to Mead that it would "put us in an awkward position with our own classmates . . . if the old effort seemed to result merely in a plaster of Paris plan and a paper commission." And to his classmate Frederick S. Allis, the college's alumni secretary, he wrote, "I got to feeling a little warm under the collar over the idea that the Commission had not been used; and indeed, I found that Mr. Mead felt the same."

Mead, ever loyal, agreed to head a revived effort, and to reenlist Olmsted. But both men had lost their earlier enthusiasm. Mead noted in a private letter to Olmsted that, while their earlier plan had been "recognized," a few years later Morris Pratt Dormitory had been built "on a site north of Walker Hall and ostensibly on one of the sites proposed by us, but without regard to the grade we had laid down. I was not consulted about the location of this building," Mead said, "and consequently got rather miffed and lost interest in the work."

Replied Olmsted, "I hesitate to accept service on your [proposed new] Commission under the circumstances only because I think a bad principle is involved in calling upon professional men to do such work without compensation." He said the pay "might be very small, proportionate to professors' salaries if you like, but the principle of compensation ought to be recognized."

A sum was agreed upon, and Olmsted continued to advise the college, sporadically, for another 10 years. Mead wanted him to visit Amherst in 1917 to discuss grading around the new Converse Library but learned from Olmsted's brother John that his friend had fallen out of an apple tree and sprained his back at his summer home in Chesham, New Hampshire. "I do not think there is the least probability that he would feel able to go to Amherst on Sept. 7th and stand about on the ground looking into the problem you refer to," the brother said.

In 1925, in correspondence with Stanley King '03, the trustee and future president of Amherst, Olmsted applauded plans for a new road defining the four sides of the old quadrangle, but he questioned whether Barrett Hall was worth preserving (it was not "architecturally very happy," he thought), and again he urged the removal of the Octagon.

At about this time the landscape architect also inspected the campus in person. King wrote him later, asking for his bill; apparently he had also asked Olmsted what had happened to the commission of 1914. Olmsted replied in one of his last known—and chilliest—letters to Amherst. The trustees' vote to establish a new commission apparently had been "a well-disposed gesture not followed up by the persistent orderly administrative action necessary to secure results," he wrote. "At all events, it seems to have died so completely that I had forgotten all about it."

As for the fee, Olmsted went on, "I do not ordinarily charge a college as much as I should a commercial land company or an industrial corporation for equivalent services, but being in a chronic condition of having more demands on my time than I have time to give to them and finding that in fact colleges are not usually very satisfactory clients (in the sense of my being able to see important physical results from the time I devote advising to them), I am unwilling to make this differential a very large one. . . .

"In this case, since I did not take the trouble to arrive at any understanding about the charges of the visit, I shall be perfectly content to send in a bill for any amount you think proper. But I shall not expect in the future, if called upon, to charge less than $150 for a day's conference and advice based on it."

King wrote promptly that $150 would be "entirely satisfactory." But it appears that Amherst never again sought an Olmsted's advice. —DCW

Olmsted to President Stearns, 1870: "Disencumber your plans"

When your college was founded Amherst was a small rural village remote from navigation or other thronged ways of men. The original college buildings were placed on the brow of a hill standing detached from the village and were made to front [toward the west] so as to appear to the best advantage from the direction in which they would first be seen by observers approaching upon or from the nearest route of general public travel. The banks of the Connecticut then held the importance almost of a seacoast, so that the region to the eastward of Amherst Hill would be often referred to as the back country.

But, when at length, with difficulty, hesitation and by successive stages an important railroad thoroughfare was established on the East Side of the village it necessarily disarranged affairs. It is already plain that the village is changing front. Not only so but an advancing movement has been forced upon it. Owing to the strongly rigid habits of the old rural inhabitants the change is of course not rapid but that it has begun and is irresistible is perfectly evident. The village is no longer rural and retired. Hundreds now take Amherst as their way and see it in passing where one did so fifty years ago, and most who have occasion to refer to the Connecticut Valley in connection with the village speak of it as "in *back* of the town." It is reasonable to suppose that before the college is much older the revolution will have been completed. There is not the slightest ground for expecting a return to the original state of things.

As to the future of the college, it must move likewise—not rapidly but surely and continuously. Even if the number of its undergraduates should not be materially enlarged, it will undoubtedly receive a more elaborate equipment and gain in all the desiderata of a seat of learning and of Science. Every ten or twenty years some notable addition or improvement will be made.

The buildings which have been recently added to the College series are much finer and make much more impression upon the mind of an observer than the old ones, which consequently, and especially as they more commonly seem now behind them, seem designed to stand in the background. None of the recent and more imposing buildings face to the westward. Clearly the college has begun to face about like the town.

In the next stop or two of your progress you may try to conform to the original theory or you may go on in a desultory way putting down a building merely according to the convenience of the moment without any concern for general effects or permanent convenience, but you can not go far in either way without running into confusion and embarrassment; the college will be lost in the midst of the village of which it will be an undivided part. The only way in which you can avoid this is to accept the necessity of a change of the old idea of a single front on the main street of the village and toward the Connecticut River, and a back yard on the other side.

Looking ahead, at all beyond our own time, the old group of brick buildings is, except for historical association, extremely uninteresting and of little value. The new buildings, including those to be erected during the next century or two, will certainly engage the eye and impress the mind a great deal more than the old ones. Some of the new ones will almost certainly stand to the Eastward of the present brick range in positions equally elevated. If there is any considerable body of buildings to the West, it will be on lower ground and will be separated from the main body by a public street. The roads or walks connecting the two bodies of buildings must be laid out mainly in a direction diagonal to their fronts which would still further tend to produce an effect of disunity of design and confusion and disorganization.

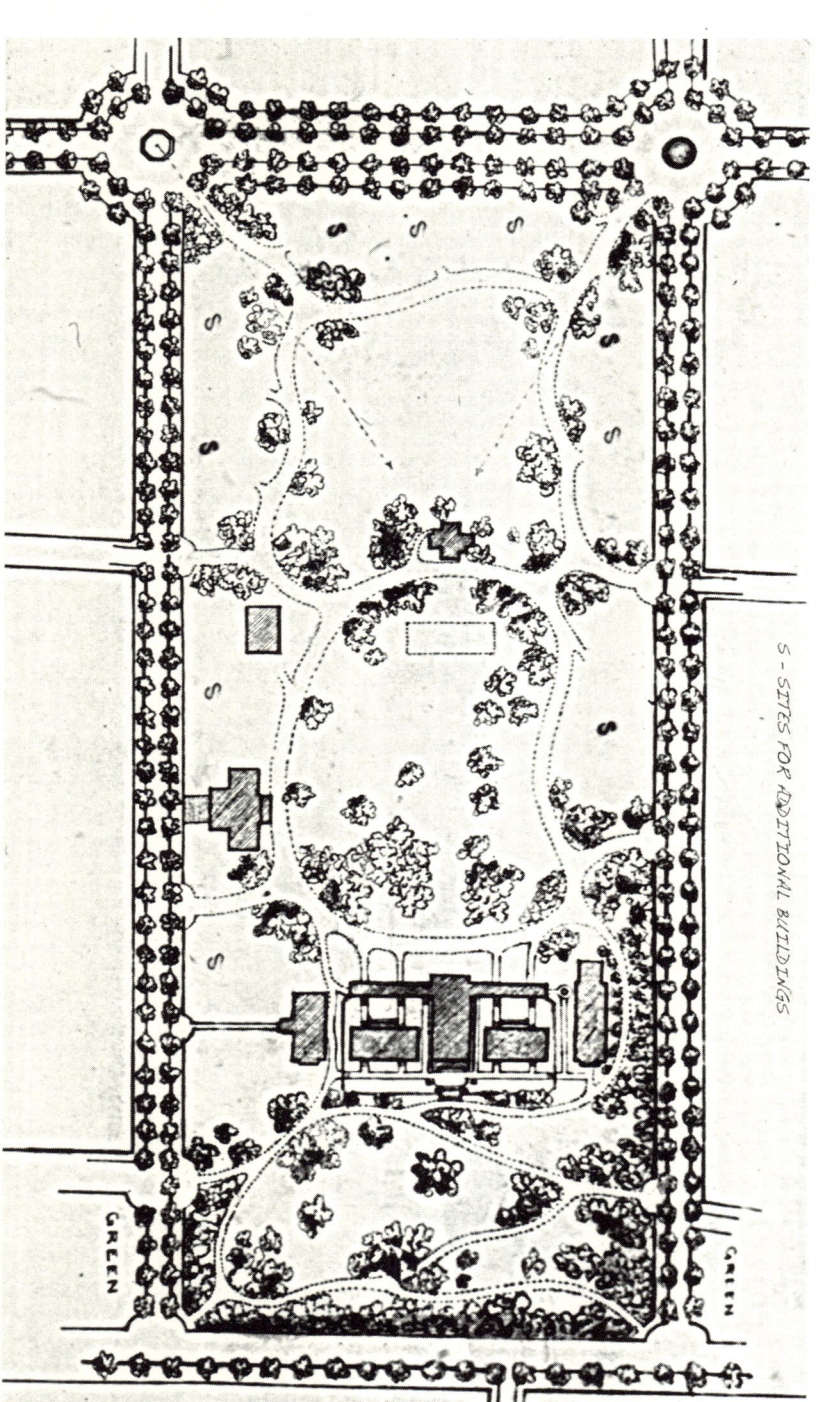

The long boulevard directly above this caption marks the northern edge of Olmsted's plan. A rectangle near the center is his site for Stearns Church. Old Chapel Row is west of it (to the right). Inside the tree-lined avenues, the letter 's' shows where buildings could be sited around a single large quadrangle extending east from College Row to the railroad (not shown, far left). *Courtesy of Olmsted National Historic Site.*

S - SITES FOR ADDITIONAL BUILDINGS

GREEN

GREEN

The remedy is to be found by freeing the mind from the association established by circumstances which have been super-ceded; disencumber your plans from regard to the few buildings—comparatively unimportant with reference to the future—which awkwardly dovetail it to the village, cut loose from the village as well as the Connecticut River and build the college up by itself about a centre of its own.

If it must be conceived of as fronting one way more than another it should be faced about as the village has been toward the railroad, approaching strangers, and the rising sun.

Let the declivity, formerly considered as the front yard but impractical as an approach, and which is now on the right of the angular entrance from the village, take the character of a quiet pleasure ground, in connection with the old village green of which it was originally a part.

Let the old range of brick buildings be regarded as the West side of a quadrangle. East of them there is a plateau and beyond it is a moderate slope to the railway. The old back yard—which has gradually taken more of the character of the college campus—might be extended in this direction toward the railway till it should be made nearly twice its present size. There would then be sides for three times as many buildings ranged around it, as there are in the whole of your present collection. Each building so placed might have a double frontage outwardly upon a public street, the other around a common center.

The principal entrance to the whole series instead of being as now in a corner and striking in diagonally between buildings from the rear of the village, should be at the middle of the East side of the Campus, which should here abut upon a broad mall and avenue laid out parallel to the railway, and intersecting the new main East and West Street of the village beyond the station and near the new Congregational Church.

If this suggestion should be approved, clearly the proposed College Church should be placed near the centre of the quadrangle, facing the Eastern entrance. Its position would be on the brow of the hill, the trees now growing there would group gracefully about it and it would stand in imposing, appropriate and beautiful relation to all the neighboring buildings and the surrounding landscapes.

—Frederick Law Olmsted

At the unhappy end of his Amherst presidency in 1923, the college's trustees agreed to one of Alexander Meiklejohn's wishes and did not give details of why they had asked him to resign. The various reports were placed under lock and key, and there they remained, the subject of mystery and blind speculation, for 59 years. Meiklejohn went on to pursue a long and brilliant career at other colleges and universities, and he was welcomed back to Amherst on two or three cordial occasions. In 1982, after he and all the other principals in the Amherst controversy had passed from the scene, the records were finally opened. They show that the trustees found the dynamic young president too cavalier with his finances and too contentious with his faculty. When this report for *Amherst* magazine, "The Story in the Meiklejohn Files," was going to press later in 1982, a few college officials did not want it printed, fearing it could reopen old wounds. But President Julian Gibbs supported the story's publication, saying he would "take the heat" if any developed. The two-part article appeared in the Fall 1982 and Spring 1983 issues. The magazine received many letters, and only a few objected to the disclosures (one Meiklejohn admirer said he was "shocked" by the first installment and hoped the second would not appear). Most of the other letters were favorable. Readers said they were glad the story was out in the open, no longer the dark, sealed mystery it had been for so long.

THE STORY IN
THE MEIKLEJOHN FILES
I. Early Trouble

A̲ᴛ ᴛʜᴇ ʀᴇǫᴜᴇsᴛ ᴏғ his friend Dwight Morrow and other Amherst trustees, Harlan Fiske Stone attended an urgent meeting in Boston in 1923. A few weeks earlier, the trustees had decided that the president of Amherst, Alexander Meiklejohn, would have to resign. They wanted legal advice, and Stone—the dean of Columbia Law School and an 1894 Amherst alumnus—was one of five men who met in a Boston law office on June 13 to discuss the situation.

Stone had traveled up to Boston from New York. On the train going home, he took out a legal notepad and wrote a summary of the main points the men had agreed upon. They believed that "sufficient cause existed for the removal of the President," and that if Meiklejohn refused to step down, they might then consider charges. Stone sent the memo to Morrow, an 1895 graduate, with a note apologizing for his bumpy handwriting. "The New Haven roadbed is pretty rough," he explained, "but I think you can make most of it out." The penciled yellow pages that Stone wrote in 1923, nearly 20 years before he became Chief Justice of the United States, are now in the "Private Meiklejohn Papers" at the College Archives.

Meiklejohn, a brilliant educator who in 11 years had won national prominence for himself and for Amherst, resigned under protest on June 19, 1923—six days after the meeting in Boston. A public uproar followed, and *l'affaire Meiklejohn* became the biggest controversy in the college's history. For 59 years, the trustees' official silence about the matter made it all the more intriguing. Last May [1982], the Board of Trustees voted for the first time to remove restrictions on the Meiklejohn Papers and make them available for inspection.

The files tell an unhappy story, showing in copious detail that the Board found Meiklejohn unfit to be president: unfit in the way that he handled his own finances and in the way he dealt with the trustees and the faculty. Before examining these files—the private letters and reports that describe Meiklejohn's deepening troubles with money and colleagues—let us look briefly at those aspects of the story that are publicly known: who Meiklejohn was when he came to the college in 1912, the lively impression he made, and the kind of education he stood for.

Amherst by most accounts was in the doldrums when, at 67, the Reverend George Harris announced his retirement from the presidency in 1911 and the trustees elected Meiklejohn to succeed him. Several of the greatest teachers on the faculty had died or retired, or were about to retire, and it was time for an infusion of new energy. Although he was only 40, Alexander Meiklejohn had made a bright name for himself in 14 years at his alma mater, Brown University, where he was a philosophy professor and dean.

It was immediately clear that the arrival of the young president marked the start of a bold new era. His inaugural address had a vigorous tone. "Surely it is one function of the liberal college . . . to give [students] an appetite for the pleasures of thinking, to make them sensitive to the joys of appreciation and understanding, to show them how sweet and captivating and wholesome are the games of the mind," Meiklejohn said. "To give our boys that zest, that delight in things intellectual, to give them an appreciation of a kind of life which is well worth living, to make them men of intellectual culture—that certainly is one part of the work of any liberal college." But more was needed. The course of study, he said, should have a design to it; a "willingness to allow students to wander about in the college curriculum is one of the most characteristic expressions of a certain intellectual agnosticism, a kind of intellectual bankruptcy, into which, in spite of all our wealth of information, the spirit of the time has fallen," he said. The curriculum should provide "a new synthesis," and this called for a special kind of faculty, because "more and more" the chairs in colleges were occupied by men who had a only a "special interest," he said, "and it is through them that we attempt to give our boys a liberal education, which the teachers themselves have not achieved."

If Meiklejohn's zeal for reform made the old guard nervous, it inspired the young. J. Seelye Bixler, a 1916 graduate and now trustee emeritus, has recalled the students' devotion to Meiklejohn. "On the platform he had personal charm, pungent wit, dazzling dialectical skill, and the eloquence of a convinced crusader. The chapel services he led were not to be missed," Bixler wrote. "We went out from chapel ready to face up to any enemy, eager to show our loyalty to a great president of a great college who had summoned us to a task that would call for the utmost in devotion. In the classroom he was without a rival. No one who took his sophomore course in logic can forget its thrills."

Among others, the reaction to Meiklejohn's youthful, aggressive intellect was not always so favorable. Bruce Barton, the advertising executive and a 1907 graduate, wrote to a friend in 1923 that he had recently talked in Amherst with prominent local author Ray Stannard Baker. Baker told him that sometimes when he called on Meiklejohn at home he would "find him with his fists up in the air, so to speak, ready to give battle on the other side of any question that might arise." Shortly after Meiklejohn resigned, alumni secretary Frederick S. Allis '93 wrote in a confidential memoir that the president had always been different things to different people: to those who agreed with him, he was gentle and charming, but to the person who "questioned his ability and his ideas," Allis reported, "there appears the dour Scot with a hard, set face."

Beyond a small group of top college officials and the trustees, almost nobody knew in detail about another side of Alexander Meiklejohn: the disarray in his financial affairs. It proved central to his undoing. Difficulties began almost as soon as Meiklejohn was first hired in 1912 at a salary of $7,900, and they reached crisis proportions in 1920–21, when his salary was $12,500 and after he had been helped out of debt with private gifts— mostly from trustees—totaling $25,460 over seven years. While the salary figures include an entertainment allowance, the Meiklejohns lived in the president's house rent-free and the college paid for their utilities. When Meiklejohn's salary was $12,500, the average full professor's salary was $3,883. The figures come from amounts given in a confidential trustee report on Meiklejohn's finances that is dated May 26, 1923. That report, and private papers of Dwight Morrow, are among the documents that have now been opened.

As early as 1913–14 Meiklejohn found that his income of $7,900 wasn't enough to cover his expenses, and he began to overdraw his salary annually and then accept private contributions from trustees to cover the excess at the end of each year. At first, some trustees quietly condoned this procedure and perhaps encouraged it. Before Meiklejohn came to Amherst, Dean George D. Olds wrote to him that he had asked President Harris about the financial demands of the job, and Olds said he learned, "as anticipated," that Harris "spent far more than his salary." (Harris's salary in 1911–12, including an entertainment allowance, was $6,400.) Olds told Meiklejohn he was certain that the trustees would "view the whole question in a large way and strive to remove every obstacle of a financial kind which may stand in the way of the untrammeled and most efficient service of its new president."

The trustee who tried to remove these hurdles was John Woodruff Simpson '71, senior member of the Simpson, Thacher, & Bartlett law firm in New York and chairman of the trustees' finance committee. In 1915, when Simpson asked committee colleagues for $4,000 to help Meiklejohn, he told them he would apply $2,450 of it "to reimburse the treasury for the President's overdrafts, and the remainder in supplying his further requirements."

The arrangement was criticized by at least two who contributed: George A. Plimpton '76, head of the New York publishing firm of Ginn & Co. and the trustees' chairman, and Charles M. Pratt '79, manager of the Pratt family's Standard Oil fortune and director of banks, railroads, and industrial companies. "Enclosed please find my check for one thousand dollars to help Meiklejohn out," Plimpton wrote to Simpson in August 1915. "Now I never parted with money with more difficulty than I do with this. There are so many ways in which I could have spent this thousand to the advantage of Amherst College; but there is no use discussing this—only I don't want ever to do it again." Pratt also sent a contribution, but he said it would be his last. He asked Simpson and the others "to excuse me from joining you again in this laudable but mistaken method of solving a personal problem."

Despite these feelings, Pratt and Plimpton made further contributions a year later, when Meiklejohn again needed money. The president told Simpson that his overdraft for 1915–16 would be at least $2,500. The year, he said, had given him "a good chance for watching income and expense, and there seems to be no question that my income is $4,500 too small. We have had no extra expense this year, no holidays except summer at the shore, no trips, no theatres or operas, no motor rides—nothing but just the expense of running this house which is our home, my office, and also general place of entertainment of guests."

In that same year an extraordinary, energetic alumnus joined the Amherst board. He was Dwight W. Morrow '95, who had left Simpson's law firm two years earlier to become a partner of J. P. Morgan & Co. The trustees appointed Morrow to the finance committee, and Simpson soon told his former associate about Meiklejohn's finances. "In April, 1917," Morrow later recalled, "Mr. Simpson told me that the President was unable to live upon his salary, that the College resources would not permit an increase of his salary at that time, and that he had been asking certain members of the Board to assist in making up the deficits. He told me that he himself was contributing $2,000 to this purpose, and asked me to contribute a like amount." Morrow agreed to match whatever amounts Simpson gave.

Overdrafts again were a problem in 1918, and Simpson decided that the trustees could not continue to patch up affairs with donations. "We have followed our late *modus vivendi* as long as we should," he wrote to the president, "and I feel now that the sooner we face the situation and work out a solution the better." Meiklejohn agreed. He pressed for increases in his salary and entertainment allowance, proposing that the total be raised to $12,500. "I beg of you to get this matter settled," he urged Simpson. "If I am not worth the amount, then let me go." Simpson replied two days later that the finance committee had voted the increase; later he wrote to a colleague that "the amount is large but it has been pretty clearly shown that the President can not do with less, so our alternative was to make the increase or prepare to part with him, which no one would wish to do."

While Meiklejohn's personal finances were troublesome, his work at Amherst was bringing the college wide and favorable recognition. Morrow's chief biographer, Harold Nicholson, observed that Meiklejohn's "efforts and his energy were, during the first few years, universally applauded." Later, the *New Republic* would say editorially that no other American college had "exhibited in comparable degree the intellectual life which has been stirring in Amherst during President Meiklejohn's regime." Meiklejohn's reputation was due largely to the contagion of his personality and ideals among the students, his success in bringing lively new teachers to the campus, and his curricular ideas.

The trustees saw that Meiklejohn was an asset. They wanted him at Amherst, so they gave him the raise he demanded. It did not seem to help. Sometimes reports reached the trustees that the Meiklejohns were remiss in paying their bills. In small-town Amherst, this was a source of embarrassing gossip. Later, when the board made discreet inquiries, it learned that Mason A. Dickinson, the local grocer, thought—"without looking at his book"—that Meiklejohn "was the only customer from whom he required a deposit in advance"; that the president at one time owed Deuel's Drug Store "for something over ten months' merchandise"; that the president had not paid bills of the physician, Dr. Nelson C. Haskell, for four years; and that Suprenant's Meat Market sold to the president's household "on C.O.D. only." The trustees learned in 1921 that the college was having to pay $1,000 or more a year for the Meiklejohns' gas and electric service, an amount "which would appear to be due to reckless waste," they were told. What was the principal drain on Meiklejohn's income? No precise answer is given in the papers at Amherst; a full answer may never be known. The president himself was rather ascetic. One luxury that the family indulged in might be expected from an educational reformer: instead of sending their boys to public schools, the Meiklejohns engaged private tutors. But occasional references in correspondence of the time also support the old and persistent report that Mrs. Meiklejohn was extravagant. Meiklejohn himself admitted that neither he nor his wife had "much business sense." And the very keenest business sense was needed during this World War period, years when the country experienced its sharpest inflation since the 1860s.

By 1919, word of the president's nonpayment of his bills had spread to alumni. Henry W. Lane '95, treasurer and manager of Monadnock Shoe Company in Keene, New Hampshire, wrote to ask Morrow, his classmate, if it wasn't "just as immoral" for Meiklejohn "not to pay his bills as it is for some other man to take the funds from an institution of savings?"

Lane also suggested that Meiklejohn was neglecting "the moral and religious life of the institution," and that "a sudden decapitation" might be best for the college.

With characteristic calm reason, Morrow replied that he had also received "a letter about the same character on the other side, insisting that the Trustees should at once decapitate certain members of the faculty who are betraying the College by libeling and slandering the President. I mention this to you to indicate that in this, as in everything else, there are two sides."

Morrow and most of his colleagues were still on Meiklejohn's side. But matters grew steadily worse in 1920 and 1921. Again, the problem was money. In 1919 Meiklejohn had asked for a paid sabbatical leave to begin in September 1920. The leave was poorly timed: the college was making plans for a much-needed capital campaign, one that would culminate in the institution's centennial celebration in 1921. But the trustees agreed to let him take his family to Europe. After all, it was understood when he was hired that he would not be asked to raise money.

The trustees named Dean George D. Olds to serve as acting president in the president's absence. And since $2,500 of Meiklejohn's $12,500 in official pay at the time was entertainment allowance, for the year Meiklejohn would be gone they voted Meiklejohn a salary of $10,000 and transferred the rest to Olds's account.

Meiklejohn accepted this arrangement. But in the year before he was to leave he again began to overdraw his salary. The raise in 1918 was supposed to end these overexpenditures, but the problem continued. In March 1920, Meiklejohn confided in a letter that one of his "reasons for wanting to get away next year is the desire to get free from the running of this establishment at the present scale of prices. It is quite impossible." He also called Morrow, who was then acting chairman of the finance committee, to ask for another raise. Morrow told Meiklejohn it would be awkward to give him one at that time, since the college was "running upon so large a deficit" and since there was "already a great disparity between the salaries of the highest paid professor and the President of the College." Again he offered to help out privately, and Meiklejohn agreed. At first he told Morrow that by July he probably would be overdrawn by $1,500; he soon revised the estimate to $3,000, and Morrow gave him that amount. As the end of the fiscal year drew closer, however, Meiklejohn found he was still overdrawn, this time by $2,476.

In the realm of personal finances, the president's single most damaging action was his handling of this debt to the college of $2,476—a sum equal at the time to almost two-thirds of the average salary for a professor. First, Meiklejohn told Morrow that he would reimburse the college for the overdraft if he was paid the customary $12,500 during his sabbatical year instead of $10,000. "I want to make this up out of next year if I can have the full salary," he explained. "I do not want help privately—though you know how much I appreciate the kindness of it."

Morrow acted quickly and sympathetically. Three days after Meiklejohn made his request, Morrow sent a confidential letter to Plimpton endorsing the idea. "If we allow him a salary of $12,500 during the year of his absence," Morrow explained, "he will really only have $10,000 because $2,500 of the amount has, I presume, already been drawn. I do not see how he could get along on less. . . . I have a very keen sympathy with the President in his inability to get along on his salary. . . . As a matter of fact, I doubt whether Mrs. Meiklejohn has ever really adjusted herself to the scale of living required of members of the Amherst faculty."

In July, Morrow went on vacation to rest up after the excitement—and to him, the disappointment—of the Republican convention in Chicago. With other Amherst friends he had worked hard to secure the presidential nomination for his old college classmate, Calvin Coolidge, the governor of Massachusetts. The Republicans nominated Senator Warren G. Harding instead, and then chose Coolidge as his vice presidential running mate.

Morrow was still on vacation when the Meiklejohns prepared to sail from New York to Italy aboard the steamship *Fernando Palasciano*. The trustees' confidential report on Meiklejohn's financial affairs, dated May 26, 1923, describes what happened next:

"Before sailing, [the president] saw Mr. Plimpton and told him he would not be able to make up the overdraft of $2,476 and still take the trip abroad, and asked Mr. Plimpton to write the Treasurer authorizing the President to withdraw the full $12,500 and let the $2,476 overdraft stand over. This was despite the fact that the extra $2,500 in his salary for the year 1920–21 had been expressly added in order to take care of this overdraft."

Under the circumstances, Plimpton saw no way to refuse. He wrote to the treasurer, H. W. Kidder: "While I have no authority to grant permission for this, yet as Mr. Morrow is away, I am willing to take responsibility with the anticipation that the action will be approved by the Finance Committee. If they do not give their approval, of course I will have to pay it myself, but I think it is the only thing to do for the present."

In effect, Meiklejohn was saying to the trustees who tried to help him: "I will keep the new $2,500 you are awarding me and remain in debt to the college for only the old amount of nearly $2,500 I owed beforehand." Nothing indicates that he thought this arrangement might now mean a total indebtedness of almost $5,000.

The trustees apparently did not realize that Meiklejohn regarded the full $12,500 as unencumbered salary until he wrote home for new advances in the fall of 1920. Plimpton replied in November that the president had used up all the money he was entitled to—that in fact the college had already advanced him nearly $16,000, "of which you were entitled to receive but $12,500, so that you owe the College $3,476." For this reason, Plimpton warned him, "there is no more money coming from the College for you until August, 1921. I am wondering whether these figures are correct. I take it for granted that you have financial resources elsewhere; I certainly hope so."

Meiklejohn immediately shot back a reply. "I infer that you intended to shock me," he wrote from Florence. "There is no doubt that you have succeeded." Actually he had not received more than $13,500, Meiklejohn said, and he was entitled to $2,500 more—for a total of $16,000—since "there is available for my trip not only the $12,500 of this year's salary but also the money [which he estimated at $3,500 more] due me for the summer of 1921." After explaining his own figures, he went on to tell Plimpton: "I am not quite so wild financially as you have made me out." But even the remaining $2,500 that he thought the college owed him would not be enough, he continued; he would really need twice that amount. "I am sorry to suggest this, but the absence had to be taken. We have worked very hard for eight years, with many circumstances of peculiar difficulty, including the financial," he said, "and it is essential that we get a genuine rest this year." As for Plimpton's remark about "financial resources elsewhere," Meiklejohn retorted, "You know that I have no outside resources."

Plimpton in December bowed to Meiklejohn's view of the salary question and added $5,000 to his letter of credit. He calculated that Meiklejohn would be overdrawn by $5,350 when his sabbatical was over, if his original debt was included.

The chairman noted in closing that "up to the present time we have raised $2,475,000 toward the $3,000,000 for the endowment, but this has not been easy work and I know that many men are making great sacrifices to help the college." The implication was that Meiklejohn wasn't.

Dwight Morrow was taken aback when he learned that the president had not used part of his 1920–21 salary, as promised, to erase the earlier debt. He wrote to Meiklejohn that he recalled having "the clear impression that the amount overdrawn for the year 1919–20 would be made up out of the salary of 1920–21." Meiklejohn replied imperturbably that Morrow was right. "The trouble was that when I came to the settling up of last year I found the situation very much worse than I had anticipated, and it was for that reason that I asked Mr. Plimpton for the 'carrying over' when I saw him in New York," he said.

Morrow was also surprised that the college's estimated deficit for the year was going to be $90,000 instead of $50,000 as originally forecast. He had taken over as finance committee chairman following Simpson's death the previous May. In a newsy five-page letter to Meiklejohn he wrote that "the amount of the deficit—whatever may be the cause of it—made us all feel that we must really take hold of the financial problem and grapple with it." The trustees had put Morrow in charge of a special committee to review the whole matter.

The president received Morrow's letter in January 1921, and quickly replied. He was "delighted to know we are moving so definitely in the direction of business organization. I have not yet forgotten the look of amazement on Mr. Pratt's face when two or three years ago I said in the trustee meeting that we had no accurate knowledge or control of our business affairs. It has been an amazing situation and I hope we are coming to the end of it."

Notwithstanding trustee concerns about his own debits and those of the treasury, Meiklejohn began urging, that winter, that the college also provide extra funds to pay him for two round trips home from Europe that he planned to make in the course of his sabbatical. As the trustees' later report told the story: "The President came home in March, 1921. . . . During his visit he asked Mr. Plimpton if the College would arrange to pay for the expenses of both that visit and the visit he contemplated making at the time of the Centennial Celebration. Mr. Plimpton told him this was not possible."

After Meiklejohn returned to Italy from his March visit, the trustees finally ran out of patience. At their meeting on April 9, 1921, they discussed the whole issue of college finances. Morrow's special committee reported that budgetary procedures on the campus had been "entirely informal"; it recommended that "a real budgetary system" be established. The board also reviewed the Meiklejohn situation, decided that something drastic would have to be done, and authorized Plimpton to call the president back home for a conference.

On April 14, Plimpton sent Meiklejohn a cablegram: "At meeting of Trustees Saturday it was considered essential in your own interest and that of College that you should come home in time for meeting of the Board May 28th. Stop I was instructed so to notify you and ask you to be here a few days before May 28th. Stop Please inform me when to expect you. Stop I will see that expense of this trip is paid." A sentence that appeared in an earlier draft of the text had been dropped from the message. The sentence was: "It seems to us that your future relationship to the college should be determined before Commencement."

Since that sentence was omitted, Meiklejohn did not know that his job was imperiled. He wrote back that Plimpton's message "of course perplexes me, and I wonder what it is all about. . . . My guess is that the budget has to be cut and that I must be there to agree to it. . . . It is good of you to assure me about the expenses of the trip. Thank you for that." Plimpton wrote to him later that the cablegram had been sent after the trustees' "very full discussion of the finances of the college and your own finances." He told the president that his overdrafts were "a real burden" for the college; the treasurer recently had told him, for instance, that there would not be enough money to send out salary checks at the end of the month unless Plimpton authorized an emergency loan. Plimpton now wanted legal advice. As the trustees would again two years later, Plimpton turned to Harlan Fiske Stone '94. He described the situation to the Columbia law dean, and later he reported Stone's opinion to Morrow. Stone, he said, thought Meiklejohn's financial affairs were "sufficient cause for his removal" and that the trustees should "give no other reason."

Plimpton had lunch with Meiklejohn shortly after the president's return to the country in May. He found the president "stirred up on finances."

Meiklejohn said he would pay back the full amount he had overdrawn and that he did not want "an issue made" at the trustees' meeting on May 28. "Was tempted to tell him that I advised to him to resign as I doubted whether it was possible for him again to have the confidence of the board," Plimpton wrote to Morrow in a brief summary. "I did say everything to him except the resignation. . . . I think he thinks if he can get the money his chances are good—but I did not promise that this will be sufficient. He has no idea of resigning. I tested him along this line."

The trustees gathered on Saturday, May 28, at the Hotel Kimball in Springfield, Massachusetts, where their meetings were often held. As the first order of business they elected Vice President Coolidge to fill the board vacancy left by Simpson. The minutes of the meeting say almost nothing about the ensuing conference with Meiklejohn, but parts of this critical session are described in a memorandum written by the trustee Frederick Woodbridge. In short, the trustees told Meiklejohn that they had lost confidence in him as president. He replied that if resignation was being considered, the trustees, and not he, should resign.

Woodbridge was an 1889 alumnus and was dean of political science, philosophy, and fine arts at Columbia. The Amherst faculty in 1912 had urged unsuccessfully that he be chosen to succeed President Harris. Woodbridge's record of the May 28 meeting reviewed the long history of Meiklejohn's financial troubles—the salary advances, the failure to clear up his 1919–20 overdraft with the extra $2,500 he received for that purpose in 1920–21, and his earlier nonpayment of bills. Plimpton had told the board that "the practice of contracting debts in Amherst ceased," Woodbridge noted. "But the President was still behind annually in large sums which were made up to him by gift." In fact, his overdraft by now had increased to $8,500.

The president "made a statement acknowledging his carelessness in the matter of overdrawing, promising that he would in the future live within his salary, and offering to repay the overdraft of $8,500 [Meiklejohn said he had already raised the amount, mostly without obligation]. . . . The board considered the whole matter in executive session and as a result appointed a committee to confer with the president and to inform him that the board had lost confidence in his fitness to be president of the college."

At this point the discussion became heated. Meiklejohn "took the ground that lack of confidence in him was no ground for an action by the

Board, that he had an obligation to the College which he was in duty bound to discharge no matter what the Board thought of his fitness as President, that if it was a matter of resignation, the Board, but not he, ought to resign. He stated again his readiness to repay the overdraft and maintained that such repayment would end the matter. He took the position that the trustees ought to allow him to continue to be President because he had, in his own judgment, a great work to perform, although in their judgment he was an unfit man to be President of the College. . . .This culmination of the proceedings only strengthened the Board in its opinion," Woodbridge concluded. In his view, the president's connection with the college was "morally severed," and now the only question to be considered was "how should his connection with the College be terminated in fact."

The trustees on the committee that conferred with the president were Plimpton and Morrow, Arthur P. Rugg '83, who was chief justice in the Supreme Judicial Court of Massachusetts, and the Reverend Arthur L. Gillett '80, a professor at the Hartford Theological Seminary. Rugg became chairman, and the group was later known as the Rugg Committee.

When Meiklejohn refused to resign in 1921, the trustees did not press the issue; instead, the Rugg Committee took many months preparing a report on Meiklejohn's finances—one of two reports that the board received in 1923 and "which were in substance charges" against the president, as Plimpton called them. Why did the trustees back off for the time being? There may have been several reasons. For one thing, Meiklejohn raised funds privately and cleared his overdrawn account with the college as he said he would, paying $8,856 to the treasury early that June. Plimpton gave other reasons in an official statement that he signed three years later: "Some of the members of the Board felt that so long as the Faculty and the students could support President Meiklejohn the Board was bound to put up with a good deal, because as time went on it became more and more apparent that President Meiklejohn was the type of man with whom a public controversy would be inevitable. Although the Board were unanimous in desiring President Meiklejohn to resign, there were some members of the Board who felt that if he declined to resign they would not want to take steps to formally dismiss him."

Stanley King '03, who was elected to the board in 1921, recalled years later that some trustees still thought "the situation could be salvaged"; he said they included Plimpton, Morrow, Gillett, Edward T. Esty '97, and "perhaps some others." Whatever held them back, the trustees felt it important to marshal their evidence. The Rugg Committee's report was not completed until 1923. It gives the outline of the story told here. The committee asked Meiklejohn to respond to their document, and his comments were included in the final printing. He corrected several minor points, and wrote among his conclusions that:

- "The increased salary and entertainment allowances voted in 1918 were adequate and would, I think, have solved the difficulty had there not come and remained the increase of living expenses incident to the war."
- "Through all the difficulties there runs the constant difficulty of my own inefficiency in dealing with personal accounts. In so far as the anxiety and distress to the trustees and the consequent harm to the college are due to this factor, I am exceedingly sorry."
- "In their later dealings with the situation the trustees have seemed to me curiously unsympathetic and at times unfair. For this, too, I am very sorry."

Those regrets still lay in the future, in a year that would see the board again lose confidence in the president when it found that deep faculty opposition to Meiklejohn was rending the college.

For now, the academic year 1920–21 ended in a festive, five-day celebration as Amherst marked its centennial. Alumni thronged the town and campus for the opening weekend, wearing purple and white badges. Before the commencement exercises on Monday, June 20, an honorary membership in Phi Beta Kappa was conferred upon Vice President Coolidge. At the Alumni Open-Air Smoker that evening, according to the report in *Graduates' Quarterly*, the main feature was "a series of stereopticon slides illustrating the athletic development of Amherst, from the early days, when sawing wood was the only major sport, to the present." On the next night the crowd was treated to a centennial pageant of 11 episodes called "Amherst Milestones," done in pantomime. A highlight occurred when "Alma Mater," played by Mrs. George F. Whicher, "arose to view and occupied the throne in the center." The celebration ended with dinner at noon on Wednesday, at which "the odd classes, then enjoying the possession of [the contested statue of] Sabrina, chanted the praises of the Amherst goddess, while the even classes wailed and rapped on the table." Dwight Morrow capped the occasion with an announcement that the centennial gift had exceeded $3 million.

Of all the speeches given in those five days, the most stirring was Alexander Meiklejohn's, on the topic "What Does the College Hope to Be During the Next Hundred Years?" The president sounded, as he often did, ahead of his time. He asked what the country should try to be in the postwar era: "Which shall it be—an Anglo-Saxon aristocracy of culture or a Democracy? . . . I cast my Anglo-Saxon vote for Pure Democracy." At the college, he said, "We may not keep ourselves apart either from persons or from cultures not our own. We dare not shut our gates to fellow citizens nor to their influence. So we must welcome boys of other stocks. And if they do not come, we must go out and bring them in. Our undergraduate life must represent the country which it serves; students must keep it free from any taint of caste or aristocracy."

He spoke for an hour and a half. "Frequent and long," said the *Springfield Republican*, "were the bursts of applause that interrupted him."

One who warmly applauded was Charles T. Burnett '95, a professor of psychology at Bowdoin College. Six days later, he wrote to his best friend and classmate, Morrow, who had given him disturbing information during that busy week in Amherst.

"The address was brilliant," wrote Burnett. "Should Amherst lose the services of this man, it seems to me, from the outside—that this loss can be no small one. I have talked but little on this subject with anyone who is his frank advocate, and that little has given to me no means of justifying, nor even accounting for, the facts you related to me the other day. The onus, however, is put upon the other half of the household, but not in a way to make me clear about it. . . . I am moved by the qualities of this centenary address, which show him to be a man of insight and culture that no college—other things being equal—can easily spare."

For the moment, perhaps, things were equal. They would not remain equal for long.—DCW

THE STORY IN
THE MEIKLEJOHN FILES
II. Final Showdown

⌒

IN LATE MAY OF 1921, Alexander Meiklejohn's financial affairs so concerned the Amherst trustees that they told him they had lost confidence in his fitness to stay on as president of the college. But Meiklejohn refused to step down, and the trustees did not force the issue until two years later.

An entirely different problem would bring matters to a critical pass. The trustees found that the faculty under Meiklejohn had split into hostile camps: one that supported the president and one that opposed him. By the time George A. Plimpton '76, president of the board of trustees, finally asked Meiklejohn for his resignation in a letter dated June 19, 1923, a day before commencement, he noted that not only the board but a majority of the faculty believed it to be "in the best interests of the College that you relinquish your administrative duties." Meiklejohn replied that he did not agree with the board's opinion that he ought to resign; but the lack of support Plimpton spoke of, he said, was "so serious that I feel compelled to tender my resignation."

What had happened? Giving his last speech as president at an alumni luncheon the following day, Meiklejohn described his trouble with the faculty in blunt words. "The thing that was in my mind, the thing I was commissioned to do when I came here, the only thing worth doing was to try to change the faculty for the better in terms of personnel, in terms of teaching method, in terms of course of study, in everything that represents the work of the institution. . . .

"May I say that it is going to be a very hard thing to improve our faculty. The faculty finds it exceedingly difficult to improve themselves and they find it exceedingly objectionable to have anyone else do it to them. Now it is essential that they be changed. I tell you that it is a tragic thing to see a faculty growing old without knowing it and resenting the coming in of younger men and younger methods and new institutions, which it needs to keep itself alive and active."

Meiklejohn's papers show that from the very beginning enormous— perhaps his greatest—energy was devoted to bringing talented young professors to Amherst. To an astonishing degree he succeeded. The trustees encouraged him in the effort and helped speed the transformation along. In 1913 trustee Frank W. Stearns '78 wrote confidentially to Meiklejohn: "I think your suggestion that when you bring in young men, [you] put them on probation for a few years with the clear understanding that if they thoroughly make good to your satisfaction they are to be jumped across some of the intermediate degrees, is a good one."

As part of the process, older professors yielded to new ones. Meiklejohn somehow arranged for Edwin A. Grosvenor '67, a professor of government, to retire in 1914, and for David Todd, the astronomer, to leave Amherst in 1917. The trustees adopted a plan requiring professors to retire at 65, with the result that three other senior faculty members—John M. Tyler '73 in biology, Benjamin K. Emerson '65 in geology, and John F. Genung in literature—also ended their teaching in 1917, the year the rule took effect.

Meiklejohn from time to time dismissed younger men if they did not meet his standards. The college he came to in 1912, he wrote several years later, was "committed to the permanent retention on its staff of several men of inferior quality as scholars and teachers, and it was rapidly becoming committed to others of the same sort."

As he moved aggressively to correct these conditions, he acknowledged that his actions were not always popular. The fact was that any president who set about decisively to rejuvenate a small college faculty needed keen diplomatic skills to succeed without hurting morale. In Meiklejohn, these skills were sometimes lacking. After his first five years as president he wrote to Dwight Morrow '95, the trustee, that he had been "pushing a rather venturesome program without hesitating to thwart other people's purposes in so far as they seemed to stand in the way of the college. The getting rid of Mr. Grosvenor and Mr. Todd, the passing of the pension rule and the application of it, the refusal of promotion to teachers, the virtual requiring that some of them withdraw, the bringing in of new men on equality with the old and in some cases above them," he wrote, "in general the insistence on an educational program which had not been entertained or practiced by the college beforehand—all these things are accompanied by strain."

Meiklejohn was a leader in educational trends of the time. Emphasis on the content of an Amherst education shifted from the classical to the contemporary as the president built up the social sciences; and emphasis in method changed from reliance on authoritarian, fixed lecture to the placement of intellectual responsibility on the student in the give-and-take of classroom discussion.

Again, Meiklejohn summed it up in his farewell address: "Some people believe that intelligence is a thing that you can have, that you can get and keep, that it comes down out of the past, that it is handed down by the teacher, that you can find it in a book, that it is there to be taken," he said. "It is not. Thinking or intelligence is a thing that you must do, it is an activity."

Through his faculty appointments and his own examples, Meiklejohn set a youthful, dialectic tone at Amherst that made it an infectious, exciting time in the college's history.

Not everyone was infected. Some members of the faculty, especially the older and more conservative teachers, were wary. One of these was the redoubtable George Bosworth Churchill '89, professor of English and Republican town moderator in Amherst. Churchill insisted that it was "not help but injury to the student to plunge him into courses for which he is not mature, or to allow an undeveloped moral nature to think that it can successfully be wholly the arbiter of its own conduct. Too many men are being graduated from Amherst today who believe that they think straight because they have many thoughts," he complained.

One person who had joined the faculty at Meiklejohn's invitation was the poet Robert Frost, who was recruited in 1916 to begin teaching at the college in the following year. But Frost decided in 1920 to "go back to farming and writing." In a letter written at the time, he explained that he was "too much out of sympathy with what the present administration seems bent on doing with this old New England college." Later, looking back on that period, he wrote to his friend Louis Untermeyer: "The boys had been made uncommonly interesting to themselves by Meiklejohn. They fancied themselves as thinkers. At Amherst you *thought*, while at other colleges you merely *learned*."

It was not just a question of intellectual style. Another matter was also at issue. To men like Churchill who still placed a high value on the early religious mission of Amherst, the new order appeared to challenge religion as well. "The college," said Churchill, "cannot afford to be irreligious. The members of its faculty, whatever their creeds, should be truly and vitally religious men, recognizable as such. No intellectual power or learning should be accepted as a substitute . . . the students should be made in all possible ways to feel that the College stands for religion as an essential in the life of man."

Doubts about Meiklejohn's support of religion ultimately reached the trustees. One member of the board, the Reverend Cornelius H. Patton '83, secretary of the American Board of Commissioners, told Morrow in 1922 that "a great many of the alumni of my generation, particularly the ministers, have lost all patience" with Meiklejohn. "They think he has no religion, or if he has any religion, that he is a non-conductor." Trustee Arthur Curtiss James '89 was appalled a year later when he saw a letter sent home by a senior. The student wrote to his father that "Prexy is said to be an atheist. Whether or not that is true, I don't know and this is my fourth year at Amherst. What I do know though is that he is a good man with high ideals and exerts a good influence at the college." Wrote James: "It is a fine commentary on the situation that a man can have been in college for nearly four years and not know whether his President is an atheist or not!"

Meiklejohn himself maintained calmly in one report that during his presidency the chapel service was "made the most adequate service that I have ever known in a college community. It is orderly, devout, and in very large measure spontaneous. The Sunday service in the Church is very satisfactory with respect to student behavior but not with respect to the quality of the service itself. I can, however, give assurance that, with the leadership of Mr. Fitch [Albert Parker Fitch, professor of the history of religion], no college community is making a more earnest and persistent effort to realize the possibilities of religious worship than is our own."

If Meiklejohn had his critics, he had his strong advocates too. "To some he is the glory of Amherst College today," lawyer Robert P. Esty '97 wrote to Morrow from Philadelphia. "We are all debtors to him, every mother's son of us, for a far-reaching and comprehensive intellectual and spiritual shaking up—at least those of us who endeavor to get at more than one side of a problem." Another lawyer, Luther Ely Smith '94 of St. Louis, investigated conditions at the college and concluded that "Amherst scholarship at the present time stands higher in the educational world than it has stood for many years, and that this result has been achieved by President Meiklejohn's leadership." Most students and recent graduates applauded Meiklejohn's influence. From medical school, Frederick S. Greene '20 wrote that "the help and encouragement I received through his dauntless idealism and willingness to seek for truth in both sides of any issue, I feel has helped me and will help me more than anything else to do my little bit for humanity as I go into the world."

In September of 1919, C. E. Kelsey '84—publisher of *Youth's Companion*— told Morrow that he had talked at the last commencement with Walter Wilcox, a classmate who was professor of economics at Cornell. Wilcox, he said, "expressed great surprise upon learning at Amherst that there was a marked split among the Amherst faculty. He stated that in the department of Economics, Amherst College faculty had been advanced from a level of incompetence to a position where her faculty in Economics was of such a high order that no other college or university in this country could even compare with it." Many signs indicated that the educational quality of the college was on the upswing, and for a long time the trustees left faculty problems in the hands of the president. But the first serious faculty dispute already had come to the board's attention. The incident began early in 1919 when a young chemistry professor, John B. Zinn, was let go over the protests of the two full professors in chemistry, Howard W. Doughty and Arthur J. Hopkins '85. Doughty and Hopkins had urged that Zinn be promoted, but Meiklejohn decided against it. Instead he replaced Zinn with a promising young alumnus, George Scatchard '13, who later had an internationally distinguished career as a prize-winning physical chemist at the Massachusetts Institute of Technology.

Hopkins wrote privately in distress to the elder statesman of the faculty, the retired B. K. Emerson, in New York. "As you are in touch with certain trustees and alumni notably Plimpton and [former President George] Harris," Hopkins said, "perhaps you might think it well to talk over with them the situation here at Amherst. . . . In the last nine months, the president has dismissed five members of the faculty—all Associate Professors," he reported. "Five men out of fifty is a pretty large percentage of a faculty to be dismissed in nine months. Of course, at this rate, in a few years, any president might hope to reconstruct the whole crowd to suit whatever his purpose may be."

Emerson was alarmed, spoke to Plimpton, and later told Hopkins that the head of the trustees "was very surprised and indignant; I went over each case with him, and I told him I condemned the plan of education, in the interest of which he was 'decapitating the intelligentsia' like Trotsky in the interest of the Soviet."

Meanwhile, another scientist—Frederic B. Loomis '96 in biology—stirred Meiklejohn's ire by complaining more openly about the treatment Zinn and others received. He fired off a letter to the trustee Williston Walker '83—a professor of church history at Yale and chairman of the board's committee on instruction—urging that there be "some regular manner in which the faculty feelings particularly in matters of appointment and dismissal might come to the Trustees." He protested that the president had made the decision in Zinn's case without consulting either Hopkins or Doughty.

Loomis notified the president of his letter. Meiklejohn—who said later that he had "thorough conference with Mr. Hopkins and Mr. Doughty"—replied testily to Loomis that his complaints appeared to bring against me charges of injustice and of disloyalty to certain members of the Faculty." Loomis, the president, Walker, Plimpton, and the trustee John W. Simpson '71 then engaged in a tense correspondence about the problem for more than six weeks. First, Meiklejohn insisted that Loomis file his complaints formally with the board, and Loomis did. Loomis

later withdrew his list of particular grievances and instead asked the
trustees to review general questions such as "the status of the faculty and
the departments in the initiation and making of appointments and
dismissals." Meiklejohn entered "formal objection" to the withdrawal of
Loomis's original complaints. Walker urged him to drop the objection.
"If you insist on an investigation you produce a controversy," Walker told
him. "It makes little difference who is right in a controversy. Its effects
are disastrous in a faculty one way or the other. . . . You can well afford to
be generous." Eventually, the president relented. A special panel of
trustees that became known as the Rounds Committee produced a 35-
page record of the Loomis incident in 1923. Criticizing Meiklejohn, the
committee said the vexing affair was "significant in revealing an attitude
of mind in dealing with matters of administration rather than an effective
handling of those matters themselves."

Attitudes were hardening on both sides. The demands of Loomis
and other professors for a voice in personnel matters eventually led to a
"conference" agreement with the president, adopted in March of 1920.
The plan set procedures under which the president sought limited advice
from the departments about appointments, promotions, and dismissals.

Meiklejohn spent the following year in Europe. When he returned,
there were further disagreements. In April 1922 the trustees told him
the faculty should elect a five-man committee to discuss the points at
issue. Of the five who were elected, Professors Loomis, Churchill, and
Harry deForest Smith, who taught Greek, and Frederic L. Thompson in
history were Meiklejohn's critics; only one, economics professor Walter
W. Stewart, was in the president's camp.

The board by now was hearing complaints from alumni. Often their
grievances were political. In 1922 Harold M. Bixby '13, a St. Louis banker,
raised one of the main objections: in a letter to Patton, the trustee, he
wrote, "I have heard from so many sources, that there can be no doubt
whatever Mr. Meiklejohn threw as many obstacles as he could in the way
of military training and participation in the War by undergraduates.
. . . He does not understand the Amherst spirit." After the World War
began in Europe, the president had urged students to examine the views
of both sides. It was true he had not encouraged the early "preparedness"
movement. When the United States finally entered the conflict in 1917,

however, he willingly made the adjustments that were needed. A unit of the Students' Army Training Corps was established on the campus in 1918, and virtually all students engaged in military drill. Meiklejohn reported to the trustees that "while the study which is done should not be allowed to become a sham or pretence, it shall unflinchingly be set aside whenever it appears that teacher or student is needed for special service in the task which now faces us as a people."

From his office on Wall Street, George B. Mallon '87 passed on to Morrow—a few doors up the street at J. P. Morgan & Company—another objection. He had heard that "several members of the Faculty are Socialists. . . . Personally I have never been very enthusiastic about [the president]," Mallon added. "I think that Meiklejohn belongs to the rapidly-growing group who cultivate 'stylish thoughts' about internationalism."

Letters like this were of little concern to Morrow. In 1923 he would get a similar complaint—about "an unhealthy atmosphere of Socialism and Bolshevism" at Amherst—from a friend in Ohio. Morrow replied after Meiklejohn's departure: "I do not think there had been unhealthy atmosphere of Socialism and Bolshevism at Amherst. There has been, however, a very bitter feeling between the old and young members of the faculty. The Board did what I think all boards should do—it tried to keep its hands off and let the faculty work it out. Despite the fact that the Board had reasons of its own for a lack of confidence in the President, it did not interfere in any way with academic policy. The situation reached a point, however, that a majority of the faculty, including some of the older men whom you knew, felt that a change was absolutely essential."

The situation reached a further point of annoyance in May 1922 with a new incident that involved the trustees. A brilliant young alumnus and one of the president's protégés, Walter Raymond Agard '15, was returning to teach Greek after two years at Oxford, where he had earned a degree in literature. Agard earlier had been an instructor, and the president now wanted him advanced to the rank of associate professor. Under the 1920 "conference" arrangement, Meiklejohn's plan to promote Agard was reviewed by Churchill and other professors of the Languages and Literature group. They acknowledged Agard's high merit but recommended that he remain on trial as an instructor for one more year. The president nevertheless went ahead and asked the trustees for the promotion, and the board's executive committee endorsed the recommendation in the spring of 1922 and passed it along to the full board for action in May.

The trustees said later that Meiklejohn had not told the executive committee about the professors' opinion. Meiklejohn recalled that he had. In either case, by the time the trustees met in May, they had heard of the disagreement from other sources. The board asked Meiklejohn about it, and according to the minutes of the trustees' meeting "the President was reluctant to state to the Board the recommendations made to him in writing by the Group of teachers consulted . . . stating that he had asked certain specific questions of the Group which had not confined itself to the answers to such questions. . . . The President was informed that it was his duty to give the Board the fullest information, and he thereupon stated that the Group was not in favor of Mr. Agard's promotion at this time." In a rebuff to the president, the board voted against the promotion.

The disputes about Zinn and Agard and the other signs of trouble at Amherst led the trustees in June 1922 to appoint their own panel to review the professors' role at Amherst with Meiklejohn and the faculty committee. The trustees on the new committee were Arthur C. Rounds '87, a New York lawyer and law professor who served the committee as chairman; another lawyer, Edward T. Esty '97 of Worcester, Massachusetts; and Stanley King '03, who at the time was vice president of W. H. McElwain, a Boston shoe manufacturing company.

So it was that by the middle of 1922 the college's board had two panels investigating problems at Amherst. The so-called Rugg Committee, established a year earlier, was preparing a report on Meiklejohn's finances; and now the Rounds Committee was to look at the faculty issue.

In an early meeting with Rounds, King, and Esty, members of the faculty committee agreed to write individual statements on a wide range of issues. The printed statements fill 75 pages and dwell at length on Zinn's departure and other grievances. Churchill, for instance, complained that Meiklejohn once ignored a unanimous wish of the Languages and Literature group to keep an English instructor on the faculty. Churchill said the president had simply told him it was "impossible." "He has never . . . offered any explanation of this attitude," Churchill objected. "When I ventured to call his attention to this fact, and to suggest that some explanation, especially of the sole, curt phrase 'it is impossible' might fairly be expected by me both as a member of the department and as an individual, the only reply vouchsafed was a smile."

The statement written by Harry deForest Smith confirmed that there was now on the Amherst campus "a situation in which we find friction, misunderstanding, internal dissension and a general lessening of efficiency and happiness." In response to these comments, Meiklejohn agreed with Smith's bleak appraisal as it concerned the individual cases. Much of the fault, he believed, lay with Churchill. The reform-minded president and the strong-willed, conservative Churchill had never seen eye to eye. Meiklejohn wrote that when he tried to hire certain prominent teachers and scholars in English, two of "the very best men in the field told me directly that the difficulty of working with Churchill was too great." Meiklejohn told the trustees, furthermore, that "Mr. Churchill's proposals of the sort of men who can work with him I cannot and will not support, so long as I am responsible for recommendations of the personnel of our teaching force." Little in these reports could have cheered the trustees.

Events began to head toward a showdown. Early in 1923 the Rugg and Rounds Committees assembled the evidence they had gathered. Morrow, the leading figure on the Rugg Committee, was drafting the review of the financial difficulties that had led to the trustees' loss of confidence in the president in 1921. Stanley King was active on the other committee.

King had a three-hour talk with Meiklejohn on February 18, 1923, and wrote about it to Morrow on the following day. He said he told the president "that in my personal opinion the situation between President and Faculty and President and Trustees was steadily growing worse; and that time was working against us instead of for us . . . indicated the possibility of an eventual smash-up, which would have very serious consequences for the college, for the members of the faculty in whom he was particularly interested, and really for all concerned."

By March, Meiklejohn had a preliminary copy of the Rugg Report. He was asked to add to it his own comment about the whole financial record. He did so, but said at the end of his statement that he thought it would be "unwise and unfair" to keep the trustees' report "as an official record"; he believed it would only "produce misunderstanding and

misconstruction." The report—marked "Private and Confidential"—
and Meiklejohn's response to it were submitted to the board at its meeting
in Springfield on March 17. No immediate action was taken. Plimpton
went over the entire situation with Meiklejohn 12 days later. Like King,
Plimpton then wrote to Morrow. He reported that the president

> recognized the fact that he does not enjoy the confidence of the
> trustees; that the faculty are divided; that the alumni are divided. The
> undergraduates, he claims, are favorable to him. He states that the
> members of the faculty who are against him hold a meeting once a week
> to see how they can bring about his removal. In other words, it looks
> to him as it does to me, as though there was to be an uncomfortable
> contest with regard to the advisability of his remaining as President
> of Amherst College. Such a controversy would mean publicity and
> general unpleasantness, with the ultimate power in the hands of the
> trustees, who are likely to be unanimous in deciding for his removal.
> He mentioned the fact that we could not remove him without giving
> our reasons; but it seems to me that the present condition of the college
> after his having been its president for ten years, and the fact that he
> is not enjoying the confidence either of the trustees or of the faculty
> would be sufficient to convince the public that the best work could not
> be done under such conditions. . . . his whole attitude seemed to be
> that he would be able to regain the confidence of the Board, reunite
> the faculty, obtain the confidence of the alumni and the friends of
> the college, and that he proposed to make a fight towards this end,
> regardless of the consequences.

Plimpton added that "of course he feels very sore with regard to his
financial record having been presented." Meiklejohn nearly two years
earlier had been forced to end the practice of drawing his salary in
advance, and the trustees had stopped making gifts to help support him
financially.

The Rounds Committee, too, was completing its study. In April,
Rounds confidentially asked Churchill what the outcome might be if
each member of the faculty was asked about the advisability of keeping
Meiklejohn on. Churchill estimated that 13 men would support the

president, and 26 would vote against him; 7 others he listed as "doubtful." As the Rounds Committee pressed forward, Meiklejohn objected that the faculty committee advising it was "thoroughly unrepresentative." He wrote to the chairman that four out of the five members—Churchill, Loomis, Smith, and Thompson—represented "a group of men who were strongly determining the policy of the college eleven years ago," and that "as to general educational interest" they were "in greater or less disagreement with the president." He also objected that the committee was concentrating on small grievances instead of asking the really important question, "'How does the college of today compare with that of eleven years ago?' What is the comparison as to endowment, as to repute in the minds of those who are watching intelligently the course of education in the country, as to the standing of the faculty, as to the success of the college as a place of study and teaching? Upon these points there has been a definite policy in the administration of the college," he said. "And there are available many valuable opinions as to the success of that policy."

Others now joined in the struggle. Meiklejohn's strongest supporters on the faculty sent Plimpton a petition, dated May 16, which charged that the problems at Amherst sprang from "the efforts of a small faculty group, led by Professor George Bosworth Churchill, to obtain political control over the College." Plimpton replied that the trustees were completing two reports that would be made available to this group if Meiklejohn agreed to it. The documents, which were ready in time for a trustees' meeting on May 26, were shown to one or two professors but were never released. Plimpton would write later that the reports "were in substance charges" against the president.

Two days before the May trustees' meeting, Plimpton sent a note to Meiklejohn saying that the president would shortly have the final reports. "Now keep cool," he wrote, "and don't get excited."

The report of the Rugg Committee reviewed what it called the "deplorable financial record" of the previous years and informed the trustees that "neither the oral conferences of President Meiklejohn with your Committee" nor his written responses had "restored the lost confidence in him as President of the College." The committee said also that it disagreed with Meiklejohn's apprehension "that misunderstanding can arise from making the final report a matter of record. It is essential that all of the facts be now ascertained," the study concluded.

The Rounds Committee in its final report said it found "an administration marked by suspicion and distrust." The board's reliance upon the president as "the reasonable medium of communication" between the faculty and trustees, it said, had "failed in important respects." Referring to the Loomis, Agard, and other cases, the report said "the wisdom or unwisdom of the actions taken . . . is of little significance compared with the fact that, in the handling of them, confidence in the President of the College has been so seriously shaken."

King drove the president to the meeting, which convened at the Hotel Kimball in Springfield. He recalled later that on the way down Meiklejohn said "that if the Board would give him autocratic power at the college for ten years, he would make it a good college." Trustees at the meeting—who included Vice President Calvin Coolidge '95 — were unanimous in the opinion that Meiklejohn should retire from the presidency; but a minority felt that if he refused to do so voluntarily, action should not be taken to dismiss him unless a majority of the faculty thought he should go.

The Rugg and Rounds reports were referred to a special, new trustee committee that included Plimpton, Esty, Morrow, and King. The new group, known as the Plimpton Committee, was directed to confer with Meiklejohn and, if necessary, to poll the faculty. To Plimpton, however, it was now just a matter of time. In a letter written the next day to Morrow, he noted that it was "definitely settled that Meiklejohn is to leave and that the committee's work is to arrange the details and make it as easy as possible for him—as well as for the College." The board president then went to Amherst and told Meiklejohn of the trustees' unanimous opinion that he should resign. He recalled later that he also discussed the possibility of Meiklejohn's "remaining as a teacher or the possibility of his being granted a long leave of absence with a reasonable payment or pension."

But the president put such questions aside. Instead, he wanted the Plimpton Committee to confer with some of the younger members of the faculty. This, Plimpton agreed to arrange. On June 9 the committee interviewed 12 men who were friendly to Meiklejohn, including Stewart,

Agard, and others who had signed the anti-Churchill petition. Most of them defended Meiklejohn and deplored the political maneuvering of his opponents.

Some of these men annoyed Morrow. He wrote later to a friend about "the eight or nine bumptious young men on the faculty who insisted that nobody thought or studied at Amherst until they came. The fine thing about them was their complete sincerity in that belief, and the imperative urge within them which led them to make it clear to the older members of the faculty that they should reform. . . . With all of my sympathy for the newer and higher civilization, and I think I have much," Morrow said, "I think it is asking a good deal to impress this civilization upon a large majority in an old New England town by the point of the trustees' sword."

On June 10, the day after the interviews, Plimpton again wrote to Meiklejohn. He now became firm. His committee had found that the situation was "much more serious than we had thought," he said; only a few of the pro-Meiklejohn men had "held out any hope of a recon-ciliation" between the two faculty camps. He said the board needed to "find out at once whether the faculty have confidence in you"; to do this, it had to receive in the next few days—by Wednesday morning, June 13, at the latest—any further written answers that the president wanted to make to the Rugg and Rounds reports. Those documents together with the answers could then be made available to the faculty. They might have to be sent to the alumni as well, Plimpton added. "The time has gone by when we can avoid hurting the College," he said; the board now had to "determine what is the right thing to do and have faith that the right action will hurt the college the least."

Meiklejohn wrote in reply two days later that he could not meet the Wednesday deadline. He agreed with Plimpton that "the college must of course take whatever consequences come from doing the right thing. I hope, however, that before [a] decision is made I may have an opportunity to talk reasonably and quietly with the members of your committee." Understandably, he did not want the Rugg report published.

Two members of the Plimpton Committee, King and Esty, met on June 13 with Harlan Fiske Stone '94 and two lawyers in Boston to weigh the legal situation. They determined that "sufficient cause existed for the removal of the President," and that if Meiklejohn refused to step down they might then bring formal charges. They also recommended that the trustees proceed with their plan to take a vote of the faculty. Stone relayed this advice to Morrow, with a draft of the questions that each member of the faculty should be asked. One question asked what likelihood the person saw of securing harmony between the president and a majority of the faculty, and a second was whether that individual had confidence in the president's administration of the college. The third was: "Do you think that the best interests of the College require that President Meiklejohn should cease to be its president?" The third question should not be asked, the lawyers counseled, unless the board was "certain that the answer will be yes by a majority."

If the trustees wanted Meiklejohn to resign with a minimum of publicity, such hopes were dashed on Thursday, June 14. The lead headline that morning in the *Springfield Republican* announced a "Crisis at Amherst College," and below it a long article filed by correspondent Louis Lyons told a story sympathetic to the president. "Dread rumors have been afloat on Amherst's campus for many days," Lyons wrote. "The seniors hear that the trustees, who eleven years ago brought Alexander Meiklejohn to Amherst to instill a new educational spirit into a traditional little New England college, are now weary of the long battle their president has had to wage for his liberal ideals in education and that, tiring under the strain, dismayed at the difficulties that become increasingly apparent as the efforts of a decade approach their full fruition, they are now ready to abandon the cause and the man they counted on to make Amherst a living college."

The story was carried across the country. Alumni were preparing to return to Amherst during the next several days for commencement and reunions; now reporters, too, began arriving on the campus. Newsmen assigned to the story included a 33-year-old editor of the liberal *New York World*, Walter Lippmann. From men like King, whom Lippmann had known in Washington during the war, he learned something about the president's problems. From students, he learned how much "Prexy" could inspire the young: "From the present student body," Lippmann reported, "he elicits a kind of devotion which I have never seen before among college men."

On Saturday, June 16, the Plimpton Committee polled 36 members of the faculty, confidentially and one at a time. When the trustees asked each person the lawyers' third question —Did the best interests of the college require that Meiklejohn step down?—24 said yes, 11 said no, and 1 did not vote.

An emotional crowd filled the College Church Sunday morning to hear the president's baccalaureate sermon. With a poetic cadence Meiklejohn talked about prophets, Christ, and the crucifixion. Prophets, he said, "cry aloud that institutions must be changed, that certain practices must cease, that certain visions must be followed. And when men hear the cry they turn to follow it. But here, alas, there often comes the break that makes the prophet weep. At Sunday times men gather to hear the message told; they take it to their hearts while Sunday lasts; but Monday comes and men are at their weekday ways again." Christ "preached a vision of what our life might be," he continued. "And men about Him, having seen the vision, turned back to dull, unseeing life again. That was his tragedy."

Plimpton spoke with Meiklejohn later in the day and afterward told his colleagues that the president did not want to make written replies to the Rugg and Rounds reports; he was willing to resign, but he wanted a final talk with the Plimpton Committee. It met with him Monday morning in the Philosophy Seminar Room on the third floor of the Converse Memorial Library. According to the committee's later report, Meiklejohn talked about the favorable reputation of the college and "asked your Committee why the Board had lost confidence in him. One member of your Committee replied, speaking for himself, that he felt that the President had failed as the administrative head of the College. The President replied that he did not recognize the competence of your Committee to pass upon his administrative fitness or unfitness."

They told the president the results of the faculty poll. The meeting recessed for the afternoon and reconvened at nine in the evening. The regular commencement meeting of the board would be held the next day. King recalled many years later that the night was oppressively hot. The seminar room in Converse was "like an oven," he remembered, "and we all took off coats to be as comfortable as possible."

An account of Meiklejohn's final unhappy meeting with the Plimpton

Committee is among the "Confidential Memoranda" of the committee at the College Archives. According to that account Meiklejohn told the group when it reassembled that "he had submitted the matter of his proposed resignation to his friends on the Faculty, that they had advised him to fight and that he did not intend to resign." The discussion was long and intense. The trustee memorandum says Meiklejohn pressed the committee about the use it might make of the Rugg report on his finances and complained that the committee "felt that they had him where they could force him to do what they wished"; the committee members said it was beyond their authority "to say into what details the Trustees might go, if required to make a public statement in connection with any subsequent action they might take." The president urged that all copies of the Rugg report be destroyed. Plimpton said he would do what he could, but he could give no assurance. After midnight, letters requesting, tendering, and accepting a resignation were drafted. Plimpton then said that "so far as it lay within his power, he would have the reports called in and no publicity given to them. . . .

"At the conclusion of the meeting the President made an impassioned address to your Committee in which he restated much that he had previously said during the evening; and concluded by saying that he would never forgive the members of this Committee. To this final statement of the President the members of your Committee made no reply."

The president then took the letters home. He told the committee he wanted to consult with Mrs. Meiklejohn before making a final decision; he would make his reply, he said, in the morning. Reporters throughout the evening had smoked and traded anecdotes while keeping vigil outside Converse beneath the lighted windows; but the president and trustees told them nothing when they emerged and headed off in the darkness. It was by then two o'clock in the morning.

The full board met at ten o'clock Tuesday morning, and Meiklejohn resigned. Plimpton's letter asking him to do so said the board also "desired you to continue in the service of the College in your present professorship of logic and metaphysics." Meiklejohn's reply said:

In response to your letter of June 19 may I say very frankly that I do not accept the judgment which you give as to the wisdom of my withdrawing from the position of administrative head of the College. I am convinced that the situation is such that my withdrawal will be harmful rather than helpful.

The lack of support of which you speak is, however, so serious that I feel compelled to tender my resignation as President of the College. Much as I appreciate the invitation to continue my service as Professor of Logic and Metaphysics, it seems impossible for me to accept it.

The board voted to accept Meiklejohn's resignation effective "at the end of the academic year 1923–4," and to grant him a year's leave of absence in the meantime, at full salary—"to be drawn as, and when, desired."

The resignation was announced early in the afternoon when the seniors, their families, and alumni were attending class exercises in the College Grove. Someone lowered the flag and tolled the bell at Johnson Chapel.

At the commencement services the next morning in College Hall, 13 seniors refused to accept their diplomas, in protest against the board's action. Meiklejohn went ahead with a scheduled speech at the alumni luncheon that afternoon in the Pratt Gymnasium. Another speaker at the table, the Reverend Willard L. Sperry, dean of Harvard Divinity School, brought Meiklejohn's friends to their feet with words from Ezekiel: "And they, whether they will hear or whether they will forbear, yet shall know that there hath been a prophet among them."

Meiklejohn's speech was now to be his farewell. He talked about education and about the faculty, about alumni, and about the trustees. "I am sure that when we have found out how to run colleges we won't have trustees," he said. "Trustees do not know what is going on, not because they are not intelligent, but because they are busy doing something else." He also said, "The point is that I am a minority man. I am always wanting change. On most of the great issues I am usually against the greater number.

"Now from that point of view will you let me say that I am amazed that the thing has lasted as long as it has. . . . I expect to be in the minority and institutions must inevitably be in the hands of majorities."

He concluded: "I differ from most of you on most of the issues of life and I am going to keep it up."

Harlan Fiske Stone in New York heard news of the resignation and wrote to Morrow the next day, "Well, I see Amherst's great liberal leader has resigned about as I expected. . . . I would have enjoyed arguing the case before the Supreme Court of Mass. but I am glad that the matter is ended."

But the trouble was not yet over, and it would take a long time for the wounds to heal. Nine professors resigned almost immediately. Agard, Fitch, Stewart, and other supporters of the president felt they could not remain on the faculty. In Agard's judgment, the trustees had "not only proved themselves educational reactionaries; they have also forsaken the real tradition of Amherst, which is a liberal tradition."

Another who resigned, Walton H. Hamilton in economics, wrote to a friend on July 3 that Meiklejohn was gone because he "gave offense to the dogmatists, who have no intellectual interest, who are unprofitable scholars, and who have spent their days and nights in academic politics." He said that "even after nearly two weeks of getting away from the event it is hard to write about the wreckage of an institution to which one has given probably the best eight years of his life."

Among Meiklejohn's critics, of course, the mood was different. Doughty wrote to Hopkins, who had been on leave, "Well, Hoppie, we have had a hell of a year, but it was worth it. The fight is over. . . . Lord deliver me from another row like it. It could not have been dirtier. The only surprising feature is that no one was physically hurt. Of a truth, New England is a wonderful country. South of Mason and Dixon's line there would have been bloodshed."

The press also took sides. Some editorial writers decided that a conservative board had removed a liberal president for political reasons. The *New York American* warned that "America is doomed if the dollar continues to dominate the colleges through interlocking directorates concerned only to inculcate in youth capitalistic opinions and to stifle all protest against things as they are which ought not to be." The *New Republic* printed "An Open Letter to Dwight Morrow," written by Felix Frankfurter, who was then a Harvard Law School professor. Frankfurter waved aside the notion that Meiklejohn was asked to leave because of faculty opposition. Harmony among scholars "is a Utopian dream," he said. "Men can work together harmoniously in a business enterprise, in a political machine, in a church, perhaps. In a college, never." No, the trustees would have to come up with a better explanation, because "no body of men are privileged to take serious action in a matter of education," he said, "without offering to the public an honest statement of their reasons."

Morrow never responded, and he and his colleagues on the board never told the full story. They simply informed the alumni that the "situation which confronted the Board was not one involving questions of educational policy, but one involving questions of essential confidence in matters relating to the adequate administration of the college."

Five days after the resignation, the *New York World* gave extensive space to the Meiklejohn story. The headline, a page wide, summarized Lippmann's view of the Amherst president: "He was lots of Woodrow Wilson and none of Lloyd George. He could inspire but could not manage. He did magnificently with students and failed lamentably with grown-ups, yet he made Amherst one of the most distinguished small colleges in America."—DCW

While Calvin Coolidge of the Class of 1895 is the only Amherst graduate ever to serve as president of the United States, historically he has not been a big man on campus. Lord Jeffery Amherst, with only the most tenuous connection to the college, gets more attention than "Silent Cal." (The college was named for the town, not for Jeffery.) Never mind: reputations often improve over time, and this may now be happening to Coolidge, whose portrait, at least, hangs in Johnson Chapel, and whose name graces one of the college dormitories. According to one biographer, Hendrik Booraem, Coolidge's first two years at Amherst were undistinguished. Fraternity recruiters found the quiet farm boy "too countrified, not a good mixer, in short unsuitable material for [their] society." But in his last two years he emerged as a strong debater and a witty public speaker. Like many other students of the time, Coolidge said that much of his intellectual development came from a popular philosophy course taught by Professor Charles E. Garman. From Garman, he told his father, he "gained a power of grappling with problems that will stand by me all my life."

COOLIDGE RECONSIDERED

Fᴏʀ sᴇᴠᴇʀᴀʟ ᴅᴇᴄᴀᴅᴇs his alma mater, like the rest of the country, has not quite known what to make of Amherst's 1895 graduate Calvin Coolidge, 30th president of the United States. Most people fall back on the stereotypes, believing that Coolidge was a silent, do-nothing, pro-business politician, dry as dust. (A detractor once said that "whenever Coolidge opened his mouth, a moth flew out.")

In July 1998, however, the college joined other organizations in sponsoring a major conference titled "Calvin Coolidge: Examining the Evidence," held at Boston's John F. Kennedy Library. Large audiences at the two-day gathering learned that, dry as he was, Coolidge has been under-appreciated.

The program of lectures and discussions drew capacity crowds of 500 people who listened first to taped welcoming remarks by Coolidge's 91-year-old son, John (Amherst 1928). From the Coolidge home in Plymouth, Vermont, John Coolidge told them: "Any fair and serious-minded person who examines my father's entire political record will be in for a surprise."

Many were. Particularly in discussion of his roles (1906–1920) as state legislator, lieutenant governor, and governor of Massachusetts, the Republican Coolidge emerged as a political activist who was popular with a broad spectrum of voters. He supported such progressive measures as a minimum wage, workmen's compensation, a 40-hour work week, votes for women, raises for teachers, and medical care for the indigent. According to Kennedy Library historian Sheldon M. Stern, "Under Coolidge as governor, Massachusetts was the most progressive state government in the country."

Speakers noted that Coolidge's most famous remark made as president, that "the chief business of America is business," has been taken out of context from a speech that went on to say, "It is only those who do not understand our people who believe that our national life is entirely absorbed by material motives. . . . We want peace and honor, and that charity which is so strong an element of all civilization. The chief ideal of the American people is idealism."

They also pointed to Coolidge's positive record on race relations. When the blatantly racist movie *The Birth of a Nation* was first shown in Boston in 1915, riots broke out and a prominent black Boston lawyer, William Henry Lewis (who graduated from Amherst in 1892), led a protest demonstration on Beacon Hill. Lewis and his followers said the film was insulting and incendiary and should not be shown. In a conference address on "Calvin Coolidge and Race," commentator Alvin Felzenberg reported that Coolidge, then president of the state senate, cast the deciding vote to establish a censorship board that could shut the film down. He speculates that Lewis brought his personal influence to bear on Coolidge as a fellow Amherst man.

In the White House, one of Coolidge's predecessors, Woodrow Wilson, condoned racial segregation in Washington, while Coolidge as president opposed it. And when the Ku Klux Klan was riding high in this country, North as well as South, Coolidge did not condemn the Klan by name but did quietly set a presidential example of tolerance, giving speeches at synagogues, black colleges, and Roman Catholic gatherings. "Compared to Woodrow Wilson," said Felzenberg, "he was a messiah." Coolidge was the last president to write his own speeches, and he crafted them well. In October 1925, not long after 40,000 members of the Klan staged a mass rally at the nation's capital, Coolidge spoke on "Toleration and Liberalism" at the American Legion convention in Omaha, Nebraska:

> [The bringing together of] different national, religious, cultural elements has made our country a kind of composite of the rest of the world, and we can render no greater service than by demonstrating the possibility of harmonious cooperation among so many various groups. Every one of them has something characteristic and significant of great value to cast into the common fund of material, intellectual, and spiritual resources. . . . Whether one traces his Americanisms back three centuries, to the *Mayflower*, or three years to the steerage, is not half so important, as whether his Americanism of today is real and genuine. No matter by what various crafts we came here, we are all now in the same boat.

Speakers at the Boston conference agreed that Coolidge was more activist as a governor than as president, but they disagreed as to why.

Coolidge was elected vice president in 1920 and became president on the death of Warren G. Harding in 1923. He was elected to a full term in 1924. One historian at the conference, Robert E. Gilbert, argued that Coolidge might have been a stronger president except for clinical depression he believes Coolidge suffered following the death of his younger son, Calvin Jr., at the age of 16. Shortly before the 1924 election, young Calvin died of blood poisoning from a blister he got playing tennis.

Gilbert, author of *The Mortal Presidency: Illness and Anguish in the White House*, said that before the son's death Coolidge was a very hardworking president who spent long hours at his desk, sent a flurry of legislative proposals to Congress, and restored confidence in government after the scandals of the Harding administration; afterwards, however, he lost interest in political affairs, stopped working closely with Congress, and took frequent naps. Gilbert quoted an observation made by Grace, the president's wife, that Coolidge "lost his zest for living," and he cited

Coolidge's own statement that "When Calvin Jr. died, the power and the glory of the presidency went with him."

Other speakers argued that Coolidge's approach to the presidency was all in tune with the times. Hugh Sidey, who covered the presidency for *Time* magazine for 40 years, said he once asked liberal fellow journalist Richard Strout, who had covered earlier presidents, why Strout liked Coolidge so much. "Back in those years," Strout told him, "we didn't really need a president, and Coolidge did it very well." Sidey added, "Coolidge said in effect, 'Just be patient. Most problems seem to run off the road before they get to the White House.' Well, I've seen that happen," Sidey noted, "over and over again."

Richard Norton Smith, director of the Gerald R. Ford Library in Michigan, said that before the New Deal era "relatively few Americans looked to Washington to solve their problems or to feel their pain." They looked instead to the states. Robert Sobel, author of *Coolidge: An American Enigma*, agreed that the quiet Vermonter was a good president for the '20s. "To be a great president," he said, "you have to be president at a time that demands greatness," and Coolidge's presidency did not face that demand. "He was the appropriate president for the times. The nice thing about Coolidge is, he left you alone. This," Sobel said, "is called freedom."

Hendrik Booraem, another speaker, noted that when Coolidge was still a student at Amherst he wrote to his father that "genius is the ability to harmonize with circumstances." That's what Coolidge appeared to do. Booraem is the author of *The Provincial: Calvin Coolidge and His World, 1885–1895.*

Coolidge left office early in 1929 and died four years later. In a tribute to the former president, Al Smith, the New York Democrat and presidential candidate, ranked Coolidge "in the class of presidents who were distinguished for character more than for heroic achievements. His great task," Smith said, "was to restore the dignity and prestige of the presidency when it had reached the lowest ebb in our history, and to afford in a time of extravagance and waste, a shining public example of the simple and honest virtues which came down to him from his New England ancestors. These are no small achievements, and history will not forget them."

For years, history seemed to forget many things about the Amherst man who went to the White House. Now that may be starting to change.

—DCW

Robert Frost never graduated from college. He spent less than a semester at Dartmouth and, later, two years at Harvard. Intermittently during a span of more than 45 years, though, students at Amherst were privileged to have him as a college professor. Frost found that he, too, benefited from the arrangement: "I've been given a certain chance here," he once acknowledged. "I was brought here in 1916, and what I was given was the chance to pursue my own honesty." In these excerpts from his book *Frost: A Literary Life Reconsidered* (1984), William H. Pritchard '53 writes about the unconventional teaching that Frost introduced in the classroom as he pursued his unique, often mischievous honesty. Pritchard entered Amherst as a freshman in 1949, the year Frost in his 70s started returning to campus to spend part of each year as a resident lecturer. Pritchard joined the faculty 10 years later, when he was completing a dissertation on Frost, and began to teach and write about modern poetry and fiction. A prominent literary critic, the author and editor of many books, Pritchard judges Frost, with T. S. Eliot, to be one of the two "most major" of the major twentieth-century poets—two who, beyond the others, produced "lifeworks of inexhaustible interest."

THE MISCHIEF OF ROBERT FROST

By *William H. Pritchard*

THE CIRCUMSTANCES LEADING up to Robert Frost's coming to Amherst College were marked by cordiality and high hopes on both sides. The precipitating agent in the whole matter was Stark Young, whom President Alexander Meiklejohn—at the suggestion of John Erskine—had brought to Amherst from the University of Texas. Young (now remembered mainly for his drama criticism) was a Southerner, an aspiring poet and novelist whose relation to the teaching of English bore little resemblance to that of scholars trained in the field. Perhaps for that reason his courses were extremely popular at Amherst, his cultivated Southern manner something out of the ordinary for a small college in western Massachusetts. Young made it his business to get to know as many important artists as possible, and it was at his suggestion that the college literary society invited Frost to read from his work in April of 1916. At the time, George Whicher was a young English instructor at the college, and 30 years later, in one of his morning chapel talks, he described his first meeting with Frost, as the curious gathered in the Christian Association Room to greet the sage:

> We found a sturdily built man in his early forties, wearing rumpled clothes and a celluloid collar, with unruly brown hair, blunt features, and eyes of seafarer's blue that had a way of magically lighting up. As

he talked, he seemed to be constantly inviting his audience to help him find just the right form of words. He spoke slowly, often rolling up a phrase with many heaves as though it were a stone to be placed in a wall that needed mending. We felt that we were watching an arduous creative triumph, the shaping into forms of ideas drawn from the dark abyss of the unconscious mind. It was a dramatic, a memorable hour that we spent with him.

Confined to the brief compass of a nine-minute talk, Whicher had recourse to metaphor to express the magic of this moment: Frost's blue eyes are "seafarer's blue"; putting phrases into sentences is mending a stone wall. Whereas the anthologist and poet Louis Untermeyer's account of first hearing Frost read and talk stressed the way he understated things, Whicher speaks of him as drawing ideas up "from the dark abyss" of his unconscious. Indeed the process becomes Miltonic in character, as at the opening of *Paradise Lost* we hear of the Spirit who "with mighty wings outspread / Dove-like sat'st brooding on the vast abyss / And mad'st it pregnant." One could carry Whicher's metaphor further and say that the students and faculty at Amherst were somehow to be made pregnant, productive of ideas, under the creative ministerings of this remarkable spirit. Frost himself grew fond of the birth metaphor, informing Untermeyer that "I put them [the students] on the operating table and proceeded to take ideas they didn't know they had out of them as a prestidigitator takes rabbits and pigeons you have declared yourself innocent of out of your pocket trousers legs and even mouth." He was not merely an impregnator, but an obstetrician as well.

One doubts that Stark Young was similarly awed. Although he took pleasure in acting as host at the Amherst reading, he had in mind the specific goal of obtaining Frost's assistance toward the end of publishing a volume of his own poetry. This poetry he read to Frost, took as truly meant the older man's dutiful response, and proceeded to send the poems to Alfred Harcourt at Holt, with what he thought was Frost's approval. In fact, when Harcourt received the book and wrote Frost to ask him about it, Frost replied with a telegram the essence of which was "Thumbs Down." But by then President Meiklejohn, and surely with Young's encouragement, had offered Frost a job as a replacement for George Bosworth Churchill of the English Department, who was about to serve a term in the Massachusetts senate. Young showed up at Frost's farm in Franconia, New Hampshire, with the offer, which Frost finally accepted in December—his teaching to begin in the following month. On December 16, 1916, he received a warm letter from Meiklejohn, looking forward to his presence at Amherst and saying that that morning in chapel he had read aloud "The Road Not Taken," "and then told the boys about your coming. They applauded vigorously and were evidently much delighted by the prospect."

Alexander Meiklejohn was an exceptionally high-minded educator whose principles and whose moral tone toward things may be illustrated most briefly and clearly by some statements from his essay "What the College Is." This, his inaugural address as president of Amherst, was printed for a time as an introduction to the college catalog. What the college was, or should be—what Meiklejohn hoped to make Amherst into—was a place to be thought of as "liberal," that is, "essentially intellectual": "The college is primarily not a place of the body, nor of the feelings, nor even of the will; it is, first of all, a place of the mind." Introducing "the boys" to the intellectual life, led for its own sake, would save them from pettiness and dullness, would save them from being one of what Meiklejohn referred to as "the others": "There are those among us who will find so much satisfaction in the countless trivial and vulgar amusements of a crude people that they have no time for the joys of the mind. There are those who are so closely shut up within a little round of petty pleasures that they have never dreamed of the fun of reading and conversing and investigating and reflecting." A liberal education would rescue boys from stupidity, its purpose being to draw from that "reality-loving American boy" something like "an intellectual enthusiasm." But this result could not be achieved, Meiklejohn added, without a thorough reversal of the curriculum: "I should like to see every freshman at once plunged into the problems of philosophy," he said with enthusiasm.

Now, five years after his address, he was bringing to Amherst someone outside the usual academic orbit, a poet who lacked even a college degree. But despite—or perhaps because of—this lack, the poet had escaped triviality, was an original mind who knew about living by ideas. For he had written among other poems "The Road Not Taken," given pride of place in the just-published *Mountain Interval* as not only its first poem but also printed in italics, as though to make it also a preface to and motto for the poems which followed. It was perfect for Meiklejohn's purposes because it was no idle reverie, no escape through lovely language into a soothing dream world, but a poem rather that announced itself to be "about" important issues in life: about the nature of choice, of decision, of how to go in one direction rather than another and how to feel about the direction you took and didn't take. For President Meiklejohn and for the assembled students at compulsory chapel, it might have been heard as a stirring instance of what the "liberal college" was all about, since it showed how, instead of acceding to the petty pleasures, the "countless trivial and vulgar amusements" offered by the world or the money-god or the values of the marketplace, an individual could go his own way, live his own life, read his own books, take the less traveled road:

> I shall be telling this with a sigh
> Somewhere ages and ages hence;
> Two roads diverged in a wood, and I—
> I took the one less traveled by,
> And that has made all the difference.

The poem ended, the boys "applauded vigorously," and surely Meiklejohn congratulated himself just a bit on making the right choice, taking the less traveled road and inviting a poet to join the Amherst College faculty.

What the president could hardly have imagined, committed as he was in high seriousness to making the life of the college truly an intellectual one, was the unruliness of Frost's spirit and its unwillingness to be confined within the formulas—for Meiklejohn, they were truths—of the "liberal college." On the first day of the new year, 1917, just preparatory to moving his family down from the Franconia farm into a house in Amherst, Frost wrote Untermeyer about where the fun lay in what he, Frost, thought of as "intellectual activity": "You get more credit for thinking if you restate formulae or cite cases that fall in easily under formulae, but all the fun is outside saying things that suggest formulae that won't formulate—that almost but don't quite formulate. I should like to be so subtle at this game as to seem to the casual person altogether obvious.

The casual person would assume I meant nothing or else I came near enough meaning something he was familiar with to mean it for all practical purposes. Well, well, well."

The "fun" is "outside," and lies in doing something like teasing, suggesting formulae that don't formulate, or not quite. The fun is not in being "essentially intellectual" or in manifesting "intellectual enthusiasm" in Meiklejohn's sense of the phrase, but in being "subtle," and not just subtle but so much so as to fool "the casual person" into thinking that what you said was obvious. If we juxtapose these remarks with his earlier determination to reach out as a poet to all sorts and kinds of people, and if we think of "The Road Not Taken" as a prime example of a poem that succeeded in reaching out and taking hold, then something interesting emerges about the kind of relation to other people, to readers—or to students and college presidents—Frost was willing to live with, indeed to cultivate.

For the large moral meaning which "The Road Not Taken" seems to endorse—go, as I did, your own way, take the road less traveled by, and it will make "all the difference"—does not maintain itself when the poem is looked at more carefully. Then one notices how insistent is the speaker on admitting, at the time of his choice, that the two roads were in appearance "really about the same," that they "equally lay / In leaves no step had trodden black," and that choosing one rather than the other was a matter of impulse, impossible to speak about any more clearly than to say that the road taken had "perhaps the better claim." But in the final stanza, as the tense changes to future, we hear a different story, one that will be told "with a sigh" and "ages and ages hence." At that imagined time and unspecified place, the voice will have nobly simplified and exalted the whole impulsive matter into a deliberate one of taking the "less traveled" road:

> Two roads diverged in a wood, and I—
> I took the one less traveled by,
> And that has made all the difference.

Is it not the high tone of poignant annunciation that really makes all the difference? An earlier version of the poem had no dash after "I"; presumably

Frost added it to make the whole thing more expressive and heartfelt. And it was this heartfelt quality which touched Meiklejohn and the students.

Yet Frost had written to his friend Untermeyer two years previously that "I'll bet not half a dozen people can tell you who was hit and where he was hit in my Road Not Taken," and he characterized himself in that poem particularly as "fooling my way along." He also said that it was really about his friend Edward Thomas, who when they walked together always castigated himself for not having taken another path than the one they took. When Frost sent "The Road Not Taken" to Thomas he was disappointed that Thomas failed to understand it was a poem about himself, but Thomas in return insisted to Frost that "I doubt if you can get anybody to see the fun of the thing without showing them and advising them which kind of laugh they are to turn on." And though this sort of advice went exactly contrary to Frost's notion of how poetry should work, he did on occasion warn his audiences and other readers that it was a tricky poem. Yet it became a popular poem for very different reasons than what Thomas referred to as "the fun of the thing." It was taken to be an inspiring poem rather, a courageous credo stated by the farmer-poet of New Hampshire. In fact, it is an especially notable instance in Frost's work of a poem which sounds noble and is really mischievous. One of his notebooks contains the following four-line thought:

> Nothing ever so sincere
> That unless it's out of sheer
> Mischief and a little queer
> It wont prove a bore to hear.

The mischievous aspect of "The Road Not Taken" is what makes it something unboring, for there is little in its language or form which signals an interesting poem. But that mischief also makes it something other than a "sincere" poem, in the way so many readers have taken Frost to be sincere. Its fun is outside the formulae it seems almost but not quite to formulate.

Frost's teaching at Amherst should likewise be seen as a move to the outside, to some road not taken by the academics around him. To do that he needed a firm structure of regular course and classroom procedures, against which he could define himself as an extraordinary phenomenon. He had no interest in enforcing classroom discipline, thinking of himself rather as "there" for those students who were imaginative enough to make use of him. One of those was Henry A. Ladd, who contributed a retrospective portrait 20 years later to an Amherst undergraduate magazine, *Touchstone*, which put out a "Frost issue." Ladd, who graduated in 1918, and thus knew Frost near the beginning of his term, recalls that the writing course he took with him met in a fraternity house in the evening, usually lasting until midnight. There was much reading of and talk about poetry, with Frost sprawled in a chair asking them questions to which, Ladd says, there was almost always no possible answer: "It would be something like 'Why do they have classes anyway?' And then the talk would begin: he would broaden it, turn it this way and that; occasionally ask questions in the middle and sometimes throw the answers out the window with contemptuous phraseology which was also picturesque so that we all laughed—on and on it would go. Then there would be long silences where some of us who were appalled at the informality and wanted things 'to go well' would try asking questions. . . ." Some evenings, Ladd recalled, not much happened; some evenings it all seemed to come together. But for a member of the faculty to ask, at an institution like Amherst College, why "they" had classes anyway, was to practice the "sheer mischief" Frost recommended as essential for avoiding boredom, in education as in poetry as in life.

Ladd also etches in unsparing terms the moral personality of his teacher, as one evening Frost began to denounce the life of "Bohemian" intellectuals in New York: "I can recall being shocked at the moral intolerance, the scorching anger behind his words. . . . I was under the assumption that he was liberal in thought, broad-minded, humanistic. I found none of this kind of thing. He had violent prejudices and hatreds; he descended to gossip with a genuine relish and abused even teachers close to him on the campus; but always with a fine turn of phrase or the selection of instances of behavior which were significant as the lines of a brilliant entertainer." This penetrating description suggests how ill-suited such behavior was to the atmosphere of the liberal college Meiklejohn was trying to nurture, with its commitment to ideas and intellectual debate and social relevance, to the disinterested search for truth and the extirpation of prejudice. Frost was such a creature of prejudice that he once insisted, "I'd no more set out in pursuit of the truth than I would in pursuit of a living unless mounted on my prejudices." Henry Ladd felt the incongruity of Frost and the liberal college, yet was also much taken with his compelling, if sometimes disturbing, performance. Here was a way of teaching "English," of teaching writing, which knew that it was necessary to talk about something besides good grammar, sentence structure, or arresting imagery. In very much his own way, Frost was as moral an educator as was President Meiklejohn. He wrote to his daughter Lesley in 1919, when she was studying at Barnard, that he was increasingly unhappy about his situation at Amherst, and complained about the pettiness of what he termed "intramural college standards," by which he meant discouragements to originality. A student of his, in response to one of Frost's remarks, had asked him, "Do they say that?"

> I told him, "no *I* say it but *they* would say it too if I pointed it out to them." They know nothing not gotten from somebody else. Quotation is the height of scholarship and scores ten. It is best if you have an idea to attribute it to someone else so that they will feel that it has the weight of authority. They are always asking Who is your authority? I suppose their attitude of mind can hardly be helped in college where acquirement is the main object. But it is deadly and deathly. How to escape it!

By the following fall he had decided to escape it by escaping from Amherst College. He moved his family back to Franconia at the beginning of February and resigned officially in the following May of 1920. On the eve of his departure from Amherst he wrote to an alumnus explaining why he would not be speaking at a dinner he had been invited to, saying that he was too much out of sympathy with what Meiklejohn was doing "with this old New England College"—even though he, Frost, had had plenty of "academic freedom" there: "While he detests my dangerous rationalistic and anti-intellectualistic philosophy, he thinks he is willing to have it represented here. But probably it will be better represented by someone else who can take it less seriously than I."

"Detestation" is the wrong word for what the high-minded Meiklejohn thought of Frost's "philosophy," but the really curious thing in the sentence is Frost's use of the word "rationalistic" to describe that philosophy. For what Frost brought to Amherst, in a very powerful form, was not rationalism, but the imagination. That imagination operated on the students who were themselves imaginative enough to respond to it, to produce an educational experience they never forgot, as can be seen from the testimonies of a number of them in the college magazine mentioned above.

One can imagine the mixture of triumph and trepidation with which Frost prepared in 1923 to return to the college he had so recently left. Writing to Wilbur Cross in the August preparatory to his return, he praised him for striking "just the right dubious note in congratulating me about going back to Amherst. I ought to have been poet enough to stay away. But I was too much of a philosopher to resist the temptation to go back and help show the world the difference between the right kind of liberal college and the wrong kind." There is a dramatic and adversary flare to this admission—or boast—which suggests how unpeacefully Frost returned. That is, he was not only firmly mounted on his prejudices, but was on the lookout for any signs of what he referred to as "Meiklejaundice," or the wrong kind of liberal education. In the satirical terms he put it to Untermeyer after his first year back, this disease meant fancying that in Amherst College you were doing something called "thinking" rather than mere "learning" (which was what they did at colleges other than Amherst). A related fancy, in Frost's opinion, was the idea that the pupil "taught himself," rather than was taught by the teacher. What he "taught" himself, in Frost's scornful view, was really only a replacing of conservative ideas with "radical" ones. So he and his students in the philosophy course Frost offered that first year back in "Verdicts" or "Judgments" inquired into what thinking really was: "We reached an agreement that most of what they had regarded as thinking, their own and other people's, was nothing but voting—taking sides on an issue they had nothing to do with laying down." "Thinking," for Frost, was deeply involved with the associative act of metaphor, of saying one thing in terms of another, of saying one thing while meaning another. When he complained that the Amherst students had been affected by Meiklejaundice, he meant that they were unable to recognize a metaphor when they saw or made one. But discounting his eagerness to lay blame on the departed president's shoulders, the complaint was inevitable from one who had committed himself to education by poetry. What Frost meant by such education—for him, the only true liberal education—was, in the language of the essay he would write in 1930, "education by poetry."

As always, the acceptance of an academic routine brought with it the wish for more freedom than was available under the existing arrangement, probably under any conceivable arrangement. And of course his insistence, in a letter to Untermeyer, that "the strength of a teacher's position lies in the waiting till he is come after," could also be construed on occasion as the hope that the students would not come after him too frequently. (If you don't bother them too much, perhaps they won't bother you, and you may be permitted to get on with writing poems—surely Frost cannot always have been above such less than high-minded impulses.)

There is then an ironic relation between public protestations—students should be responsible for their own education; a teacher should wait until he is "come after"—and private feelings (the teacher is disinclined to spend time marking student papers; the teacher desires to be let alone rather than be pestered by the eager young). But to judge this divergence of motive as hypocritical on Frost's part, or to regard it solely with cynicism, one must be very clear and fairly inflexible about what constitutes *real* as opposed to "symbolic" teaching—the kind Frost said he did. A number of his colleagues on the Amherst faculty were perfectly clear about the matter and wondered just what the duties were for which he drew a salary. That feeling grew stronger after he returned in 1926 from his one year, last-shot flirtation with the University of Michigan, and took up once more the position he would fill for the next 12 years. A full professor, he was expected to be in residence only during the 10 weeks of the winter term (later, when Frost began to go to Florida in December, the time was changed) and to have no official duties beyond giving an occasional lecture or reading. One can imagine the sort of grumbling this arrangement produced among those not so favored, and how any discrepancy between what was professed and what was practiced might be eagerly seized upon as evidence of bad faith. Yet, in a sense, there was no discrepancy at all between belief and practice; Frost professed a sort of academic laissez-faire and also carried it out.

After his final stint at Michigan, he returned not to farming (except in his special sense of that activity), but to Amherst College under an arrangement which could hardly have been bettered. The course catalog for 1926–27 carried, at the end of its section of English departmental offerings, the information that "During the winter Professor Robert Frost will be in residence to conduct special classes in English and to hold informal conferences with the student." This was an artfully worded piece of information, making clear that he was no ordinary professor and that students should not expect the usual thing—whatever that was—in their dealings with him. The English classes he would conduct were "special" ones (part of their specialness consisted in their not meeting very often) and the conferences he held with students would be "informal" ones. And he could look on this special status as corroborative of his insistence that in a classroom one should rise above issues of right or wrong, yes or no, true or false.

The college's alumni include a U.S. president, a Supreme Court chief justice, distinguished teachers, preachers, poets, doctors, philanthropists, business leaders, scientists, lawmakers—the list is long. But among these, paradoxically, the most accomplished graduate of all may be one of the least known: the lawyer Charles Hamilton Houston of the Class of 1915. Houston has justly been called "the legal architect of the modern civil rights movement." He was born in 1895, a year before the landmark Supreme Court ruling in *Plessy v. Ferguson* that upheld "separate but equal" race segregation. The court eventually overturned *Plessy* in rulings that culminated in 1954 with *Brown v. Board of Education*. Speaking at Amherst in 1978, Thurgood Marshall cited Houston as "the engineer of all of it." "When [*Brown*] was being argued . . . there were some two dozen lawyers on the side of the Negro," he recalled. "We very carefully went from one to another, and there were only two who hadn't been touched by Charlie Houston." At Amherst, Houston majored in English, music, and French, and was elected to Phi Beta Kappa. Robert L. Carter is a senior U.S. District judge for the Southern District of New York. Like Marshall, he was one of Houston's protégés who argued *Brown* before the Supreme Court. This article (without its original 42 footnotes) is reprinted from the *Harvard Law Review* of June 1998.

TRULY A GREAT AMERICAN

By Robert L. Carter

Charles Hamilton Houston was totally committed to—indeed, consumed by—a singular mission: finding and wielding levers of change to free black Americans from racial oppression. Houston believed this goal could be accomplished principally through court decisions that would accord the Fourteenth Amendment its intended meaning as the guardian and insurer of equal citizenship rights for black Americans. He determined to reach this result by carefully conceiving test cases to persuade the courts to adopt his view of the Fourteenth Amendment as a guarantor of racial equality. These cases were to be undertaken particularly in the critical areas of education, employment, and voting rights.

Houston believed that black lawyers had to assume primary responsibility for making real the Fourteenth Amendment's guarantee of racial equality. Thus, the education and training of a top-flight cadre of black lawyers was a priority. His conception of the black lawyers' role in the fight for equality was not the result of jingoism or nationalism. On the contrary, Houston was fully committed to integration: he maintained that the black community must seek the support of whites and that white awareness of widespread discrimination against blacks would stimulate sympathy and support for the effort to eliminate segregation. Still, Houston believed that blacks themselves should be at the forefront of the fight to end racial oppression. In Houston's view, the development of a consciousness among blacks that racial injustice was unconstitutional, together with black leadership against racial oppression, was vital: he expected that the leadership and consciousness of individual blacks would be contagious, inspiring the entire black community to engage in acts of public protest against segregation.

Houston's agenda was a daunting one for one man to undertake. It is a measure of his greatness as a scholar, lawyer, writer, public advocate, educator, and "social engineer" that Houston accomplished so much of what he set out to do before his untimely death at age 54, and that he left such a rich legacy upon which those contemporaries he inspired, as well as future generations, could build to complete the tasks that he did not live to finish.

From what origin did such a visionary arise? Houston was born in Washington, D.C., on September 3, 1895. Both of Houston's parents were schoolteachers; his father was a principal. However, upon settling in D.C., Houston's parents had pursued other vocations. Houston's mother, Mary Hamilton, gave up teaching for the more lucrative tasks of sewing and hairdressing for Washington's gentry. His father, William, took a job as a War Department clerk, while at the same time studying law at night at the Howard University Law School. Upon admission to the bar, the elder Houston opened a law office.

After graduating from Washington's public schools, the younger Houston enrolled at Amherst College at age 16. After completing Amherst [in 1915] and teaching in D.C. for two years, Houston enlisted in the army, seeking training as an officer in the artillery corps. However, because of racial discrimination, black officers then were being trained only for service in the infantry. Thus, Houston became a first lieutenant in the infantry, but resigned this position in June 1918 to attend artillery school. In September 1918, he won his commission as a second lieutenant in artillery. Houston was mustered out of the army in April 1919.

In the fall of 1919, he enrolled in Harvard Law School, where Felix Frankfurter became his mentor. After earning an LL.B. degree, Houston remained at Harvard to secure a doctorate in law, an S.J.D. In 1923, with Frankfurter's help, Houston was awarded a Sheldon Traveling Fellowship that he used for study in Spain, where he earned a Doctor of Civil Laws degree from the University of Madrid.

In 1924, Houston returned to Washington and joined his father's law firm, a move that placed him in the upper echelon of the nation's lawyers. Houston worked in this firm for five years, while also teaching part-time at Howard Law School. As a law professor, he taught his students that the Fourteenth Amendment held the key to eliminating racial discrimination and to securing equal treatment for blacks, and that a revolutionary change in race relations could be accomplished through the law. In 1929, five years after joining the faculty, Houston became vice dean of Howard Law School.

At the time that Houston became vice dean, Howard Law School trained the majority of blacks who entered the legal profession. However, the law school was a marginal enterprise lacking accreditation. Its faculty, most of whom were employed part-time, was weak. Neither were its students well trained; most held full-time day jobs and attended law school at night.

Houston changed all of this. During the course of his tenure at Howard, Houston transformed the law school into a well-respected institution. He closed the night school, dismissed the weak faculty that he had inherited, and replaced it with a group of talented young black scholars and advocates. By 1931 he had secured both accreditation for the law school from the American Bar Association and its membership in the American Association of Law Schools. Perhaps the most significant change that Houston achieved was making courses in civil rights law a special focus of the basic curriculum. These courses revolved around Houston's thesis that the Thirteenth, Fourteenth, and Fifteenth Amendments were the guarantors of the personal, economic, and social freedom of the black community. This emphasis on civil rights law was not merely an academic exercise. Houston encouraged graduates of Howard Law School to embark on their professional careers by returning to their local communities and instituting test cases designed to undermine racial discrimination and engage the black community in various forms of advocacy and self-help. Moreover, under Houston's leadership, selected members of Howard's student body and law school faculty became partners with the NAACP in devising and developing legal strategies to level race restrictions. These efforts brought respectability to the black bar: until Houston arrived, the NAACP's legal cases had been brought by white lawyers.

The cases involving Houston and these lawyers are legion. A few are illustrative of the significance of their endeavors. In 1932, Houston, as NAACP counsel, sought to prevent the extradition of George Crawford, a black man from Massachusetts, to stand trial in Loudoun County, Virginia, for the murder of two white women. Houston argued that the systematic exclusion of blacks from the grand jury that had indicted Crawford had fatally tainted the indictment against him, warranting denial of the extradition request. That battle was won at the trial level but vacated on appeal, and Crawford was taken to Loudoun County to stand trial. Houston, along with Leon Ransom, who had graduated first in his class from Ohio State University Law School before joining the Howard faculty, and Edward Lovett, a Howard graduate who was one of Houston's protégés and later a partner in Houston's firm, were Crawford's trial attorneys. Loudoun County had never seen black attorneys of their caliber. Indeed, they were probably the best-trained group of black lawyers that had ever appeared in a Southern court. The case was lost, but the jury surprised everyone by recommending life imprisonment instead of the death penalty. In rural Virginia at the time, this sentence was a singular victory.

In 1935 Houston joined the NAACP as its special counsel. In that position he developed the blueprint for the legal strategy to outlaw the separate but equal doctrine in education, which would be the organization's primary target for the next 20 years. Instead of a frontal, all-out attack, Houston's strategy was to proceed with caution. He decided to start at the state-supported graduate and professional school levels, where public education was available for whites but not for blacks. If the law were to require such states to make equal provision for the education of blacks at professional and graduate school levels, Houston surmised that the small number of blacks seeking such training would make it grossly financially inefficient to operate separate institutions for blacks. Thus, states operating dual school systems would be forced to admit blacks into the existing segregated state institutions.

Houston also had hopes that judges would have little difficulty un-derstanding that a segregated law school was inherently an unequal institution. Assisted by Thurgood Marshall, Houston instituted three cases in the early 1930s: first, *Pearson v. Murray*, in Maryland state court, seeking the admission of Donald Murray to the University of Maryland Law School; second, *Bluford v. Canada*, in federal court in Missouri, seeking the admission of Lucille Bluford to the School of Journalism of the University of Missouri; and third, *Missouri ex rel. Gaines v. Canada*, in Missouri state court, seeking the admission of Lloyd Lionel Gaines to the University of Missouri Law School.

Pearson was important because it was the first such case in the country and because it resulted in Murray's being ordered admitted to the university. *Gaines* was even more significant, because the Supreme Court's 1938 decision in that case placed strictures on the separate but equal doctrine that doomed it to extinction. The Court held that the constitutional validity of racial separation was conditioned on the state having provided equal facilities for blacks, and that states could not meet their obligation to provide blacks with equal education facilities by providing them with out-of-state scholarships.

The day before Houston was scheduled to argue *Gaines* before the Supreme Court, he presented a preview of his argument before the students at Howard University Law School. This was the start of a tradition that continued for at least 30 years—NAACP lawyers giving Howard law students a preview of their appearances scheduled for the next day in the Supreme Court. The tradition was firmly ensconced when a justice asked Houston a question that one of the students had put to him the day before. Notwithstanding the pragmatic function of the tradition, Houston, always the educator and motivator, enthusiastically engaged in this exercise to demonstrate to students how to make an appellate argument and to encourage them that they, too, could someday appear before the Supreme Court if they challenged themselves despite the racial discrimination that they were forced to endure.

I was present when Houston made his argument before the Court on behalf of Gaines. One scene from that day I will never forget: that of Houston rising to go to the podium to begin his presentation and of Justice James C. McReynolds, who was sitting to the left of Chief Justice Charles Evans Hughes, simultaneously spinning his chair around so that his back was to Houston throughout the argument. It is a comment on the times that there was no stir in the courtroom at this deliberate insult and no comment about it among ourselves afterward. Seemingly, no one who witnessed the incident regarded it with distaste or outrage. Thus, this deliberate showing of bias toward blacks by a member of an institution responsible for serving the interests of all Americans, if not commonplace at the time, was not unexpected. That incident provides a clear picture of the climate in which Houston conceived and began to effectuate his plan to transform American race relations. It is probably an indication of the progress in race relations that Houston helped the country achieve that my reflections on that incident of some 60 years ago are far more emotionally charged today than were my reactions at the time.

After leaving the NAACP, Houston continued to garner ground-breaking victories as a civil rights lawyer in private practice. For instance, in *Steele v. Louisville & Nashville Railroad Co.*, Houston made ground-breaking labor law by obtaining a holding that the union representative of a collective bargaining unit was under a duty to provide fair represen-tation for all members of the unit, both union and nonunion members. Houston was also instrumental to the success of the Negro Alliance, a Washington, D.C.–based group that picketed and urged boycotts of com-mercial operations situated in the black community that refused to hire black employees. After a court injunction was sought to enjoin the pick-eting of the Alliance, Houston garnered a signal Supreme Court victory for the organization when the Court held that the Alliance was engaged in a labor dispute which, under the Norris–La Guardia Act, could not be enjoined by the courts. In addition, Houston helped devise the legal strat-egy for, and argued, *Hurd v. Hodge*, which, along with *Shelley v. Kraemer*, outlawed the enforcement by the courts of restrictive covenants.

Although this tribute focuses on Houston's work as a lawyer and legal scholar, it is important to note that Houston's role in the struggle for civil rights extended beyond this realm. In fact, much of what progress has been achieved in alleviating racial oppression was either generated or fur-thered by him. Houston was a member of the President's Fair Employ-ment Practices Committee, a body created by executive order of President Franklin D. Roosevelt for the purpose of eliminating discrimination by companies holding government contracts. The FEPC was the precursor of antidiscrimination agencies that came into being after World War II. In addition to conceiving the strategy that culminated in *Brown v. Board of Education*, Houston was a strong advocate of black community activism. While no sit-ins or marches by blacks occurred on his watch, we can infer from his efforts to galvanize the black community to action that he would have applauded the 1960s sit-ins by college students in Greensboro, North Carolina, and elsewhere, as well as the nonviolent civil disobedience campaigns led by Dr. Martin Luther King, Jr.

Actually, it is difficult to think of any aspect of black Americans' struggle for civil rights that has not been influenced by the thoughts and actions of Charles Hamilton Houston, or by those directly or indirectly under his tutelage. Throughout his professional life, Houston devoted all of his energy, thought, and skills to the goal of freeing the black community from the burdens of racial discrimination. He was in truth a great American.

One pleasure of editing a magazine is having good articles arrive unsolicited "over the transom." Several pieces reprinted in this volume were just that kind of unexpected windfall for the Amherst quarterly—among them this story sent in by John S. Lancaster '51, in 1988. Lancaster, a public relations executive in California and an active alumnus, had a lover's quarrel with his alma mater on many issues, but his lasting affection for the college can be seen in this reminiscent essay. The college has an important place in the history of baseball. Amherst and Williams played the country's first intercollegiate baseball game, in Pittsfield, Massachusetts, in 1859. In that early contest, in addition to home plate, there were four bases instead of three, and batters and pitchers were called "strikers" and "throwers." The confrontation went on for three hours, and a sportswriter marveled that "the [unnamed] Amherst thrower lasted the whole game. More faultless and scientific throwing we have never seen." The final score was stratospheric: Amherst 73, Williams 32. Lancaster's 1948 game was not as historic as the Pittsfield encounter, but for one man, Stuffy McInnis, it was momentous.

A GOOD DAY FOR STUFFY McINNIS

⌒

By John S. Lancaster

JUNE 2ND FELL on a Wednesday in 1948 and came during the period between the end of spring semester classes and the beginning of final exams. Ordinarily, students would have stretched out on the grass in front of their fraternities or dormitories, making a pretense—if not a serious effort—of preparing for finals.

But the lawns were clear that afternoon. To the surprise of the most dedicated Amherst baseball fans, who usually shared the bleachers with three-score spectators, at best, hundreds of students—singly, in clusters, even in droves—were pressing through the gates of Pratt Field. Even the small ranks of faculty members and staff who regularly watched Amherst teams perform—men like Dwight Salmon and Ben Ziegler, Bill Wilson and Scott Porter—were joined by a large number of colleagues. Eventually about 1,000 people were in the stands to watch the day's event, a game between the Lord Jeffs of Amherst and the perennial New England powerhouse, the Crusaders of Holy Cross.

The undergraduate body that year was unique in the history of the college. The 1,150 students included large numbers of veterans of World War II, some of whom had spent as many as three and four years under arms. In the classroom they sat beside fuzzy-cheeked 18- and 19-year-olds whose sole exposure to the war had been via newspaper and radio. The baseball squad reflected this mixture: 14 of the 20 members were veterans, although, interestingly, there was only one senior on the team, catcher Jack Forte, originally a member of the Class of 1947. Despite the differences in age and maturity, it was a congenial group whose members respected one another's talents, understood and forgave their foibles, and learned to recognize the signs of too long a bout at the fraternity bar the night before. The team members have remained close over the years despite broad geographical dispersal.

This was not to be an ordinary game, and although the reasons had not been trumpeted about the campus, the underground system that only students are able to implement had reached into the deepest corners of Converse Library; even those who knew little more about baseball than there are nine men on a team wandered to Pratt Field to see the next-to-last regularly scheduled baseball game that would ever be played there.

The game was to bring together on the same diamond for the first time in over 30 years Holy Cross coach Jack Barry and Amherst's coach, John "Stuffy" McInnis, who had once been teammates on Connie Mack's Philadelphia A's. Barry was now in the 28th year of a coaching career that was to extend over 40 seasons at Holy Cross. His teams ultimately compiled an incredible .808 winning percentage. Not one of those 40 teams ever suffered a losing season, and the Crusaders were regularly conceded the collegiate baseball championship of New England (no official designation or playoff system existed). On top of that, Barry had come to Holy Cross in 1921 at the conclusion of a fine Major League career that reached its high point in the years 1911 through 1914, when he played shortstop in Connie Mack's storied "$100,000 Infield" in Philadelphia. Even today it is widely acknowledged by baseball historians that no other Major League infield unit has ever come close to matching the skills of the A's infield of those years.

"Stuffy" ("That's the stuff, McInnis," his teammates used to call to him when he was a 14-year-old playing ball with men 15 and 20 years his senior on diamonds in his hometown of Gloucester, Massachusetts) was the first baseman on that A's team, and to the casual fan it was hard to tell why. Most first basemen stand in excess of six feet, have long arms to grab errant throws and sharply hit ground balls, and possess long-ball power. McInnis was barely 5 feet 8 inches tall. Size alone must surely have restricted his range, yet the record books tell otherwise. His attire was always the same—a maroon cardigan sweater, black street trousers, and athletic shoes (his only acknowledgment of his role as coach), with a slight bulge under the sweater.

Quiet, somewhat reserved, and not well known beyond the team, Stuffy had arrived on the Amherst campus in March, well after baseball practice had begun in the Cage. Amherst's longtime coach, Paul Eckley, had suffered a heart attack while playing squash early that February, only a few weeks before practice began, and a frantic search was mounted to find a qualified baseball man to step in immediately. Stories have it that athletic director and head football coach Lloyd Jordan telephoned his old friend Joe Cronin, then general manager of the Boston Red Sox (and later American League president) for suggestions. Cronin talked about Stuffy McInnis, who had coached baseball at a small prep school north of Boston. Soon, Stuffy was hired to coach that one season.

Although Stuffy was not particularly well known to younger baseball fans in 1948, the Amherst players quickly searched the baseball archives and record books and discovered that Stuffy was no ordinary baseball man. He was a member of five other Major League teams after his tenure with the A's: the Red Sox, the Indians, the (then Boston) Braves, and the Pirates; then he managed the Phillies for one year, in 1927. He had played on six pennant winners, and all but one of them had gone on to win the World Series and be crowned world champions. He had completed his career with a .308 lifetime batting average and a .990 lifetime fielding average. These kinds of numbers would qualify most big leaguers today for the Hall of Fame.

Stuffy was a graceful athlete, said a veteran fan who had seen him play. Nevertheless, how could a man that short perform so flawlessly as a key member of Connie Mack's infield, and in the years thereafter? "It was easy," said Stuffy. "Those three guys—second baseman Eddie Collins, third baseman Fran 'Home Run' Baker, and Barry—never made a bad throw. Anyone could have played first base for Mr. Mack in those days and never made an error."

As old baseball fans know, following the As' loss to the Braves in the 1914 World Series, Connie Mack broke up the team that had won three straight world championships in 1911, '12, and '13. Mack not only managed the A's, he owned the club as well, and he was losing money, despite fielding four consecutive league champions. The A's were so good that interest waned and attendance dwindled. He broke up the club after the 1914 season not because the team lost in the World Series that year but because he was slowly going bankrupt. Collins, Barry, and Baker were all traded; Mack kept McInnis for three more years before trading him to the Red Sox in 1918.

At Amherst in 1948, with no coach at hand as the March 10 starting date for spring practice arrived, second baseman Dave McNeish functioned as the team leader until Stuffy arrived. The team practiced every afternoon in the batting nets, awaiting his arrival. He had become a mysterious legend. Though anxious to meet him, the squad went about the everyday business of preparing for the season as best it could—in the Cage while snow outside gave ground to spring only slowly.

One day, Ivar Rosendale '49, the team's 19-year-old co-captain, who was to lead the team in hitting that year, was swinging at pitches in the batting nets.

"Why don't you adjust just a little bit and follow through like this," a voice said. Rosendale glanced up. Stuffy had arrived.

That first moment with Stuffy was the way it was to be over the next few months. There were few instructional meetings. Informality prevailed, with Stuffy offering tips, dispensing praise and encouragement freely, always pleasant and upbeat. His style was to instill confidence. "He believed in me and stuck with me," says Ezra Bowen '49 today. Bowen was the first baseman, struggling to master a new position. The team developed confidence, had fun, and looked forward to practices which on many college campuses today are repetitive, dull exercises of the fundamentals: hitting the cutoff man, practicing rundowns on the basepaths, learning intricate signals (Stuffy had none; if he wanted a man to steal, he waved his hand from the bench). The team developed a special camaraderie; players pulled for one another and overlooked teammates' mistakes. Practice sessions were well organized, however, and quiet discipline took hold.

Loyalty and commitment to one's teammates were two qualities Stuffy admired and encouraged. He expected his players to do their best at all times, and he was constantly calling "Good play" or "That's the way, boys." But if Stuffy was almost always taciturn and easygoing, he also could be tough and unbending. During one game early in the season, Stuffy decided that the situation called for a pinch hitter, and as the Amherst player due up to bat moved toward the batter's box, Stuffy called him back and sent a pinch hitter to the plate. The replaced batter muttered under his breath as he passed the substitute on his way back to the bench: "I hope you strike out." Only one other player heard the exchange. And Stuffy.

The next day Stuffy called a team meeting before practice began. The players assembled in the Pratt Field stands. This was pretty unusual. He did not waste words: he confronted the player before the others and although he did not refer to the specific incident of the day before, Stuffy dressed him down for a few scathing minutes, then concluded: "You should be ashamed of yourself. You don't belong on this team. Turn in your uniform *now*." And the player, a regular, never played another baseball game in an Amherst uniform. Even today, some members of that '48 squad do not know why Stuffy ejected him from the team.

Barry and Holy Cross had high hopes of winning the game against Amherst and maintaining their annual supremacy in New England. Once again, their record was a winning one, and a victory at Amherst would assure them of another championship. Chances are, Amherst was considered another easy win for the Crusaders, a team that included no fewer than six players who would ultimately be signed by Major League teams. Four would play in the game. (In those days, Major League baseball clubs rarely signed college players at all.) For the Amherst players, the game was a big one, a chance to test their strength against a bona fide baseball power. True, the Williams game coming up a week or so later was the important one, but this one was also special.

Whether Stuffy had ever heard of the Little Three before he came to Amherst is uncertain; but he wanted to beat Holy Cross, and his old teammate Jack Barry, badly. For Barry, victory over Amherst would be the 450th of his career at Holy Cross. McInnis, on the other hand, had never coached at the college level until this season. Though they were former teammates, Stuffy, then 57 years old, aimed for the Holy Cross game as the season progressed.

Amherst carried an 8–4 record into the game. "Rosie was the only guy who hit for us all year but he batted over .400 and carried us offensively," said co-captain Charlie Murphy '49 recently. "We won on good fielding and good pitching." Clarke Rainey, who could "throw smoke," and Murphy, a left-hander with a sharp-breaking curve ball, formed the nucleus of the starting staff. It was Charlie's turn to pitch, and Stuffy tossed him the ball.

Barry and McInnis met for the first time in many years that day as the players warmed up. Dave McNeish '49 was taking batting practice when the former greats greeted each other. After a few opening pleasantries, Stuffy said in response to a question from his former teammate: "Jack, Amherst is really great! You ought to see the training table here. I never imagined kids in college ate like this. The athletic facilities are terrific; I swim every day. And you should see where I'm living [Stuffy's wife had remained at their home in Gloucester during the few months he was at

Amherst]. I've never lived anywhere like this before. They treat me like a king. It is just unbelievable!"

Barry kept mumbling things like "Holy smoke! You're kidding! I never heard of anything like this! I can't believe it!" He was impressed. One of those who couldn't—and didn't—believe it was McNeish. He knew there was no training table at Amherst, that Stuffy ate his meals quietly, often by himself, at a corner table in Valentine Hall. Furthermore, Stuffy couldn't swim. His "house" consisted of a small room in North College where he was constantly bothered by noisy students who apparently never slept. Professor E. Dwight Salmon asked Stuffy once how he liked living in North, and Stuffy replied, "Not bad. It's like livin' in a bowlin' alley." Alone much of the time, Stuffy frequently lingered at the corner of Main and North Pleasant Streets, where he developed a series of friendships with various townspeople, regaling them with stories of Connie Mack, Ty Cobb, Tris Speaker, Babe Ruth (with whom he roomed for one year), and the other baseball giants. At night, unable to sleep, he often joined the town policeman in his squad car as he made his rounds.

The game began, left-hander Murphy of Amherst against another southpaw, Al McEvoy, who would sign a contract with the New York Yankees a few weeks later. Neither team scored in the first, but Holy Cross began to peck away at Murphy, who was having control problems, in the second. The Crusaders scored single runs in the second, third, and fourth innings and tallied two more in the fifth. Unable to score in the second, Amherst matched the opposition's scores in innings three, four, and five. It was 5–4 Holy Cross after five, and the Crusaders failed to score in the sixth.

This was not going the way Barry had planned. After all, he had thrown his best pitcher at the Jeffs and . . . well, it was a typical Murphy game. Murphy fit the description of a standard left-hander in those days—a lot of stuff, but no one was ever sure where the ball was going, including Murphy. Slender, graceful, and extremely competitive, Murphy had been an infielder in high school before coming to Amherst, where Eckley had converted him to a pitcher.

"John Bergin, our best reliever, was throwing in the bullpen every inning that day. He pitched an entire game but his name never got into the box score. The game was a long one for those days (2:40), and John sweated every one of those 160 minutes," says Murphy. By the time the game ended, 19 Crusaders had reached base. Murphy gave up eight hits (all singles), issued six bases on balls, and hit three batters. In addition, two of Amherst's three errors allowed Crusader batters to reach base.

Murphy typified southpaw pitchers, if not all pitchers, in another way as well: he would rather talk about his hitting than his pitching. It is still true today: "In that game, I hit the hardest ball I ever hit in my life. Right between the left fielder and the center fielder, and I figured I had a home run or a triple, easy—there was no fence at Pratt Field. As I rounded first base, I had to break stride to avoid hitting Calvin, their first baseman; and by the time I got straightened out, I couldn't make it beyond second. I had played ball for Barry for two summers in the old Blackstone Valley League and he taught his players every trick in the book. It was no accident Calvin was in my way, and although it was obstruction, the umpire missed it. That Barry was a tough competitor!"

Jack Jordan '50, Lloyd's son, led off the bottom of the sixth and smacked a ground ball out past short for a single. Forte reached first when shortstop Bill Porter, later signed by the Boston Braves, batted his ground ball. First and second, none out. Murphy struck out, but Dave McNeish, the team's sparkplug hustling as he always did, beat out another ground ball. Now the bases were loaded with one out. First baseman Ezra Bowen was due up.

Barry called time and walked slowly to the mound. True, even though Amherst had the bases loaded, none of the balls had been hit solidly this inning. His team had already scored five runs in only six innings and Murphy was in trouble all the time. Given all this, how come the tying run was on third with one out and a possible winning run was on second? A brief discussion ensued, out went Major League prospect McEvoy, and in came another Major League prospect, Dick Shellenback, soon also to sign with the Braves.

Like every Amherst player on the field that day except Rosendale, Bowen was a veteran. He had suffered a serious injury while in the Navy and had been discharged with a 50-percent disability allowance. Despite his physical problems he had earned a regular spot on the team through hard work and hustling. He was batting second in the order. Bowen swung at the first pitch and missed. The second was high and outside. Bowen watched the third pitch go by, taking it for a strike. One ball, two strikes.

"I figured Shellenback would throw me an outside, letter-high fastball," Bowen recalled. "His first two strikes were like that. And I was ready for the next one." Bowen swung and smashed a solid line drive up the alley between the left and center fielders. The ball could not be caught, and Jordan, Forte, and McNeish all scored. Bowen made third standing up. The score was now 7–5 Amherst.

(Nearly 40 years later, reminiscing about the game, Bowen said: "Two days after the game, I received a telephone call at the fraternity house; it was some guy from the Veterans Administration in Washington, D.C. He said: 'Bowen, I picked up the sports page yesterday and I read where you're playing baseball up there, running out triples and winning games. I'm not only taking you off 50-percent disability, I'm taking you off *all* disability. For good!' So we had a long discussion and finally he says: 'Okay, okay, 25 percent is okay but that's it.' He had read an Associated Press story about that game. I wish I knew who wrote that story; it has cost me a lot of money over the years," he concluded with some animation. I did not tell him that, since the AP could not assign a reporter to the game that day, a student representative of the Amherst News Bureau filed 400 words and a box score to the AP. The student was Harry Dalton '50, who later became general manager of the Milwaukee Brewers.)

Sophomore Bill Genovese '50, who was to anchor the Amherst infield for four years as the team's third baseman, then beat out an infield single, scoring Bowen. Rosendale, who had two hits that day to extend his consecutive batting streak to 13 straight (he was to hit in every game that year but the last one), flied out, and Lew Hammond '49 approached the plate.

Lew had become the team's regular center fielder only after the season had begun, missing the first few games to attend spring football practice. Not particularly athletic in appearance, Lew was a tough competitor, and he seemed to thrive on pressure. Now he waited for Shellenback's delivery. Though the Crusaders had fallen behind, Barry had relieved his top starter with his best relief man. There were still three innings to go, and anything could happen—particularly in view of Murphy's wildness. Hammond was a key man to Barry.

Hammond rifled the first pitch into left field. It went for two bases and Genovese scored: 9–5. Dave Gold, the ninth man up in the inning, flied out. But the five runs scored that inning were enough. By now, Murphy had begun to settle down and he shut out Holy Cross in the seventh and eighth innings.

An odd event occurred in the Amherst seventh. Murphy was struck on his "funnybone" by a pitch from Shellenback, and Stuffy called time to ask his old teammate if he would agree to allow Amherst to use a "courtesy runner." Despite his misfortunes of the day, Barry readily agreed, and Ed Lonczak was inserted as a pinch runner for Murphy. By the end of the inning, Murphy had shaken off the tingling sensation in his arm and returned to pitch a scoreless eighth.

Amherst scored once more in the eighth, making it 10–5. The Crusaders made a final push in the ninth, scoring twice. But Murphy had it all together now and struck out third baseman Joe Cunnane, his 13th strikeout victim, to end the game. After the game, Stuffy, despite his New England reserve, seemed downright ebullient. "Nice game, boys!" he said. "Good game." Was his smile a little broader? Was there a quaver in his voice?

Amherst went on to defeat Colgate in Hamilton, New York, on June 5, then lost to Williams in the season's finale at Pratt Field, 1–0, a loss that cost the Little Three Title. When the Williams game ended, the players left the field and walked the one block to the gym where they changed before and after each game. When Stuffy arrived, he went directly to his locker, removed his cleats, and put on his street shoes. He reached into his locker for a small duffel bag. He put his cleats into the bag, zipped it shut, and without a parting word walked away.

McInnis went on to coach the baseball team at Harvard from 1949 to 1954. He died in Ipswich, Massachusetts, on February 16, 1960, at the age of 69. He set all-time Major League records for fewest errors in a season (150 games or more), 1; most consecutive errorless games by a first baseman, 163; and most chances accepted by a first baseman in a season, no errors, 1,300. He set those records in 1921. Sixty-seven years later, they had yet to be broken.

Several of the men who played for Amherst in the Holy Cross game contributed to this story. At the time, Ezra Bowen was a senior editor with Time, Inc. Jack Forte was a Superior Court judge in Boston. Bill Genovese, retired, was formerly assistant vice president of Commercial Union Insurance Company. Lew Hammond is the president of Hodge and Hammond, in New York. Dave McNeish owned a venture capital firm in Wellesley, Massachusetts. Charlie Murphy was signed by the Brooklyn Dodgers following his graduation, pitched one year in the minor leagues, and then was associated with the advertising firm of McCann-Erickson in New York. "Rosey" Rosendale was in the mortgage banking business in Solano Beach, near San Diego.

When Amherst fraternities reached a heyday in the nineteenth century, unsophisticated young men like Calvin Coolidge had trouble finding any that would accept them. In his Coolidge biography Hendrik Booraem reports that the "countrified" Coolidge at first was considered unsuitable for membership. That elitist fraternity system lasted up until World War II, but after the war the college sought improvements, finding fraternities "hurtful" to many excluded students—especially Jews, blacks, and others considered different from everyone else. Reforms were instituted, including one that required houses to disavow any discriminatory clauses in their national charters. "Unfraternal Conduct" tells of one fraternity that faltered at first but then led the way to embrace the spirit of inclusion. Under a new, more democratic system, fraternities enjoyed nearly three more decades of acceptance. Then, with the college's admission of women, their days were suddenly numbered. The remaining houses became enclaves mostly of sophomore males; increasingly, fraternities were known for boisterous all-campus parties, vandalism, and anti-intellectual activity. A trustee committee concluded that "on occasion [they had] been the venue of gross social behavior which is no longer tolerable." They were finally abolished in 1984. Still, there had been proud years in the college's fraternity history—none prouder than 1948.

UNFRATERNAL CONDUCT

AT AMHERST, 1948 began with a quiet offer of brotherhood and ended in a blizzard of headlines and controversy. Before it was over, one party to the dispute was charged with "unfraternal conduct," the other with the "taint of Ku-Klux Klanism." The year became a test of commitment for a surprised group of undergraduates, and for the college itself.

The story told here is based on archived material and on recent reminiscences about that time, long ago, when the local chapter of Phi Kappa Psi was not only the first fraternity at Amherst, but also one of the first in the nation, to pledge a black student. Later, following the civil rights movement of the 1960s, the "Phi Psi Affair" became little more than a footnote to history. At the time, it was an important moment—not only at Amherst but nationwide.

In the fall of 1947 Thomas W. Gibbs, of Evanston, Illinois, was among 254 freshmen who entered the all-male college in the Class of 1951. He was one of two black students in the class; the other was Mercer Cook III, of Washington, D.C. When Director of Admission Eugene S. Wilson '29 visited Evanston Township High School in the fall of 1947, a homeroom teacher urged Gibbs to talk with him. Gibbs remembers that Wilson told him Amherst "was looking for a wider geographical representation and more minority representation," so he applied.

World War II had ended two years earlier, and Amherst, like the rest of the country, was eager to move beyond the war years to fresh beginnings. The college adopted a curriculum of new courses for freshmen and sophomores. It also sought reforms in student life outside the classroom, and one question was whether or not to allow fraternities to reopen. The fraternities had been closed during the war. Greek-letter societies had existed at the college since 1837, and by the time they were shut down in the early '40s there were 13 chapters at Amherst.

Many opposed their return. Professors complained that the fraternities had been "anti-intellectual and undemocratic," and a majority called for their abolition. In 1945 this was also the recommendation of an Alumni Committee on Postwar Amherst College, chaired by Charles W. Cole '27, a professor of history at Columbia University, a year before he became president of Amherst. In its report, "Amherst Tomorrow," the committee said the fraternities' "sense of exclusiveness and social preferment" was "hurtful to the young men who are in the fraternities because it gives them a false and undemocratic sense of superiority. And it hurts the students who are outside the fraternities by giving them a wholly unwarranted sense of being inferior and of being social outcasts."

The committee also said it seemed "impossible to defend a condition in which the College accepts a student on the basis of one set of standards but no fraternity may elect that student because of the existence within it of a different body of standards. If, for example, the newcomer is from one of the minority racial or religious groups in American society, or if he is not sufficiently prepossessing in appearance or manner, or if he is too poor to feel able wisely to assume the expense of fraternity membership, he is on all these counts too likely to remain outside of the fraternity fold." The report alluded to the fact that several fraternities' national organizations had rules excluding Jews, blacks, and others.

Other Amherst groups wanted fraternities reopened. In a survey conducted by mail, 666 alumni voted in favor of fraternities and only 195 voted against them. And the executive committee of the Alumni Council was unanimously in their favor.

In June 1945 the trustees voted to let the organizations reopen but only under certain conditions: comparable housing should be made available to upperclassmen who did not belong to fraternities; fraternities could not have their own separate dining facilities; national dues should be "drastically reduced"; a new House Management Committee should create "a system of faculty adviser for each fraternity"; and so on. Ten months later the trustees added another condition: That, "on or before October 1, 1948, each chapter shall formally advise the Board . . . there is no prohibition or restriction by reason of race, color, or creed affecting the selection of members of such chapter." (Eventually the deadline was extended to February 1951.)

When the organizations were reestablished, five houses still had discriminatory clauses in their national regulations. Phi Kappa Psi was not one of them.

Many Amherst students at this time were war veterans, and Francis C. Newton '47, a Phi Psi member, notes that "ex-servicemen, at least in the north, generally had little sympathy with segregation. We were generally older than the average college student of other eras and were, on the whole, more cosmopolitan." But the test for admitting a black student to a fraternity at Amherst did not come until the Gibbs case in 1948.

Jewish students were invited to join the reopened fraternities and it did not seem to cause a big stir. M. Wallace Rubin '48, who believes he was "the first practicing Jew ever admitted" to Phi Kappa Psi, remembers that in 1947, when one of the members harassed a pledge because of his religion, the rest of the house "jumped all over him." "They decided that they didn't fight a war to come back and 'childly'—their exact word— abuse others," Rubin says. "From that moment on, Phi Kappa Psi at Amherst became a different organization. I was accepted as a person and as a brother, and the way was paved for Tom Gibbs the following year."

By the time the rushing season began in the spring of Tom Gibbs's freshman year, the newcomer from Illinois had already made an impression on upperclassmen at Phi Kappa Psi. Richard Quaintance '50 recalls that his "congeniality, quiet leadership skills, and performance as a student and athlete were plain to all who knew him." Gibbs was active with the cross country, track, and debating teams. Francis Newton remembers that another Phi Psi, Harry G. Barnes '49, "asked me whether I would have any objection to the house pledging a black student. I told Harry I had no objection to Tom although I didn't know him. I'm sure I said if he was acceptable to Harry and/or the other students, he was acceptable to me. I never heard any objection, and Tom's pledging became a fact."

Amherst fraternities "rushed" freshmen in the spring, issuing bids to students they wanted. One member could blackball a nominee, so the choice had to be unanimous. If the student accepted a bid, he was then "pledged" to the fraternity, but he and his pledge class were not initiated into membership until the following fall.

The spring of 1948 was a busy season, filled with athletic competition and student politics. Along with Hugh M. Hamill Jr. '51 and John W. McGrath '51, Gibbs was elected to represent his class on the Student Council. The fraternities were caught up in social activity. Phi Psi began planning a "Knave of Hearts" party to follow the big spring prom, billed as a "Lobster Quadrille" with a "Mad Tea Party" featuring the Dormouse and the Mad Hatter selling beer and other refreshments.

After 52 years it's not surprising that men now in their 70s, who were members of Phi Kappa Psi at the time, have different recollections of that 1948 rushing season. Some now say people knew immediately that pledging a black student would be political and controversial—that it might cause trouble with the national. Others say it hardly occurred to them. One freshman invited to join Phi Psi that year, Nesbitt Blaisdell '51, believes the students knew the significance of the step they were taking. "I think we realized that spring when we all were pledged, what a momentous decision the upperclassmen had made in deciding to pledge Tom, especially given the midwestern roots of the fraternity's founding," Blaisdell recalls.

Many other Phi Psi chapters were southern, and Francis Newton says that the Amherst group was "well aware of [this] and knew if we pledged a black man there would be trouble." Harry Barnes recalls that "some members had reservations because pledging a black student would be a break with tradition. But when the final decision was made, there was no opposition. My recollection is also that we did not consult the national fraternity, feeling that it was within our rights to determine whom we wished to select." Gibbs does not recall any hostility during rushing. "It was all very courteous," he remembers. "There was nothing to make me think I was out of place." Only later did he learn from black upperclassmen that black students had never gone through the process before: "I didn't know that, by tradition, I wasn't supposed to!"

Because Phi Psi was not one of the houses with restrictions against minorities, the trustees' anti-discrimination edict of 1946 was not a direct factor. "I knew that we had no discriminatory clause," Frederick Greene '49 recalls, "so that wasn't an issue at Phi Kappa Psi. I didn't anticipate initially that this was going to be a big deal. In any event, we were not doing it to 'make a statement.' The people who knew Tom thought he would fit in well, so let's have him."

Some felt it was prudent, though, to consult the president of the chapter's alumni corporation, which owned the fraternity's Georgian Revival residence on College Street. He was the prominent Harvard paleontologist Alfred S. Romer '17. A year later, in an article in the *Atlantic Monthly,* Romer recalled that a member of the rushing committee alerted him to its plans in March and asked if alumni brothers would approve. Personally," Romer wrote, "I told him, I would approve, and I felt sure that at least a fair percentage of the alumni would also. But . . . [this] was a pretty radical step, even if in line with college policy," he added, suggesting to the undergraduates: "Better think it over carefully, and get plenty of advice."

Francis Newton reports that an older graduate, then a college chaplain in Pennsylvania, visited campus and tried to stop the brothers from moving forward. "I recall him sitting on a couch in our common room and making a big pitch urging us not to pledge Tom, for the good of the fraternity," Newton recalls. "He told us that, if we did, we were sure to be kicked out of the [national] fraternity, and he didn't want that." The brothers didn't want it either, but they stuck to their plan, and Gibbs joined the pledge class that April.

Officials of the national fraternity soon heard the news. Romer reported what happened next:

> There arrived a deputation from the national fraternity headed by an ex-president, Harry S. Gorgas, a New York lawyer. Its object was to persuade the chapter to withdraw the pledge to Gibbs. The boys refused. Both morally and in fraternity law, they were on firm ground. The deputation withdrew—pointing out, however, that the Amherst chapter would encounter strong opposition at a national convention of the fraternity to be held in Colorado in early July. The undergradu-

ates, they said, had better poll their alumni to sound out their sentiments on the matter, and state their case by circular letter to the 50 or so other chapters of the fraternity.

Here was trouble, but not, it then seemed, too great difficulties. [Amherst's Phi Psi] alumni were polled—some 500 graduates stretching back over half a century. They overwhelmingly supported the chapter—90 percent for Gibbs, many enthusiastically. Letters were sent to inform the other chapters.

Officers of the Amherst house and a few other members now planned to attend the national fraternity's summer conference at Estes Park, in the Colorado Rockies. Fred Greene '49, president-elect of the chapter, remembers that—perhaps naively—they thought reason would prevail, especially since Phi Kappa Psi had no discrimination clause. "We went out with the purpose of convincing them," he recalls. "We wanted to present the issue to the convention and get a vote, or at least discuss it." Ward Burns '50, a Phi Psi representative to the college's House Management Committee, agrees: "I thought we had a chance of winning," he remembers.

In the meantime, the two students who had spearheaded Gibbs's invitation to join the fraternity, Harry Barnes '49 and Donald Sibley '51, got in touch with Gibbs early that summer to tell him there could be trouble. "They wanted to make sure I'd stick with them," Gibbs recalls.

The Amherst delegates headed west to the convention. Richard Quaintance, whose home was in Katonah, New York, linked up with his roommate Robert Huggins '50 in Rochester and rode to Estes Park in Huggins's 1932 Model A Ford. Along the way they picked up brothers Robert Doane '49 and Sumner Powell '46, an alumnus, who jostled along in the rumble seat. Greene, meanwhile, met up with James Bandeen '49, an ex-marine who had been president of the fraternity that spring. Bandeen's father owned a Chevrolet dealership in Michigan, so they drove to the Rockies in a new Chevy Powerglide. At Estes Park the Amherst groups were joined by Ward Burns.

Under other circumstances, the Amherst group might have looked forward to a good time. Instead, "it became very serious," Greene recalls, "as soon as we got there." Older fraternity "boys" socialized at the conference with the student representatives. Harry Gorgas was very much in circulation. Greene remembers that the brothers referred to him as "Gorgeous Gorgas." There was also the national executive secretary, "Dab" Williams, described by Burns as "a benign, jovial older fellow" who "tried to be nice to everybody." Winston R. Tate of Kansas City, Missouri, was the national president.

When the Amherst men arrived they were surprised and alarmed by what they discovered. The fraternity's executive council had voted that Tom Gibbs could not be initiated. It would require a two-thirds vote of the convention to overrule the council, but support wasn't there, and the men in charge were determined to avoid an open discussion. Writing in the following year, Romer reported that officials at the conference also made it clear that "should the Amherst representatives show signs of recalcitrance, there was ready for introduction on the convention floor a resolution to revoke their charter and summarily throw the chapter out of the fraternity."

Greene recalls that the Dartmouth and Cornell delegations, but not many others, sympathized with Amherst. Quaintance remembers "conversations in hallways where we learned the extent of [opposition from] Bible Belt and southern membership but also the sense of threatened privacy pervading northern and western chapters as well." He heard, for instance, "that the Phi Psi chapter at Brown University . . . wanted to feel it could welcome a brother from any other chapter in the nation to stay overnight—but could not so welcome an African-American. That kind of sentiment seemed pretty general."

National Secretary Williams "was interested in trying to maintain some level of harmony," Greene says, "but Gorgas's and Tate's idea of harmony was, 'Stop doing this.'" Greene also remembers, word for word, the extraordinary remark by one official that "The greatest intolerance is intolerance of intolerance."

Soon the national officers tightened the screws further, demanding that Gibbs be de-pledged. The Amherst delegates were in a quandary. If they held their ground, the house could be voted out of the national, and they did not feel they had authority from their brothers back home to precipitate such a drastic action. So they agreed to an unpleasant compromise: they would buy time by de-pledging Gibbs if the fraternity's leaders would withdraw their threats against the fraternity and erase the record of the steps they had taken. The house would then take up the issue again with its alumni and the other chapters.

The conference ended without a public showdown, and it was all kept out of the papers. Sobered by their experience, the Amherst delegates headed home. Greene and Bandeen stopped at Tom Gibbs's house in Evanston and explained the awkward situation. "I recollect we left the convention agreeing to pick up Tom Gibbs's pledge pin on the way home and telling him that what ultimately was to happen was going to be decided by the house," Greene says.

Ward Burns recalls that the national officers "knew our objective was still to pledge Gibbs. We made it very clear to Tom that this was a technical thing. As I recall, we said it would enable us to start with a clean slate, that we were doing some negotiating, that he was going to be pledged." In fact, reports Greene, "I didn't regard the de-pledging as a big matter. It was a technicality in the process of getting him into the fraternity. We told the national, okay, we will pick up the pin until we can get back to the college to discuss this with the chapter. We were not really lessening our commitment; we were suspending things so we could acquaint the house and our alumni with the situation. I was concerned about keeping the alumni informed, and keeping the house unified. I don't think any of us had the sense we might reverse our position." Gibbs recalls that he was "disappointed" about being de-pledged. It meant the weeks ahead would be difficult. "I remember wavering," he says, "as to whether it would be worth going through with it."

In his *Atlantic* account later, Romer quoted from a Phi Kappa Psi newsletter that circulated after the convention: "Before the convening of the Grand Arch Council," it said, "a great many alumni were advised that one of our chapters had pledged a Negro. Thanks to the fearless, diplomatic leadership of President Winston R. Tate and the able assistance of his Executive Council associates, the problem was settled at the G.A.C. without discussion on the floor." At Amherst, the "problem" was far from settled. When students returned to campus in September, Greene acknowledges, "quite a few people in the house were cross when they learned Gibbs had been de-pledged. But I think they quickly understood we didn't view it as a reversal but simply a temporary suspension."

As trouble intensified, Gibbs sought the advice of his scoutmaster back in Illinois—a man named George A. Sweatt. Racial difficulties had occurred in Gibbs's high school days when he was the Eagle Scout chosen to represent his region at the Scouts' international Jamboree in Moisson, France. Gibbs went to the festivities—but at home there had been protests, even hate mail. "So I had encountered that kind of thing," he says.

Sweatt advised him to avoid responding to criticism, to keep a low profile—and to accept support "without much comment," Gibbs says, "so my words couldn't be twisted." Gibbs followed the advice. Burns recalls that he "was absolutely stolid. He never showed any emotion. You'd tell him something and he'd say yes, meaning he understood." Another Phi Psi, George Calvert '50, says he believes Gibbs was "keeping his distance for self-protection. I don't blame him for that."

At Amherst the administration, too, kept its distance—sympathizing with the plan to pledge Gibbs but letting the fraternity work things out for itself. The president and trustees were already on record opposing discrimination. "It was benign support, not active support," Burns remembers. "They were all in favor of what we were doing but let us do it." Elsewhere on campus "the general feeling was one of support," he recalls.

Gibbs says he encountered "more pressure to stay than to withdraw." Encouragement and support came from fellow students, especially his own classmates, and from many others, including Professors Gail Kennedy of philosophy, Ralph A. Beebe '20 of chemistry (a Phi Psi alumnus), Albert E. Lumley, who was Gibbs's cross-country coach, and Admission Director Eugene "Bill" Wilson.

George Calvert '50 remembers that "the house meetings were intense, with a couple of guys in my [sophomore] delegation very much against taking a stand against Phi Kappa Psi national." While Greene, on the other hand, does not remember "much factionalism," he also notes that some of the brothers "had stronger ties to the national, through parents, than others. Some cared about the national quite a bit."

In his 1949 account Romer reported that initially the house seemed "irrevocably split" between those who wished to temporize with the national and those who wanted to initiate Gibbs that fall regardless of the consequences. The latter included most—perhaps all—of the pledges. As one of them, Nesbitt Blaisdell, remembers, "we voted secretly and unanimously to turn in our pledge pins—i.e., resign as pledges—if Tom's was not given back." John Walker '51, another pledge, recalls that this left the rest of the house with a difficult choice: "They did not wish to lose

their entire pledge class—a financial disaster—but they did not want to
lose their national affiliation either." Gibbs recalls "there was an element
that did regret the decision the house had taken. But everybody was very
civil. So, on the surface, the house was united."

If opinion at Phi Psi was not united when college reopened, it soon
coalesced. The house wrote to ask its alumni for advice; once again, an
overwhelming majority of respondents favored pledging Gibbs. The
house wrote to the 54 other Phi Kappa Psi chapters around the country
and received 18 responses: half of them were opposed to Gibbs's membership, a third were in favor, the rest noncommittal. Looking back, John
Walker believes "the letters of condemnation that we received (some
filled with unbelievable filth) came far more from the Midwest than they
did from the South."

Still, nothing had been in the papers.

The fraternity initiations would be held, as always, on Williams Weekend, which would be November 13 and 14. Gibbs had now been repledged.
Letters were still coming in from other chapters, but the Phi Kappa Psi
brothers resolved their differences and voted unanimously to initiate
Gibbs with the rest of the pledges. "The morality of sticking to our guns
became important," Greene reports. As chapter president he prepared to
notify the national fraternity about the decision in a letter to its newly
elected president, Howard L. Hamilton, secretary of the faculty of arts
and sciences at Ohio State University. The letter would rehearse the
events of the summer and reiterate that there was no fraternity prohibition against blacks becoming members of Phi Kappa Psi. It would also
tell the organization's leaders, ahead of time, about the planned initiation. It said this would not occur until November 23. "The house was
strongly in favor of doing that," Greene recalls. "What we were doing
was right. From my standpoint, sending them this letter meant they now
had to do what they had to do. We put the ball back in their court."

"We realized," Ward Burns says, "that Fred's letter was not going to
do much to mollify the national—though we hoped it would." The letter
included responses Phi Psi had received from chapters around the country. "Among others, we would particularly call to your attention the letter
from Mississippi Alpha which indicates the belief of the members of that

chapter that our membership is our own concern and that they expect us to act in the best interests of the fraternity—a thought echoed, as you can see, in the communications from several other chapters."

The letter went on to say that the brothers at Amherst felt the national's executive council at Estes Park had "contravened the established criteria for membership in the fraternity by introducing qualifications outside the realms of character and ability." It also said, "We particularly feel that the national officers have all along treated this situation as a problem to be disposed of without really having faced squarely the principle involved: whether race is to be a criterion for membership in Phi Kappa Psi. . . . The problem is of such magnitude and nationwide concern that once undertaken, it cannot be lightly thrust aside, but as a matter of basic conviction and principle must be pursued to a definite conclusion."

The letter was dated November 3, but the fraternity did not mail it immediately. The brothers still hoped to hear back from more chapters. Gibbs stayed in the background. "I think it helped my studies," he says, "because I concentrated on them more, as a way of escaping from the pressure."

November 3 was Election Day, and in mock balloting the Amherst student body voted 66 percent for the Republican presidential candidate, Governor Thomas E. Dewey, 10.6 percent for the Socialist, Norman Thomas, and 9.3 percent for the Democrat, Harry Truman.

There still had been no publicity about the events at Phi Psi. Not even the *Amherst Student* had covered the story. But that was about to change. Russell J. Collins, a reporter for the *Boston Globe,* got wind of what was happening and wrote a dramatic, front-page story that appeared in the *Globe* on November 7. It was quickly picked up by other media.

Phi Psi's letter had not yet reached the national, and the fraternity's leaders were now likely to get the first word about plans to initiate Gibbs from news reports. Howard Hamilton and others would not be pleased. The *Globe* headline said "Amherst Frat to Admit Negro, Defy National Rule," and the article said the Phi Psis at Amherst were "convinced they will lose their national charter. They feel, though, that the principle involved is worth it."

On November 8 the *Amherst Student* broke its silence with a front-page news report and an editorial, written by Paul E. Bragdon '50, deploring the *Globe*'s intervention and going on to say "it is not for the national fraternity to impose limitations, particularly unseemly racial or religious restrictions."

On November 12 the Amherst members received word from the national that President Hamilton and the executive council had unanimously suspended the Amherst chapter "on grounds of unfraternal conduct." Now the story was everywhere, and reporters descended on the Amherst Phi Psi house. Burns recalls that one of the brothers, Jay Geraghty '50, a burly football player, "wanted to take them on one by one, but we restrained him." Campus police directed reporters to the college news bureau, headed by Horace W. Hewlett '36. Hewlett's office had already begun issuing press releases describing the trustees' antidiscrimination policy and providing other background information.

The local chapter and Amherst were applauded in the national press. On November 15 *The New York Times* editorialized: "In this episode we will see the real meaning of a liberal education. An Amherst degree has always been respected. It will be more respected now." On November 21 the *New York Herald Tribune* published a scorching letter addressed by national columnist Ernest K. Lindley, a member of Phi Kappa Psi, to his fraternity's national president. "The condemnation 'unfraternal conduct,' applied to Massachusetts Alpha, is a grotesque perversion not only of the English language," Lindley wrote, "but of all the fine principles for which our fraternity, in common with many others, professes to stand." He urged Hamilton and the council to reconsider. He said that "in these times, and those ahead, any white American who cannot meet on the basis of social equality with members of other races is, in that respect, a liability to his country . . . the suspension of the Amherst chapter pollutes Phi Kappa Psi and every one of its members with the loathsome taint of Ku-Klux Klanism."

In the "Talk of the Town" feature for its Thanksgiving week issue of November 27, *The New Yorker* said simply: "At this season we are thankful for the Amherst chapter of Phi Kappa Psi, which has decided to explore the nature of brotherhood, against its parents' advice."

Phi Psi quickly accepted its orphaned status and became a local fraternity renamed Phi Alpha Psi. The "new" house finally initiated Gibbs and the others at a dinner ceremony held at the Wiggins Tavern in Northampton on December 4. Alfred Romer and President Cole were the featured speakers. There, essentially, the story ended. Before long the national leaders of Phi Kappa Psi summoned officers of the Amherst fraternity to a Christmas holiday "trial" in Chicago, where they expelled the chapter once and for all and ordered a two-year suspension of Quaintance, Bandeen, Burns, Greene, and Huggins from their memberships in the national.

Journalists continued to write about the story. A correspondent for *Collier's* magazine asked President Cole: Why all the fuss? In real life, after all, private clubs discriminated all the time. "Institutions of learning ought to pick and choose the best parts of our culture, not the *worst*," Cole replied. "College students ought to set the pace. If they make enough headway with the democratic idea, the country clubs and the business clubs will come along later."

Amherst fraternities came along in the meantime. Phi Delta Theta was the last house at the college to get rid of discriminatory language in its membership rules. After repudiating the national's discrimination clause in 1952, the chapter was dropped by its parent organization the following year and became a local house, Phi Delta Sigma.

To a reporter who wrote for *The New York Times Magazine,* President Cole said he was proud of the Amherst Phi Psis: "I admire them both for the action they took and for maintaining their stand against pressure. They handled the situation in an able and dignified manner. It is a tribute to the house, and it augurs well for the future of Amherst."

Today Tom Gibbs reflects that, "for me and, I think, for much of the [pledge] delegation, we learned something about the maturation process. We had to support each other. We had to grow up more quickly than we might have otherwise." Gibbs was elected president of Phi Alpha Psi in his senior year. He later became an Episcopal priest and served for 18 years as dean of the Cathedral Church of All Saints on St. Thomas, U.S. Virgin Islands.

Looking back, Fred Greene is pleased with how everything ended. "We didn't do this to further civil rights, to further some cause, to take a step to further racial justice," he says. "But in retrospect I agree that, having gone through it for all those months, it was worth doing. I never regretted it. We did the right thing."—DCW

Thanks to initiatives taken by his longtime friend and colleague Professor William H. Pritchard, two books of essays by Professor Theodore Baird (1901–1996) have been published by Amherst College Press. They are *The Most of It: Essays in Language and the Imagination* (1999), and *English at Amherst: A History* (2005). In them Baird's highly original voice conveys something of his genius and eccentricity. Baird is best remembered, though, for his work with younger faculty in shaping and teaching the college's unique English 1 course for freshmen. In words combined from two related passages in *English at Amherst*, Baird said teachers in the course would "take a question, something like this: 'What is conflict?' and 'What was it like when you felt conflict?' . . . The student and teacher were on the same footing. They were both perplexed and they were both putting what mind they could on the immediate problem: how do you tell, how do you put into words, such an experience as this?"

One of those teachers, Walker Gibson, wrote the following article which appeared in the Fall 1986 issue of *Amherst* magazine, excerpted from a chapter that Gibson, now emeritus professor of English at the University of Massachusetts, wrote for *Traditions of Inquiry*, edited by John Brereton, ©1985 by Oxford University Press, Inc. It appeared in *Amherst* under the title "The Influence of Theodore Baird."

AT WORK AS A TEACHER

By Walker Gibson

No account that I have ever made conveys what the
course is like day by day and in the students' papers. It
is probably both better and worse than you think.

—Theodore Baird

T<small>HEODORE</small> B<small>AIRD</small> was born in 1901, graduated Hobart College
in 1921, and in 1929 received his doctorate from Harvard. After brief
tenures at Western Reserve and Union College, he began his long career
at Amherst in 1927. For the next 43 years he engaged in the varied
chores required in a small department with a strong literary tradition,
including a very popular course in Shakespeare; during most of these
years he occupied the Samuel Williston Professorship. His reputation
today, however, rests not so much on his teaching of literature as on
his leadership in the teaching of freshman composition. For a quarter
century Baird was director of English 1–2, the year-long required course
in freshman writing. It is for this course that he himself would want to be
remembered, and it is this course and its development under his guidance
that concern me in what follows. . . .

Two things to clarify at the outset have to do with format or structure.
First, the course was team-taught in the sense that every instructor was
expected to take part in its planning and development at every stage.
Second, the course offered its students an integrated sequence of assignments (different each year) that began somewhere and more or less
logically led somewhere else.

That the course was team-taught does not mean that a group of people
met a few times and went their several ways, nor that they participated

directly in one another's classrooms. In English 1–2, teamwork meant something else and something fairly rigorous. A draft of assignments was composed over each summer by a member of the staff (often Baird himself); this draft was then discussed, amended, agreed to in a trial form. Staff members (8 or 10 individuals, that is, a majority of the department) met weekly during the academic year for a couple of hours or so, and absence from these meetings was unthinkable. The agenda for every meeting was the same: how to edit and rephrase the next week's assignments so as to elicit some worthwhile response from students.

Baird's faith in this form of teaching-by-consensus seems to have originated in the 1930s, when with four other young teachers he participated in an earlier composition course known as English 1c. An article he wrote for the college's alumni magazine in 1939 concludes:

> The only virtue of English 1c is that five teachers are engaged in a common effort to see to it that the freshmen do as much writing as we can read and that the writing is as decent, as clear, as sensible, as intelligent as we know how to make it. And the five teachers come together to make one course, not for the appearance of uniformity but because by an exchange of ideas, by self-criticism, by argument, we can define our objects more clearly and use the best methods for achieving them that we know about.

It should be added that the cooperative give-and-take Baird describes as English 1c had to have been different in important ways from the later cooperative efforts that became English 1–2. It is one thing for five young peers to meet and agree on a common procedure. It is quite another thing to meet with twice as many who range in sophistication and experience from the newest departmental recruit to the senior director himself. And in English 1–2 there was a senior director, and he did direct, though he also made conscientious efforts to involve everyone democratically in the decision making. There are, of course, limits to the uses of democracy in educational planning. Dull people meeting in equality together will produce dull materials unless led by an individual with energy and imagination. In English 1–2, no one doubted where the energy and imagination were finally coming from, and no one doubted who was in charge, for all the genuine cooperation and consensus that did go on.

In any event, for the dozens of young instructors who passed through this regimen (and I was one), the experience was heady in the extreme. Most of these instructors (though not I; my years there date from 1946 to 1957) labored under a three-years-and-out-you-go rule that was cruel treatment, but most of them left feeling that their minds had been permanently changed—and for the better. More of that later.

The second feature of the course into which Baird put all the strength of his convictions concerns the assignments themselves. First, there was the sheer number of them, over 30 per semester. Directions for writing a short paper (one to three pages) were distributed at every class meeting, due at the next class. These papers were read, commented on (without grades), returned to the students and discussed at the following meeting of the class. (The teaching labor may sound intolerable, but it wasn't, not quite. Beginning instructors taught three sections of from 20 to 25 students each. Others taught a single section as part of a normal three-course load. Only one instructor, to my knowledge, actually cracked up.) The schedule of assignments was followed precisely by all sections of the course, which meant that over any given 48-hour period the entire freshman class (300 young men with outrageously high SAT scores) was engaged in solving the same set problem. That this resulted in a good many dormitory seminars among students was inevitable and probably beneficial.

More important, the agreed-on assignments were sequential: they led from one place to another. During the first semester (English 1), they were concerned with some aspect of the students' nonacademic or extracurricular experience; in English 2, attention was directed to their classroom experience, specifically in history and in science. No text or reader was ever used; selections from the students' written work, mimeographed and distributed, became what text there was. The electronic copier, of course, was not then available; it would have been invaluable.

Sets of assignments, particularly in English 1, were organized around some concept or *key term*. One early year the term was *technique*, and the main question was, How can you say how it is that you do something you know how to do? (The conventional label "process paper" was never mentioned.) How can you describe in words the special feel of a successful serve in tennis? Answer: You can't. What can you describe? An order of actions? Baird used this example in a piece he wrote about the course in 1952, addressed to parents and alumni:

> A student who is a good tennis player sets out to write a paper on what he does when he serves a tennis ball. He knows he knows what he is writing about, yet as he begins to address himself to his subject he immediately encounters the inescapable fact that his consciousness of his own action contains a large area of experience quite beyond his powers of expression. The muscular tensions, the rhythm of his body as he shifts his weight, above all the feel of the action by which he knows a stroke is good or bad, all these and much more lie beyond his command of language, and rendered almost speechless he produces a mess. He knows in the sense that he can perform the action, but he does not know in the sense that he can communicate this action to a reader. At this point the teacher tries to get him to distinguish between these two levels of experience, to become aware of them, to generalize about them. The next step is for the student to take for himself by recognizing that a part or an element of his experience can be communicated to another person when he isolates the order in which he throws the ball into the air, raises his racket, and so on, and that the order of his actions as distinguished from the action itself is the subject of his writing. The student may even perceive that between the order of movements as he sees them and the order of words in a sentence some relation can be made, and that when he has made this relation he knows what he is talking about.

Other organizing themes in other years included the experiences of puzzle-solving, of playing games (What is a game?), of reading a road map. Glancing at such a list, it is perhaps no wonder Amherst people despaired of making the course appear serious and sensible to the outside world, and what the outside world picked up about English 1–2 did Amherst's reputation no good. "Oh you teach at Amherst," a professor at a neighboring college once said to me. "You teach at Amherst, do you?

That's the place where you tell your freshmen how to read a road map."
This was said contemptuously. And yet I remember fondly that sequence
on the road map. Students were issued an oil company's map—and
other maps too—a textbook for once, and assignments were generated
around that text. "What is a road map?" we finally asked, and the answer
(of course) was that it is a set of directions, a guide for certain kinds of
human action. It is not an expression of terrestrial reality. Many weeks
of effort were required to arrive at this revelation, commonplace though
it sounds. Meanwhile our neighboring colleges thought us frivolous and
silly, and no doubt we sometimes were.

The map is not the territory, the great semanticist Alfred Korzybski
has memorably told us. We did not mention *Science and Sanity* to our
students, but Korzybski's dictum underlay much that went on in English
1–2. The word is not the thing. . . .

[The assignments asked] a good deal of the student, and Baird always
took advantage of his advantage: namely, a captive audience of highly
motivated, decently prepared, and reasonably smart young men. That
he saw his deep responsibility in this situation goes without saying. The
assumption he made, in the very tone of his assignments, was a generous
one: You and I are intelligent adults, eager for education, and I take it for
granted that you will be as concerned and excited and good-humored as I
about this business we're embarked on. (*E.g.* English usage.) But was this
a fair assumption? Not always, of course. In moments of gloom—and
Baird allowed himself occasional attitudes of exaggerated gloom—he
confessed his doubts about that assumption:

> I see plainly where I have gone wrong—if wrong it is—in assuming
> that our students are better than they are, that they can be talked to
> from the level of adult interest (whatever it may be), that the best ideas
> I have are not too good for them. Plainly a strong case can be made
> against me, for with this really nice set of assignments I had many
> students asking, what's the idea of this course? And without shame!

(That question, needless to say, has been asked by people other than
students and without shame. What is the idea of this course? How is it
different from other composition courses in purpose or goal? One answer

is that it isn't different at all. For what do we want of our students? A critical attitude toward language? A recognition that the world they live in is the world they express in words? That control of that world and of themselves depends considerably on their control of their own words? Things like that. In such formulations we can feel the insidious creep of "correctness," the blur of our pious abstractions. Still, this is the sort of thing we all believe. This is surely what all composition courses are all about, and English 1–2 was no different. "It is probably both better and worse than you think.")

But Baird never remains gloomy for long, and a few lines later he turns it around: "You mustn't think I say I am wrong. I couldn't do it on any other terms."

At any rate, the fact seems to be that, for very many students, Baird's influence was crucial to their understanding of their education. For most of the instructors who passed through his hands, as I have said, the same was true. (A partial list of men who have worked with Baird includes [1985] a number still at Amherst—G. A. Craig, Benjamin DeMott, John Cameron, William Heath, William Pritchard—as well as a large number who have taken some part of Baird with them to other pastures— Reuben Brower, C. L. Barber, W. V. Clausen, Julian Moynahan, Roger Sale, William R. Taylor, Jonathan Bishop, John F. Butler, William Coles, myself.) . . .

But not everyone was favorably impressed by English 1–2, and there were those, both students and faculty, who were thoroughly hostile. Many, of course, didn't "understand." Baird's good friend Robert Frost was one of these—he said it was "kid stuff"—but then, as Baird ruefully remarked, we couldn't undertake to educate Frost. Some faculty members saw the course, quite rightly, as a threat to their own way of doing things. (Here are the facts, boys; learn them.) An important exception was the physicist Arnold Arons, director of Science 1–2. It is not too much to say that freshman English and freshman science enjoyed for some years a rapport and a common intellectual approach that must have been unique in American education.

And then the assignments themselves seem to cry out for parody, friendly or unfriendly. They were often burlesqued in one student publication or another. The course figures largely in Alison Lurie's *Love and*

Friendship (1962), an irreverent novel about faculty life at "Convers College":

Assignment 11

Here is a photograph, an airview of Convers College.

(a) Let us assume you are now somewhere in the middle of the area contained in the photograph and you recognize this as a photograph of the spot you are now on. What do you do to recognize this?

(b) Define, in the context of (a) "the spot you are now on."

(c) What difference do you see between this spot and the one in the map in Assignment No. 10?

If this assignment, evidently lifted from an actual series, looks far-out or silly in Lurie's novel, it was anything but silly in the context of the series, where the student was invited to see that "the spot you are now on" can be both anywhere and nowhere.

Actually, Baird's assignments are hard to parody successfully because their language is so modified by self-ironies and admissions of final failure that take the ground out from under the parodist. If you ask questions to which you do not know the answers, you are relatively invulnerable to a burlesque that does the same thing.

"This freshman course has been the center of my entire intellectual life, and more than that, for to it I have brought whatever I have learned as a human being." So wrote Baird to the college president toward the end of his teaching career. The question arises, What were the origins of English 1–2? What had Baird encountered in his reading of experience—"as a human being"—that could account for the particular character of the course? I certainly can't presume to answer that with any assurance. Baird himself has recently remarked, "I would say that all my teaching was in rebellion against my own formal education and my elders." I *have* mentioned Korzybski, certainly an important influence, but there must have been hundreds of others in and out of books, for Baird has always been an omnivorous reader as well as a sharp observer. Occasionally, he distributed a list of suggested reading to his staff, and I don't suppose anyone actually looked up all those things—I know I didn't—but the lists did at least suggest what *he* was reading. They are not the sort of lists we hand out nowadays to our graduate seminars in rhetoric and teaching. One, dated 1946, for instance, in addition to Korzybski, includes three titles by the physicist Bridgman and two by the historian Collingwood. William James is prominent. There are a number of books on how the mind thinks: Polya, Wallas, Wertheimer. And there are also titles to remind us that Baird was acutely aware of what was just getting under way in linguistics and the study of grammar: Fries, Hayakawa, Marckwardt, Ogden, and Richards.

A later list (1954) begins with E. D. Adrian's *The Physical Basis of Perception* and ends with J. Z. Young's *Doubt and Certainty in Science.* Take that, you young English teachers. In between appear again Bridgman, Collingwood, James, Korzybski, several linguists. Among current titles there is one that made a big hit at Amherst at that time, McLuhan's *The Mechanical Bride.*

To such lists ought to be added one name possibly omitted as too obvious: Henry Adams. At one period (before my time) the entire freshman course was organized around a close reading of *The Education.* That book was surely formative in Baird's own education, and one can perhaps feel in his own prose style some echoes of Adams.

Authors such as those I have mentioned, together with the general procedure of the course, have suggested to some that there must be a specific intellectual source to all this, perhaps even a *secret* somewhere. In one of the very few published critiques of English 1–2 that exist, James H. Broderick undertook to find such a source in early-twentieth-century American philosophy. ("A Study of the Freshman Composition Course at Amherst: Action, Order, and Language," *Harvard Educational Review* 28:1 [Winter 1958].) Broderick mentions, quite plausibly, logical positivism, operationalism, pragmatism, John Dewey's instrumentalism, and, of course, semantics. No doubt there is a lot to it; no doubt connections can be drawn. But it's important to recognize (as Broderick did recognize) that such language was not part of the vocabulary of the English 1–2 staff and most emphatically did not appear in the classroom. This was an English course and not a course in philosophy, though, like everything else worth talking about, it had its epistemological biases. Perhaps the staff could be faulted for a certain disingenuousness in making so little of grander philosophical relations. But no, it was an English course, and I think we were so caught up in our concern for our students' expression of their experience that our place in intellectual history (if any) rarely occurred to us.

One suggestion of Broderick's, however, in that 1958 article, is worth emphasizing: namely, that English 1–2 was most essentially American. This, too, was not a claim I can recall anyone making at a staff meeting, but it seems to me now exceedingly true. It's hard to imagine another country or another culture where such an enterprise would be likely. Perhaps among other things it was an exercise in patriotism. . . .

Baird remains very much a respected and familiar figure in the Amherst community today, though he is probably, for most people, respected at a little distance. In both social and professional interchanges, he has always suffered from the handicap of saying what he thinks. He has no small talk, hates cocktail parties, and couldn't endure committee and departmental meetings. (English 1–2 staff meetings, of course, were something else.) He complained often about his juniors, and he fought constantly with college administrators. "This is the worst year I ever saw at Amherst: all the fools are now in command"—that remark might have done duty for almost any year. He frightened some people, including those in command. Yet what was always available, if you gave him half a chance, was the most generous and sensitive awareness of others and their feelings. Caring so deeply about the course, he cared deeply about all those who worked with him. Here is a note he wrote to a young and anxious teacher who had finally got to the point where he could compose a halfway decent assignment for English 1. "Do I ever say with sufficient emphasis to carry how much pleasure and admiration I feel when I see you at work as a teacher. We do take each other for granted and expect as a matter of course the understanding from others—at least in this course—which was hardly come by for the individual himself. I feel I have been especially dull lately and have taken everything for granted. Let me make acknowledgement now and in a loud voice."

At work as a teacher—that is the *key term*. It is his own work as a teacher we acknowledge now—and in a loud voice.

Many details of this evening in October 1959 did not remain etched in my memory decades later. But they were written down a day or two after I observed them and then copied into the occasional journal I kept as a student—copied from a letter I wrote to my parents. I did not telephone them in Indiana to tell them about the experience; in those days they were skittish about long-distance calls, and they knew they would learn more about my adventures from the weekly letters they expected me to write. And what a night this was to write home about! I was thoroughly enchanted by the occasion, and it never occurred to me that Robert Frost was other than the wise beloved old poet I saw and heard that evening at the Commagers' house. For a different portrait, and one describing an earlier Frost, see "The Mischief of Robert Frost" by William H. Pritchard, on page 143. Years after the 1959 occasion I was disconcerted to see the old Commager house standing vacant. I asked a friend, poet Susan Snively, if she knew of any poem that gave the sense of an abandoned place haunted by memory. She suggested "Walking to Sleep" by Richard Wilbur '42, and that gave me a place to start.

REACQUAINTED WITH THE NIGHT

Nor must you dream of opening any door
Until you have foreseen what lies beyond it.
Regardless of its seeming size, or what
May first impress you as its style or function,
The abrupt structure which involves you now
Will improvise like vapor.
                        —From "Walking to Sleep"
                        by Richard Wilbur '42

THE 140-YEAR-OLD Commager house has stood vacant at 405 South Pleasant Street since 1995, the year Professor Henry Steele Commager, frail and sweet-tempered, moved out of faculty housing and into a condominium. Without asking questions, Pete Joy, the campus police officer, took me to the back of the house, unlocked a door, and let me in.

What would be in the dusky space? Vapors of memory? Specters? I wasn't sure.

No feelings awoke at first when I looked at my innocent student journal entry for the night of October 14, 1959, then went to the house to look at the pale, empty room and tried to quicken the past. Not only had all the partygoers dispersed long ago: every one that I remembered had died. Robert Frost. Commager—and his wife, Evan, the hostess, long before him. Steele Commager, the son. Harriet Whicher. Rolfe Humphries. John Moore. Merrill Van De Graaff, too. Leaving me to recompose the lustrous evening alone.

Mrs. Whicher, who in her widowed 60s attended the party, once quoted Frost, the guest of honor, as having said that composition ends up "saying as you go more than you hoped you were going to be able to say, and coming with surprise to an end that you fore-knew only with some sort of emotion." Would I meet with surprise? Ultimately the exercise of reading the journal and then revisiting the room, of looking back,

back again to a magical evening, "improvised" like vapor indeed. Things turned out to be not what they seemed. Other Amherst people remember similar evenings, have stories of spellbinding hours with Robert Frost, of Commager hospitality, or of both together. It was only one evening of many, in a faraway time. But how could I forget it.

No doubt Mrs. Commager reached me on the pay telephone in South dormitory with the invitation. Frost was in Amherst on his annual fall visit and they were having him over Wednesday night with some other people; come to the house at 8:30, and bring a friend if you'd like. The Commagers knew my family in Indiana and were good about entertaining homesick students with faculty. I decided to bring a fellow sophomore and Phi Psi fraternity brother, Merrill Van De Graaff—a quiet, talented friend from Utah who wrote poetry for the campus literary magazine. Merrill had a big toothy smile and a perpetual air of credulity. He was thrilled.

The evening came and we walked half a mile to the boxy, white clapboard house and knocked at the door. The windows were aglow; cars were parked in the drive. Evan Commager welcomed us cheerily and put us at ease with her soft southern voice. She wore a long gown and was tall and maternal. Her hair was drawn up in a pompadour; she belonged— the house belonged—in a Victorian time. We were led into the back living room crowded with people and voices, upholstery, overloaded bookshelves, after-dinner drinks and laughter. A fire burned on the hearth. John Moore, beloved professor of classics, was there, speaking shyly in a voice softer than Mrs. Commager's. Merrill and I were delighted to see, too, one of our favorite teachers, the poet Rolfe Humphries—tall, hollow-cheeked, bald and furrowed, his impassive face betrayed by a gleam in the eye. Then who could miss the effusive host, the historian Commager, bobbing out of his chair to pitch logs on the fire or snatch books from the wall. Pugnacious and merry, he rasped away in a singsong tumble of words—"Why, how clever!"—and—"Surely you remember Santayana's observation—!" But we focused most of all on the Guest of Honor. There he was: the old god Kronos himself, in a great chair. The leonine white head, craggy brows, and gruff melodious voice were unmistakable. Were we introduced? Did we get to shake the hand? Here memory fades; we were young and entranced.

The older guests had come in from the dining room and were buzzing in small conversations, an audience before curtain time. The 85-year-old Frost soon removed his glasses, which were equipped with a built-in hearing aid. This meant that he was about to do more talking and less listening. He quipped later that he liked to know what was being said, and that if he did all the talking it wasn't a problem. The individual conversations died out and Frost became the center of attention. In the mesmerizing near monologue that followed, he changed topics quickly. He and Commager had been arguing about Bertrand Russell. The poet dismissed the philosopher, saying he did not have much regard for agnostics, while Commager admired Russell for rejecting things "unevidenced." Other appraisals followed. The poet brought up Emerson— saying that his only lack was storytelling—and then came to Poe, who fared poorly. He amused us with the question: was Poe's Annabel Lee a maiden "whom you may know" for the purposes of the poem?—"Or perhaps you've met her?" Homer's *Odyssey*, he told us, was "the greatest novel ever written." He added that he himself could never write an epic because he would not be able to concentrate on a single theme throughout. At another point Frost recited his adage that "poetry is that which gets lost in translation." Another wonderful coin, still in mint condition. I stashed it, too, in my journal.

Had I been a brighter lad, a different aspect of the moment would have struck me. There sat Rolfe Humphries, after all, best known for his major translations of Ovid's *Metamorphoses*, Juvenal's *Satires*, and Virgil's *Aeneid*. But the circumstance struck me now, more than 40 years later.

Frost said education is learning there's "a book-side to everything," and I knew of a certain book, *Poets, Poetics, and Politics: America's Literary Community Viewed from the Letters of Rolfe Humphries, 1910–1969*, edited by Richard Gillman and Michael Paul Novak. Would the book reveal more? Yes, there it was in the Introduction: a reference Humphries once made to "that tired old *traduttore-traditore* cliché, or the maybe-malice-made mot of Frost's that Poetry is that which gets lost in translation. . . . So [Humphries wrote] here I am now, look you, a poet translating a poet, not some frayed but polite border functionary wearily exchanging the scrip of one republic for that of another." *Translator-traitor? Maybe-malice-made mot? Border functionary?* Things had occurred that evening I hadn't seen. (And was it Rolfe Humphries who joked later, in one of our classes, about the writer who had his works translated into a foreign language because they "lost something in the original"?)

Frost's monologue that evening went on. Some fraternity boys, the night before, had asked him to name the four greatest Americans, and he said he had done so: Washington, Jefferson, Lincoln, Emerson. Diversity was not the mantra. Martin Luther King, Jr., was still relatively unknown, nor did anyone at the Commagers' throw the names of Albert Einstein, say, or Susan B. Anthony, into the contest.

"What about Mark Twain?"

The sudden interruption came from Humphries—maybe (I now wonder) stirred up about the translation jibe. If there were going to be parlor games, he was willing to play. (With a characteristic baseball metaphor Humphries once advised a young poet: "move the ball around, change up on 'em every once in a while.")

Frost would have none of it. Twain? "Not that stuff," he said gruffly.

Ball one—maybe even ball four, because their matchup had begun years before. In 1939, in what he called his "leftish" days, Humphries had written for *New Masses* a review of Frost's volume *A Further Range*, saying brutally that "when you call him a reactionary -------, or a counter-revolutionary --- -- - ----- you have in essence, said it all." Frost swung back the same year, calling Humphries a "bargain-counter revolutionary." They had gotten their danders up early and kept them there.

The book of letters revealed more. Humphries, a 1915 Amherst graduate, joined the faculty in 1957. Frost by then was returning to campus twice a year as the Simpson Lecturer. When Humphries began teaching that fall he found (he wrote Theodore Roethke) "R. Frost here, and putting on his act, which is fascinating in spots, also embarrassing. I don't think it is good for people (never mind him) to sit around the feet of greatness this way and think even the most troglodytian politico-reactionary remark is the profound and simple wisdom of the bard of the folk." Well, there Merrill and I were, two years later, spellbound by the dangerous bard.

The spell wavered at last, not long before midnight, when guests stirred to leave. Coats were claimed. Mrs. Commager thanked us for coming; it was nearing the end. Suddenly Frost asked if anyone was walking back toward the Lord Jeffery Inn, where he stayed. A pause, then Merrill blurted that we'd come on foot. So—miracle of miracles—we were chosen.

The night must have been fair, perhaps even one of Amherst's brilliant autumn nights with its pinprick legion of stars. But under the trees it was dark. The old poet moved slowly and could not see the path. We walked at each side of him, steering the way. Our luck emboldened us to speak. I had heard a story, and asked Frost if it was true, that he had once given a talk at Columbia University where Lionel Trilling introduced him in an endless, pedantic fashion, analyzing Frost's work and concluding, finally, with speculation about the meaning of the poem "Stopping by Woods on a Snowy Evening."

"And tonight," Trilling's said to have said, "perhaps Mr. Frost will tell us exactly what he *really* meant when he wrote 'But I have promises to keep, / And miles to go before I sleep, / And miles to go before I sleep.'"

Was it true that Frost went to the microphone then and declared: "Why, I suppose I was tired, and wanted to go home"? He did not confirm it. But I remember a smile in the dark. Then he stopped in the leaves, beyond the golf course. "You remember how it goes," he said, and recited the poem from beginning to end.

> The woods are lovely, dark and deep,
> But I have promises to keep,
> And miles to go before I sleep,
> And miles to go before I sleep.

I still hear the gruff melodious voice dropping to granite on "woods," then rising to a bell tone on "promises."

"Now, for instance," he concluded, "this evening is pleasant and peaceful, but in the morning we'll have other things to do."

So much for the deeper readings. His conclusion was the one we foreknew.

When Frost died three years later, even Humphries felt the loss. He wrote to Richard Gillman: "His cantankerous sides are not going to be readily forgotten, and I think this is all to the good, so that when we think of his best it will really shine. . . . My own private service consisted of reading a poem as far back as *North of Boston*—the one called 'After Apple-Picking,' and thinking of his wry tone."—DCW

The Amherst catalog today lists more than 130 administrators. The student who wants help with a personal problem will find 20 counselors to turn to: 11 of them deans of various rank, plus 5 psychologists, 2 psychiatrists, and 2 health educators. In 1950, when the indomitable Maude Miner was in her heyday at the campus switchboard, there were 22 administrators, and only 5 appeared to be directly involved in student services (3 deans, a business manager for student activities, and a registered nurse). It was a smaller college and a simpler time. In this sketch of Mrs. Miner we see her pitching in to give help and advice to students. Lean staffing meant that skilled, dedicated, and energetic people like Maude Miner shouldered many responsibilities. In her case, these included secretarial support for departments, holiday meals and hospitality for students, informal advising, and, of course, operating the switchboard. She worked at the college for 34 years, retired in 1967, and died in 1993 at the age of 94. Her husband, Harry, died in 1966. They had no children.

THE LONG AND HAPPY REIGN
OF MAUDE MINER

⌒

Maude Miner smiles right away when visitors come to see her these days at the Cozy Corner Nursing Home up in Sunderland, eight miles from Amherst.

"I'm an ordinary person," she declares. "I'm the way I always was." The second remark is true. At 92, Mrs. Miner has the same brisk, friendly, take-charge air about her that she brought to her 33 years as the college's telephone switchboard operator—a position she held from 1933 to 1967.

The other remark is false, because the peppery, cheerful presence who also found time all those years to give faculty and administrators a sympathetic ear, who served students as advisor, guide, troubleshooter—and sometimes *in loco parentis*—is not "an ordinary person" and never was. Small anecdotes here and there form a pattern, and the pattern reveals an optimistic and strong-willed person who was always there to enjoy and help others.

Like scores of other students, Fred Luddy '51 worked the night shift for Mrs. Miner at the switchboard. He remembers her as one of those strong and indispensable women in the "man's world" that Amherst was at the time. "You came up to them on tiptoe," he says. Ted Bacon '42, who worked 15 years as an admissions dean in Johnson Chapel, remembers that Mrs. Miner's control room off the chapel's main corridor "was a busy intersection, and her door was always open." Theodore Baird, emeritus professor of English, recalls not only her telephone service but other work she performed: "How simple the college was. The English Department didn't have a secretary," Baird says, "they had Maude Miner at the switchboard. She did an awful lot of typing for us. She was always friendly and helpful."

Today Mrs. Miner reminisces happily about those days on the Hill. "Every day there was something different, and to me it was something humorous—because that's the way I looked at things. It's the way I look at things now. Oh, professors came in with some choice stories," she laughs. "And students would tell you things that would raise your hair, if you were that kind. But they knew I wouldn't tell."

Former President Calvin H. Plimpton '39 still speaks of Mrs. Miner with awe. "She knew everything that happened," he marvels, "and she never leaked a thing." John C. Esty '50, who was a dean for 10 years, says people called her "Chief."

Mrs. Miner's own recollections are full of small incidents that suggest business and pleasure were almost one and the same. There was the time that she accepted the student offer of a kitten that a group had been hiding in one of the dormitories in violation of college rules. "They had kept it moving from one room to another, but they told me: 'We don't have any rooms left, and we think the maid is beginning to get wise.' I had him for 17 years. We called him 'Mugsy,' because his mug looked funny."

Mrs. Miner helped students in other ways. One day, she recalls, a popular freshman came to her in despair and said, ' "I've had a bid from 13 fraternities and I don't know which one to join.' I said, 'Well, you sit down and we'll talk about it.' " She guided him through a careful process of elimination: a few of the houses charged more than he could afford, he did not feel at home in a few of the others, and so on. "When we got it down to just three, I said, 'Go out for a walk now. Go alone, and think about it.' The next morning he came in with a big grin and said he'd made up his mind." Another time, as part of their initiation, pledges at a fraternity had to identify the locations of odd objects throughout campus and town. These included a specific local gravestone, and one of the students decided that the best way to start was to talk to the Chief. "I told him: 'You're in luck, I know just where it is,' " she recalls. "I suppose they thought he'd never find it."

Mrs. Miner found whatever anyone needed. She was famous for locating "nice rooms" in town where out-of-town dates could be housed overnight. That's one reason that a black member of the Class of '52, Ulric Haynes, Jr., appreciates Mrs. Miner to this day. He says that it wasn't easy, back then, to locate townspeople who would make a room available to a black visitor; but Mrs. Miner kept making calls until she found one. "She did it for me without any condescension or patronizing whatsoever," Haynes recalls. "As a black student I had some challenges, but Maude never let a challenge go by without facing it down."

On another occasion she counseled a student who had been kicked out of class. The professor told him not to return. When the student came to Mrs. Miner for advice, she told him to take his seat in class the next time it met, say nothing at first, and then slowly join the discussion. The plan worked. Nothing was ever said, and the student passed the course. She says she enjoyed her counseling sideline. "Sometimes Dean Porter [C. Scott Porter] would say to a boy, 'Go see Mrs. Miner, she'll help you.' I said to him once, 'Listen, I'm no psychiatrist.' He said: 'Maude, I don't know what you're doing, but keep it up.'"

She and her husband, Harry, who worked for the light company, often invited students, secretaries, and the daughters of local families to parties at their little house just down the road from College Hall, on Route 9. "It wasn't for dates," she explains. "I wouldn't have them matched up one-for-one. It was just to have a party." Foreign students, and others far from home, received invitations to Christmas dinner, and other special concern.

Mrs. Miner began her career in Amherst in 1917, working for the local telephone company. When she moved to her college job in 1933 there were 25 telephones on the campus. When she retired in 1967, there were 350. Someone calculated that she had said the words "Amherst College" about 2,000,000 times.

She doesn't have much to say about big historical events, like the 1938 hurricane or President Kennedy's visit in 1963. She remembers that the hurricane struck when her husband was out of town, and that students showed up at their house to be sure she was safe. And she remembers the Secret Service inspecting the campus before Kennedy's visit. "Two men with black suits on, very businesslike, came to look everybody over. I suppose other people were very respectful because these men worked for the president," she shrugs. "But I didn't care who they worked for. I just told them I was perfectly peaceful."

Mrs. Miner doesn't tell "war stories" about important phone calls or switchboard emergencies. "I could handle them all," she says firmly, "and since I could handle them, they weren't emergencies." She would rather talk about the people she saw every day—especially students. "We were such an informal bunch," she says. "It was that kind of job, and I liked it."—DCW

In a professional lifetime a professor touches the lives of hundreds, sometimes thousands of students. This impact is often acknowledged years later, when alumni are startled to read that a favorite professor has died. Their letters to the college magazine are then often the warmest tributes made at the time, perhaps at any time. So it was when John A. Moore, a much-loved professor of classics, died in 1972. It was not Moore's *pro forma* obituary but a personal appreciation written by one former student, and a poem written by another, that recalled Moore's special qualities. The first writer remembered Moore as "a true Hellene," a rigorous intellectual who gave "jewel-crafted talks" on Homer, Aeschylus, and Thucydides. In lines of blank verse the other recalled an examination period: "At something past the hour Professor Moore said: / Gentlemen, if I may shake the tree . . . / What a way for a professor to talk!" The following reminiscence is by still a third alumnus, one who was moved to write about Moore many years later. Richard F. Teichgraeber III '71 is a professor of history and director of the Murphy Institute of Political Economy at Tulane University.

WITH RESPECT TO JOHN MOORE

By Richard F. Teichgraeber III

THIS IS THE RIGHT time and place to offer a belated memorial to John Andrew Moore (1918–72). Twenty-five years out, I now believe, in some moods, that he was the most important of several great teachers I had at Amherst. Class of 1880 professor of Classics and department chair when our class graduated, he died during the summer of the following year, at the age of 54, of a massive cerebral hemorrhage. I had two courses with John Moore: in spring semester 1970, Colloquium 36: Ancient and Modern Literature; and in fall 1970, Classics 97, a directed readings course on Shakespeare's plays. At the time of the first class, my academic record was lackluster, and I was looking for a way out of my then political science major, hoping to ignite some intellectual fires. (I had taken all but one of George Kateb's three courses in political theory, and what remained of other departmental offerings looked uninspiring.) In the fall of 1970, I became an English major. I mention all this at the start to make it clear that my credentials here are those of an admiring bystander, not one of John Moore's distinguished or favorite students. Even so, he was a teacher who changed my life.

The air at Amherst is always full of talk about great teaching, about what President Tom Gerety called in his 1994 inaugural address "the peculiarly human relation of the teacher to the student, the one who knows and the one who would know." My own career as a teacher, however, has taught me that part of what makes this relationship peculiar is that generalizations about excellent teaching are always suspect, because no one formula manages to capture the practice of every successful teacher. John Moore in fact violated many of the techniques we usually think of as essential for effective teaching: in a room full of students, he seemed shy and nervous; he spoke softly and quickly, and only reluctantly made eye contact. During meetings of Colloquium 36, which he team-taught with Joseph Epstein of the Philosophy Department, he appeared content to let the more openly confident Epstein take center stage. Where Epstein was an aggressive performer, Moore seemed to want to teach less by talking than by listening intently when others talked.

John Moore may have been the only self-effacing teacher I had at Amherst. Yet when we first met he also was the subject of a well-established myth that gave his diffidence an unusual aura of authority. Moore himself probably never knew of the myth, and I don't remember how I first came across it. There's little question, however, that it was spawned and kept alive by student gossip concerning an apparent lacuna in his professional training.

Before joining the Amherst faculty as an instructor in 1947, Moore had received his B.A. (1938) and M.A. (1940) from Harvard, where he was a member of Phi Beta Kappa and wrote a senior honors thesis on Sophocles and Arete that was selected for publication (Harvard University Press, 1938) by a faculty committee. In 1938–39, and again from 1940 to 1942, he pursued graduate studies at Wadham College, Oxford. Moore interrupted his academic training for four years to serve as a civilian decoder in the U.S. Department of the Navy, and then returned to Harvard in 1946–47, after his election to the prestigious Society of Fellows.

Glittering credentials, to be sure, but John Moore never went on to finish his Ph.D. Why not? The answer, countless Amherst undergraduates of his era appear to have told themselves, had something to do with the cryptographic work he did for naval intelligence during World War II. The story we heard and passed on to others told of a heroic defeat: after he had broken an important and extremely difficult Nazi code with several days of solitary and exhausting work, John Moore then had an emotional or psychological breakdown himself, and this somehow had prevented him from getting on with his doctoral thesis.

As with many undergraduate myths, this one, I've learned, reflects little of the truth. Moore's work on decoding involved locating repeating mathematical patterns in nightly encryptions sent by Japanese submarines, not by the Nazis. He also didn't work alone, but as part of a team that included Richmond Lattimore, the distinguished translator of Homer, and Helen Bacon, later a professor of classics at Smith and Barnard. As for the actual reason for Moore's missing Ph.D., well, it turns out that the guiding idea of Harvard's Society of Fellows was to free gifted academics from the now unchallenged tyranny of the Ph.D. lockstep. Junior Fellows were known for following their own noses—in Moore's case, one of the results was *Selections from the Greek Elegiac, Iambic and Lyric Poets* (Harvard University Press, 1947)—and in the 1940s most of them managed to gain teaching positions without taking a Ph.D. The more famous Richard Wilbur '42 and C. L. Barber (who also taught at Amherst during John Moore's era) are two other examples.

By any measure, my single most important (and altogether accurate) memory of John Moore remains that of a voice I first heard while reading comments he wrote in the margins of a journal I kept as one of the requirements for Colloquium 36. This course was a remnant of Humanities I–II, a "Great Books" sequence required for all Amherst freshmen as part of the post–World War II "New Curriculum." Until the faculty abolished the requirement in 1964, Moore had served regularly as the head of the team that taught Hum. I–II, although he never mentioned this during the time I knew him. (The debate about the fate of "Great Books" did not begin to rage until the mid-1980s.) There were 29 students in Colloquium 36 in 1970—others included Bob Elliot '71, Rick Goggans '71, John Hendricks '71, Ed Merves '71, and Wendy Wasserstein (then a junior visiting transfer from Mount Holyoke and not yet the famous playwright she later became)—and we met in Converse on Monday and Friday afternoons at 2 o'clock to discuss "Great Books" like *The Odyssey*, *Oedipus Rex*, *The Republic*, Keats's *Letters*, *Anna Karenina*, and *Death in Venice*. Here is Moore's first comment, about a long journal entry in which I offered some obviously overheated responses to Homer and Thomas Mann:

> This is a highly *personal* reading of the books, and in a sense that's good—it reminds us that these characters are images of actual lives. This gives reality to the act of reading. But there's a danger (and per-

haps a certain clumsiness) in always asking "Am I Odysseus?" "Am I
Aschenbach?" The answer can never be unqualified "yes"—these are,
after all, ideal artistic types. And it is almost futile (and although helpful to a degree) to ask the same questions about the people we know
(*e.g.*, you and I can never know as much about Prof. Commager as
Mann knew about Aschenbach, because Mann *invented* Aschenbach)—in a word, fiction can give us intuitions and glimpses into the
potentialities of lives, our own and others; but not too direct nor too
unequivocal ones, because no author knows all there is to know about
man in general. The mystery remains.

During my first two unimpressive years at Amherst I hadn't managed
to elicit anything quite like this: a reassuringly thoughtful set of comments—critical, to be sure, yet at the same time encouraging and
relaxed. Moore was a teacher who apparently not only thought that I—at
long last—had something substantial to say, but he also spoke back to
me in an authoritative but kind voice which hinted that somehow I might
find my way to become his peer.

Here's another example of Moore's voice—his comments on my naive
egalitarian railing against Plato's elitism—I still find wonderful to listen to:

My trouble here is, that though I largely agree with you that Plato has
too scant a regard for the complex creative potential of each human
individual, I find that lack diminishes only slightly my great admiration for the *Republic*. The question to which he mainly addresses himself was particularly acute at that historical moment, but it is also a
perennial question—is there any rational alternative to the morality of
unlimited self-aggrandizement which is advanced by Thrasymachus?
This is a theoretical issue which may not interest you, but has very
important practical consequences. You seem to assume that individual
initiative can only be creative & valuable. If we look at the society
around us, with its devotion to wealth, power, and pleasure, and its
deep impieties toward the environment and the general good, we are
apt to reconsider.

Once more criticism conveyed with respect. There's no hint of the disdain undergraduates dread and find so devastating, but instead quiet and decidedly un-condescending encouragement to think again, to get it right.

I have no doubt that it was not John Moore's intention to steer me toward an academic career. But almost in passing that, I suppose, is what he did. Today I remember little about how exactly he helped me become a more careful and honest reader of Shakespeare's plays. What I do remember is that, during the first semester of my last year at Amherst, in the course of our weekly meetings in his office in Grosvenor House, his intent listening to my thoughts about the plays inspired me with an unexpected determination to proceed on my own: first to an honors thesis on *Othello* in the spring of 1971, then on to graduate training in intellectual history at Brandeis. Another way of putting this would be to say that John Moore's most effective work as a teacher, in my case, was probably done neither in Converse nor in his office, but in the Robert Frost Library, where I spent countless hours on my own, reading and annotating texts and listening to recorded versions of Shakespeare's plays, entirely without his supervision, gradually coming to believe that I too had the stuff one needed to be a teacher and a scholar.

Henry Adams once defined great teachers as individuals who "effect eternity," because they can never tell where their influence stops. Sounds like a bromide, but only if you can't come up with examples of what Adams may have had in mind. When the Amherst class of 1971 meets for its 25th reunion, John Moore will have been gone for almost 24 years, but his influence has yet to stop in my case. For on the shelves of my office at Tulane, I still have in easy reach both the journal I kept for Colloquium 36 and the annotated volumes of the Arden edition of Shakespeare's plays that I discussed with John Moore. The sight of them evokes remarkably clear memories of my days as his student, and sometimes these same memories help to fortify my occasionally wobbly sense of self.

Horace Porter started life in 1950 in the rural hamlet of Midland, Georgia. He was one of nine children in a weathered farmhouse without running water or electricity. As a boy he worried about hellfire and damnation, and about stories of the Ku Klux Klan. But he also listened to whippoorwills at night and he lived in springtime among pink-and-white plum trees. He was an exceptional student and a voracious reader. In 1959 the family moved to Columbus, Georgia, where, in high school, Porter read a college manual written by Eugene S. Wilson, dean of admission at Amherst. He began writing letters to Wilson, which sparked an encouraging two-way correspondence. Impressed by Porter's wide reading and his hunger for education, Wilson admitted him to the Class of 1972 on a full scholarship. Porter majored in English and American Studies and wrote an honors thesis on black literary figures of the Harlem Renaissance. After completing graduate work at Yale, he taught at Dartmouth, then Stanford. Now professor of English and American Studies at the University of Iowa, Porter is the author of books about Ralph Ellison and James Baldwin. Professor Allen Guttmann, his Amherst thesis advisor, says that the books "demonstrate the same very personal engagement with the topic that characterized his undergraduate writing." This essay on Porter's Amherst experience originally appeared in *Change* magazine in 1977 and was reprinted in *Amherst* magazine.

REFLECTIONS OF A BLACK SON

By *Horace Porter*

THERE COMES A time when every young man leaves his father's house. I left my home in Columbus, Georgia, on the second of September in 1968. It was a day marked by three extraordinary events in my life: I boarded a plane for my first flight; I left the South for the first time; and that afternoon I walked across the campus of Amherst College.

Late in the day I met my roommate from Grosse Pointe, Michigan. After the usual introductions and small talk, Brian asked me about my religious views. I told him I was a Baptist, a Christian. He stated emphatically that he was an atheist. We assured each other we would not allow the difference to lead to conflict. That night, however, in a scene reminiscent of Queequeg and Ishmael at the Spouter Inn, I got down on my knees to say my prayers. Brian asked if something were wrong. I told him that I was saying my prayers. He nodded, amazed. That was the first and the last night I said my prayers on my knees at Amherst. I reasoned it was time to bring to an end that particular practice of my Southern boyhood.

Yet I pondered the events of the day for several hours after my prayers. I thought of my parents. Like many Southern blacks born during World War I, neither had made it through high school. Neither had, of course, gone north to college. And neither had heard of Amherst until I spoke about it. At boarding time that morning, they had assured me that they

would pray for me, and they asked me to pray and trust in the Lord. As
I lay awake, I wondered why my parents had found it necessary to pray. I
had expected them to be as ecstatic as I was. I was not, after all, like many
of my unfortunate friends, on the way to the battlefields of Vietnam. I
was going to college.

It took me a few years and many wakeful nights to understand that
my parents had few assurances of my safety and success. They had only a
belief in my capacity for perseverance and an inviolable faith in the
benevolence of God. As the years passed, I came to understand the reasons why my parents prayed for me. Having heard numerous accounts of
handsome Johnnies who went away to college and were led astray—into
the world of drugs, wild sex, political militance, or any of the confusions
of that raucous decade—they prayed that I would continue to serve God
and remain a loyal member of the family. For they also had heard tales of
black Johnnies who eventually discovered reasons to stare at their own
birth certificates with contempt. My parents prayed that after the novels
and the teacups, I would still be their loyal, humble, and God-fearing
son. A remembrance of my parents' reactions surely stirred my emotions,
my intuitions, something inscrutable within me. And I prayed silently
and alone from time to time.

I needed my prayers. Amherst was like a foreign country those first
few months. The college itself was undergoing significant transition.
Compulsory attendance at chapel had been terminated the year before.
The faculty had voted to change the old curriculum (in which certain
core courses in mathematics, physics, and English were required) to a
system marked by the glorious freedom of distribution requirements in
the three major divisions. But Amherst of old still asserted itself. We had
to declare ourselves "independent" to avoid fraternity rushing. We were
expected to escort young ladies home to Smith and Mount Holyoke at the
stroke of 12. And, of course, Marge and Isabelle came to make our beds
each morning.

The students all appeared wealthy, articulate, and atheistic. Clad in
faded bell-bottom jeans and wire-framed glasses, they discussed the war
and the coming election with what seemed to me expertise. Everyone, or
so it appeared, discussed books I had not read. No one discussed books I
had read. I had spent nights, dawns, and hot summer days reading the

Bible, Shakespeare, Austen, Melville, and Twain. Richard Wright, James Baldwin, and Norman Mailer had aided me in effecting a truce with the barren and brutal reality of my last three years in Columbus. But their styles were not as influential as those of the nineteenth-century writers. Therefore, my vocabulary and diction manifested many vestiges of nineteenth-century rhetoric.

Moreover, with many words I had merely lexicon acquaintance. I had never heard them come alive in speech. That curious state of verbal affairs occasioned one of the memorable joys of Amherst: during those first weeks words I had known for years via the page emerged in my world of sound. I soon became comfortable enough to pull out a few of my own stops. I used my favorite words without feeling embarrassed and without baffling those with whom I spoke.

However, I still had not read Hesse, Kazantzakis, and Beckett. Everyone, it seemed, had already met Godot. I had read some of Sartre, but God knows I had not heard of Marcuse. Menaced by my sense of intellectual insecurity, I read books and examined journals and periodicals with a diligence I have not since been able to surpass. It was during that unforgettable season of intellectual passion that I read Ralph Ellison's *Invisible Man*, a novel that shook me with the force of an earthquake. Given the temper of the times, I readily identified with the nameless protagonist who proclaims: "I was my experiences and my experiences were me." I was driven to explore my own hidden name, my own complex fate.

I read W. E. B. DuBois, James Weldon Johnson, Carter G. Woodson, Jean Toomer, and numerous other Afro-American scholars and writers. Theirs was a valuable legacy for me. In times more trying than my own, they had worked and thought well. Some, like DuBois and Woodson, lived and wrote during the heyday of what came to be known as scientific racism. The notion of the innate inferiority of the black race suffused the air they breathed. But by dint of their indefatigable wills and their discipline, they wrote novels and histories that spoke eloquently of the souls of black folk—long before my time, even before the time of my parents.

Ironically, those black writers and thinkers helped to bring about the first long, snowy winter of my discontent at Amherst. Only a few Amherst professors had even heard of them when I arrived. No one on the faculty was primarily committed to a study of the Afro-American experience.

The one black member of the faculty was a mathematician. That greatly disturbed me. After those initial months of awe and a trip home at Christmas, I began to consider the social and political dimensions of my love for books, words, and ideas. What, I wondered, was in store for me if I decided to make my love my profession? What peculiar problems would I encounter as an Afro-American intellectual? I asked myself what was the real beast in the Afro-American intellectual jungle. My attempt to answer those questions led me to the realization that I owed my soul to the Bible, the Constitution, and the Declaration of Independence, to Shakespeare and Melville, to Freud and Marx, and to the English language in which I thought, spoke, and wrote.

This awareness proved very troubling at the time because of the obsession among black students with all that was unique to the Afro-American experience. Black pride was regarded as inextricably bound with a black consciousness, a black aesthetic, and black English. Intellectually, the assumption was, of course, highly problematic. But discussion was rarely dispassionate during those years. In fact, if one were black and did not use the black vernacular from time to time, one ran the risk of being labeled a "Negro." That was one of the most pejorative epithets a black student could use to describe another brother, or sister, an elegant variation of the "oreo" of a decade later. On a deeper level, the question was whether Afro-Americans were being forced to learn what—in many cases—amounted to an alien tongue. It was frequently pointed out to me that many Afro-Americans speak a variant of American English. I knew, of course, that my family's English was very different from the English of Amherst, that each time I boarded a plane to return home for a short spell, I had to weed out of my vocabulary much of the verbal flora I had cultivated. I did not want to sound like a guest in a strange house. I had to get down, as it were, into the black vernacular. I had to tune my ears to a different subjunctive and accept, once again, the fact that inflections can be marvelous adverbs.

The two languages were indicative of two vastly different worlds. And the trips, over the years, back to the world from which I came, made me bitter and frustrated. I occasionally encountered high school friends back from Vietnam. A few had been wounded and they held me spellbound with their stories of the war. Other classmates had been bruised and disfigured on the streets of America. One friend—peace to his adventure-some spirit—was murdered. And I saw friends, relatives, and neighbors—some of the most responsible, hardworking, and patriotic people I know—who were getting on, although facing daily, to use Mailer's phrase, "the dirt and dark deliveries of the necessary."

I flew back to Amherst after those trips, back to a room of my own, back to the quiet and comfort of the Robert Frost Library. I felt somewhat guilty because there was no black community in which to work or play in the town of Amherst. I began to take perhaps too seriously the charges of militant black nationalists and other critics of the American society who argued that black students at prestigious colleges and universities were being bought, that our loyalties were being subtly besieged by the "system," that life in ivory towers was a luxury we could not afford at such a late hour, that it was the responsibility of my generation to destroy "Faulkner, Dick, Jane, and other perpetuators of evil."

Those arguments, along with the fact that the faculty and administration approached Afro-American and black studies with the same reserve and circumspection they brought to all important matters, shook my confidence in the scholarly process. To be sure, I had learned the value of reasoned discourse. I knew how precious the goals of academic freedom and objectivity were to the academy. But I also realized that courses concerning Afro-Americans were no different from others; any course could become partisan or ideological depending on the teacher and the students. I recognized too that some scholarly and artistic work necessitates years of contemplation, but I reasoned that a commitment to the black struggle was not necessarily incompatible with such endeavor. I wanted the Afro-American presence asserted at Amherst. I wanted the Afro-American voice heard immediately.

I had become a victim of the rhetoric of the time. The charges of certain glaring deficiencies in the Amherst curriculum were valid enough. But I started to associate too many of the ills of American society with what took place at Amherst. Since I assumed that we were some of the most intelligent and promising men of my generation, it seemed to me that Amherst was failing. It was not teaching its students, who would some day wield significant power, the duty of making a new America. The failure of white students and minority students to interact significantly was a salient example. In this matter of race, I frequently asked, why is there so much of the society and so little of the mind at work here at Amherst?

American society at large was as much a cause of my malaise as Amherst College. There were so many palpable evils to be eradicated. To speak out and rebel seemed, at the time, the only right thing to do. I became one of the more prominent members of the Amherst Afro-American Society. I petitioned and protested. I signed angry letters addressed to the Amherst administration and the world. I encouraged the rebellious imperatives of my newly politicized self: I went on strike, I sat in, I fasted, I wept. I prayed.

In many ways, my situation was hardly unique. Professors frequently boasted that they were teaching students to forget the parental world of unexamined obedience and programmed cant. We were urged by Dean of Students Robert Ward to "be your own man." And with the odd combination of insanity and perspicacity that marked the rhetoric of our time, we tried to do exactly that. We asked our teachers, our mentors, our distinguished visitors, how could we be our own men in a system that was racially and politically rigged? How could we be our own men when we were expected and could be called upon almost any day to throw away our lives foolishly defending a rice paddy in Vietnam? How could we be our own men when the courses we took were basically the same ones taken by the men who sat in our nation's highest councils of power?

Every year the student body faced a series of crises and rallying causes. One after another they came, in lockstep: Kent State, Jackson State, My Lai, Calley, Carswell, Angela Davis, George Jackson, Attica. And the war that went on and on led along with the other crises to numerous expressions of moral outrage. We had two moratoria my first year and a major "takeover" by black students and a general strike my second. We sat in at Westover Air Force Base during the spring of my last year. Moreover, the state of things, the times, forced a number of my classmates and other students away from the college. Some did not return. Others tripped on drugs and never really came back. I, too, was frustrated and tired. I longed for a nonpolitical space for myself.

I grew nostalgic at times. Columbus, Georgia, had been a world of black and white (though sometimes unpleasant) certainties. I missed the communal warmth and encouragement of relatives, friends, and neighbors. I missed Sunday mornings in Columbus—New Providence Baptist Church and the hours of praying, singing, and shouting. Those Sunday mornings had shaped my sense of my self and the world. Yet I now had to admit grudgingly that Sunday morning had been robbed of its hallowed traditions. My singular compulsion had become the Sunday issue of *The New York Times*. I communed quietly with Russell Baker, and the whole galaxy of New York literary personages. Thus, my Sundays became a symbolic critique of my religious past. I now looked at the world with new inner eyes. Furthermore, I was forced to admit that my parents' Christian vision was limited, that it had been impaired by history, circumstances, and time.

But as Faulkner reminds us, our pasts are never really past. In spite of my intellectual attempts to become something other, Christianity was in my blood. My father and grandfather are Baptist deacons. So when I communed with my own heart each Sunday morning at Amherst, I sometimes felt like a sinner—or worse, a backslider. Something deep within told me that it was neither right nor sound to turn my back on the traditions of my forebears, that I was not only being a prodigal son but also a foolish one. I was reminded, too, to use my grandfather's oft-quoted expression, that my arms were too short to box with God.

My teachers, fellow students, and occasional guest lecturers helped me through those days of nostalgia and frustration. George Johnson, Wilburn Willams, Sixtue Vusi, Calvin Ward, Gregory Domingue, and Gary Kornblith—all brilliant, if ruthless, intellectual sparring partners—spent hours arguing with me about almost everything. We talked until dawn; then, sensing Truth's everlasting elusiveness, we went to bed. But days at Amherst were not a time to sleep either. Teachers like Theodore Baird, Earl Latham, and Benjamin Ziegler had served the college so long and excellently that they had become living legends. Others, like Norman Birnbaum, Henry Steele Commager, and Benjamin DeMott—prolific commentators on American culture and politics—contributed to what was called "the Amherst experience." But a good college, like a thinking man, sometimes grows preoccupied. During my years, the heart and the mind of Amherst pondered the "ideal of goodness and wisdom." Leo Marx, George Kateb, and John William Ward were at the college's center.

Marx and Kateb could draw a crowd at midnight. The word merely had to get out that one or the other or both had decided to speak on, say, the Vietnam War, the Constitution, or amnesty for the draft evaders, and we would all come. Neither quoted vintage Pericles and Lincoln with the oratorical flourish of Henry Commager—no one this side of heaven can!—but their courses were extraordinarily rewarding.

I started watching Kateb while I was a freshman. In a moving charge to the graduating class of 1969, he warned that radicalism was getting out of hand. Yet he assured them that "your decency is incandescent." And the radical class rose applauding. During the spring of 1970, when students were striking across the country, Kateb walked through a noisy crowd and took his stand. Convinced that the academy was endangered from without, he stated movingly: "I consider Amherst and places like it a haven, a haven where thought—that fragile, weak, precious thing— can go, if only to hide."

I enrolled in his course, American Political Thought, the following year. The course met in Amherst's best lecture hall, the Red Room in Converse Hall. (It is a red-carpeted room with swivel chairs, pedestaled ashtrays, and soft light.) Kateb urged us to listen, not to take notes. However, his lectures were too good to go unrecorded. Each brought another note of sweetness, another gem of light. He quoted the greats: "When men are void of purpose, the void becomes the purpose," he said, recalling Nietzsche. "Of the Gods we suspect, of men we know, that as a consequence of their natures, they rule wherever they can," he said, citing Thucydides. Occasionally, he referred to his late teacher C. Wright Mills. But even Kateb was a target for scathing criticism during those years. Once a sophomore called him a "whore to reason."

Leo Marx also lectured in the Red Room. Marx's great pedagogical device was his practice of effecting an aura of spontaneity. If we were discussing *Moby Dick*, the Red Room suddenly became the *Pequod* at sea. And we saw Ahab's "topmost greatness and topmost grief" as we sailed upon the bosom of Marx's mimetic eloquence. One morning Marx lectured on Mailer's *Why Are We in Vietnam?* It was the best lecture I ever heard as an undergraduate, a sermon of sorts. That lecture forced me to see that, in many ways, I was as American as DJ and Tex. Sometimes while listening to Marx lecture, I wondered whether his teachers, Perry Miller and F. O. Matthiessen, had been as inspiring.

There were other professors I shall never forget. Theodore P. Greene taught me to avoid long quotations, insisting that what mattered were my own thoughts. When I was a sophomore, Tillie Olsen was our writer in residence. She read my stories with care. She encouraged me to keep a journal and to continue writing. Allen Guttmann, my advisor, became my friend and my guide to clear thinking. He suggested works by black writers of whom I had no knowledge. He taught me how to read novels critically. He was never too busy or too indifferent to read assorted essays that I stuck in his mailbox. He made no secret of the fact that he disagreed with my politics, but on many occasions he invited me home for dinner.

If a student grew bored with the Amherst faculty, many visitors and lecturers—kooks and false prophets as well as eminent scholars and writers—served to dispel his ennui. I shall always remember the day during my freshman year when Ralph Ellison came to Amherst. I had read his novel a few months before and was eager to talk to him. I did not want to appear uninformed in the presence of the man whose novel had changed the way I viewed myself in relation to the world. Consequently, I asked him several questions. "Who is your favorite writer?" I inquired. He assured me that he admired many authors. However, I wanted to know his favorite. He finally answered, "Dostoevsky." I asked him why he had chosen to end the novel in the manner that he did; he responded at length, shrewdly forgetting the name of one of his characters. I promptly provided it and he continued. He was generous and kind. A few other students and I talked with him until dinnertime. I had brought my paperback edition of *Invisible Man* along, but I lacked sufficient courage to ask for an autograph. John William Ward, detecting my shyness, called the writer back. Without hesitation Ellison inscribed that tattered paperback, now the most precious of all my volumes. After dinner he lectured to a crowd in Johnson Chapel, discussing race and American literature without notes for well over an hour. Calvin Coolidge stared, seeming to hear all, from a portrait above his shoulder.

That was one of many great days at Amherst. But I was unhappy much of the time too. For I had come as one of the last black delegates of the Civil Rights Era, an era brought symbolically and dramatically to a close by the assassination of Martin Luther King, Jr., a few months before.

I had come, that is, with a definite sense of personal and historical purpose. Thus, I readily internalized and was willing to act upon Amherst's motto, *Terras Irradient*. The behavior of my peers was at times disheartening. They will do nothing to change America, I often thought and said. Yet I remained because I saw that in its own groping way Amherst was about changing our collective mind and heart. I saw, too, something of the possible beauty and glory of life there. I learned the value of critical and dispassionate discussion. I came to treasure most forms of artistic expression. I experienced the pleasure of leisure time. Many sunny afternoons I leaned and loafed with my friends on the grass of Memorial Hill. Many snowy nights, I danced until dawn. Yet my love for Amherst was tortured by an inarticulate hate, my hate by an undeniable love.

My feelings were similarly contradictory on commencement day. The months of my senior year passed in a flash, and before I knew it I was marching along with my classmates to our seats facing the Robert Frost Library. Faculty members, deans, and various dignitaries stared down at us from the platform that had been constructed on the library's patio. I had spent most of my 21 years frantically preparing for that day of graduation. Perhaps I was dazed by the bright magic of the occasion. I still do not know; but something happened. My mind's ear closed itself to the speeches, the names, the applause. And I watched my classmates, one after another, accept their diplomas.

Amherst College was sending forth another class of its sons to "illumine the land." And those purple-ribboned diplomas had great significance. They meant that one's sensibilities had been caressed by some of the finest minds in America. They meant that one had been taught some of the best that had been thought and said. They meant that one had experienced profound sweetness and light. But they did not mean that one had an understanding of those brutal truths taught by the university of adversity. They did not mean that one had intimate knowledge of the "fires of human cruelty" or that one had gained an acute awareness of what it means to be disadvantaged, both by law and custom. Perhaps Amherst could never teach that. Perhaps no liberal arts college could. I did not know. But the world of my father's house had taught me much about those particular facts of life. That knowledge distinguished me from most of my classmates. And my mind seized the moment to make it clear.

Then it was my time to stand. I stood and turned, catching my moth-er's eye. And as I walked toward the platform a poem by Langston Hughes I had memorized years before mysteriously came to mind. I heard a voice, a sweet Southern voice, saying:

> Well, son, I'll tell you.
> Life for me ain't been no crystal stair.
> It's had tacks in it,
> And splinters. . . .

I walked across the platform. I accepted my diploma. I started walking back. But I still heard that voice:

> So boy, don't you turn back.
> Don't you set down on the steps
> 'Cause you find it's kinder hard.
> Don't you fall now—
> For I'se still goin', honey
> I'se still climbin',
> And life for me ain't been no crystal stair.

John William Ward, a professor of history and American Studies at the college, became Amherst's fourteenth president in 1971, when there was growing campus unrest over the country's continued prosecution of the war in Vietnam. Concern rose to new heights in the spring of 1972 when President Nixon ordered renewed bombing of North Vietnam and the mining of the harbor of Haiphong. Ward received a standing ovation when he announced to an overflow audience in Johnson Chapel that, exercising his rights as a private citizen, he would join students and faculty who were planning to block traffic in a nonviolent protest at the Westover Air Force Base in nearby Chicopee, Massachusetts. The next morning, Thursday, May 11, he and his wife, Barbara, and nearly 400 Amherst students and professors were arrested and charged with disturbing the peace. Ward and his wife pleaded no contest to the charges and were each fined $10. Meanwhile, the president's action received national news attention and stirred lively controversy, especially among the alumni. Eleven days after his arrest Ward talked about civil disobedience in an *Amherst Student* article published on June 1. Following are excerpts from the interview, conducted by the paper's political editor, Peter E. Scheer '73.

THE CIVIL DISOBEDIENCE OF
JOHN WILLIAM WARD

STUDENT: CAN YOU sum up what has been the general tone of faculty, trustee, and especially alumni response to your recent act of civil disobedience?

WARD: I don't have the benefit of any objective survey, and I also never much cared for Lyndon Johnson's way of measuring his popular support by weighing favorable against unfavorable mail. But my mail is nevertheless my only real source of alumni opinion and I am invested in that sampling of opinion even if I am not willing to judge what I did on the basis of it. I was surprised, really surprised, to find that the letters that have been coming in are running about 8 to 2 in support of my act of civil disobedience, or at least my right to have committed it. I actually had every anticipation that alumni response would be the other way around.

STUDENT: Which particular group, of all those associated with the college, have been the most responsive and/or supportive?

WARD: I've received a lot of letters, at least 100 so far, from parents of students presently enrolled at Amherst. These give me the most pleasure. Only a few of those, as I remember, were unfavorable; even they weren't beating up on me, but were seriously concerned about the kind of model I might be holding up to their sons. For the most part, letters from parents were restrained and concerned, but not angry. Many of the parents who wrote were, as I suggested, only partly supportive. They often began by saying that they were glad that their son is at this place, that my action has helped them to understand him better, and that though they didn't necessarily agree with what I did or my motives for doing it, they were proud that I had the courage to do what I felt I had to do.

STUDENT: What kinds of things did your critics criticize in what you said and did?

WARD: Not surprisingly, the supportive letters were usually very brief and friendly, "thank you for what you did" and so on, and it was the critical letters that were generally the more reasoned, long, and detailed. Of course, I am excluding the rather sad, threatening, and obscene letters that were always written anonymously. I'm simply throwing those away; I don't care to listen to anyone who doesn't have the courage to sign his own letter.

As for the serious critical letters, though . . . all seem to cluster their criticisms around two points. The first is the possibility of distinguishing between my office as the president, and anything I want to do; and the second condemns my breach of the law, whether civilly disobedient or otherwise, as completely unacceptable under any circumstances. . . .

STUDENT: How does [your frustration about the war in Vietnam] justify civil disobedience?

WARD: It is directly related to what I perceived to be the impotency of words to protest a war which has been governed by 18 years of unexamined and misguided assumptions. All along the way, the men who held the power to make decisions about this war were locked into a certain mind-set. And I don't mean to make this sound like an exclusively anti-Republican criticism. Kennedy had it, and so does Mr. Nixon. The premises which underlie the conduct of American foreign policy in Southeast Asia have never been seriously questioned in 18 years, and I don't think that my words or letters at this late time in history are going to be able to enlighten our leaders or change those assumptions. . . .

STUDENT: Isn't it pretty clear, though, that because Nixon can go to China and to Russia that he recognizes Vietnam is, finally, of only secondary importance—if not completely dispensable—to our national interest? Certainly he believes that it is not of the same strategic significance as Berlin, for instance. What makes the continuation of the war and its most recent escalation so frustrating to me is that Nixon understands just how peripheral Vietnam is to our security interest, and yet is willing to risk so much for so little.

WARD: I really wish I could believe that. I wish I could credit Nixon with that kind of comprehension of the situation, but I am afraid he takes even more seriously this concept of national honor and pride which is invoked again and again. I don't see how anybody can take pride in what the United States has done in South Vietnam. . . .The day I was arrested I received a number of very angry phone calls—and these were very difficult because in a way it's better to be able to see whom you're talking to—and again and again at some point in the conversation the angry caller would say, "I wish we hadn't gotten into this war, but now that we're in it we've got to see it through." My response to that, and this didn't please people very much, was that that is not a very adult kind of reasoning. If you really do think that the policy is wrong, then to advocate that we pursue it simply because we have already invested some quantity of pride and honor, is like kids' play. "I can't admit I'm wrong." And that does seem to me to be awfully immature. Somewhere lurking in the back of our president's mind is the notion that I am not going to be the first president to lose a war, and so on.

STUDENT: Yes. Well, what I was suggesting was an even more Machiavellian perception of Nixon: that he did not really fear that any pride or honor was at stake in Vietnam except insofar as he kept saying that it was at stake, but really only feared for his own political future, and so was willing to do anything short of nuclear war to insure it.

WARD: Yes, that's possible. You know I was in Paris when the bombing began and came back a week early just in time for the mining of Haiphong harbor. And when I was in Paris a number of Parisians would say to me, "If you want to protect the lives of the last remaining troops, obviously the best protection of their lives would be to get them out of there." And clearly that's true. De Gaulle did it, and France was much more involved historically in Indochina than the United States has ever been. . . . And when Nixon came in I think he could have negotiated a settlement at only a negligible cost of honor and pride, however he measures such things.

STUDENT: Certainly the terms he is offering now to North Vietnam and Hanoi would have been considered more than generous in 1968.

WARD: It depresses me a little, no, not a little, it bothers me an awful lot that after so many years there is not clear public understanding of the motives and consequences of the war. I came to Amherst in 1964 and that very year we taught a course in American foreign policy, and the second term turned into a full semester's study of Vietnam. And at that time, some eight years ago, I came to the decision—not decision, none of us has ever been able to make any decisions—but I came to the judgment that the assumptions that were controlling our foreign policy in Vietnam had never been questioned and were in fact wrong. . . .

STUDENT: To return for a moment to the circumstances surrounding your arrest, I wonder if you could elaborate on the distinction that you made between your public and private roles, and especially how you have replied to criticism on that score.

WARD: Ironically, many of my critics and supporters both deny me that right: to disassociate my presidential office from actions motivated purely by individual conscience. Supporters will say, "What you've done is great and is significant because you acted as president and had the courage to exercise your conscience as leader of a college. Don't get yourself all schizophrenic about it, but take pride in the fact that you are the president and still have the capacity to act morally." And the critics, on the other hand, insist that precisely because I am the president I have to forgo the kinds of political protests that an individual, speaking for himself alone, is free to undertake. For the moment my judgment about this dilemma is really a pragmatic one; that is, I don't feel that I have a completely intellectually satisfying answer to the tension between self and role. But until I can arrive at one I am not going to allow myself to be wholly absorbed by the constraints of a particular office. Many who have criticized me have said that I lost the privilege to act as an individual when I took the office of president because the public world would not understand the difference between my self and my role. That is true; the public probably will not understand that distinction. But that hardly settles the dilemma. The individual, I am told, cannot speak because he will involve the institution in which he works or lives. So, one turns to the institution and gets the answer that each has a special function in our complex society and that the institution therefore cannot take a stand on matters of general public, political, and moral concern. When one asks,

"Who is responsible?" it turns out that no one is. The result is precisely the frustration and alienation which lead either to a cynical privatism or sudden outbursts of mass action. There should be, of course, one institution that solves the problem: government. But Congress is nearly impotent. I think that the major item on our political agenda is to ask how we might extend the idea of citizenship from the single self to the anonymous institutions which exercise power in our society. But until that difficult question is resolved, I cannot reasonably be expected to surrender myself to the job, to ignore my mind and conscience while waiting on a collective personality, whatever institution it may be, which we also say must be silent.

STUDENT: But of course part of your motivation for committing civil disobedience was your position of relative power and influence. You said in your address the night before your arrest that writing another letter would be like "throwing a paper plane against a blank wall." And by the same analogy the act of civil disobedience by a student or even a professor is probably just as ineffectual, but the act of civil disobedience by a college president could conceivably carry some political weight.

WARD: Yes, that's true. But it's also true that the address, which found its way from the working press to the op-ed page of *The New York Times* and a large number of other papers, carried some force or weight with an awful lot of people because of the little epigraph at the end that explained that I was arrested. It's important that if I had written an abstract intellectual piece about the war or the need for civil disobedience, many people would have read it and perhaps been intellectually interested, but probably not very emotionally moved one way or the other. The words have a kind of topical interest but also an emotional force because they are linked with an action. There's a moment when words standing by themselves on a page gain an emotional authenticity because one has borne witness to them. Certainly there's no denying that my office added further emotional weight to what I said, but even more important was the willingness to invest something of myself, to substantiate my ideas by acting on them.

STUDENT: So, then, you don't see a hard and fast distinction between your role as president and your role as a thinking and moral individual.

WARD: No, I certainly do not. I know it's nearly impossible to maintain that distinction, but it's the consequence of not trying that worries me; the consequence of voiceless but powerful institutions that force personally injured or outraged individuals into frustration, privatism, or occasional outbursts of mass action. Amherst College cannot take an institutional stand on the war; one would have to prove that such a stand was fundamentally related to the educational function and purpose of the college for it to become involved in such an issue. . . .

STUDENT: Didn't the faculty, as a body, declare its opposition to the Cambodian incursion in 1970?

WARD: Yes they did, but they spoke only for the faculty. Then the question becomes one of "Who speaks for the institution?" And, legally, the only people who can are trustees. But you see the whole logic that criticizes what I did founded its argument on the liberal notion that government—and not leaders of institutions acting as individuals, and not specialized institutions themselves but government—is responsible for addressing matters of general public, political, and moral concern. But things are finally getting critical. To put it softly, this country is being torn apart, and people are beginning to turn to each other and ask, "Where is everybody? Where are the people who are supposed to exercise power and responsibility in society?" How are these people's voices being felt, or are they being felt at all? I just don't think they are. It's that kind of conundrum that makes it necessary for me to consult my conscience and act on it as an individual. . . .

STUDENT: Under what circumstances would you feel that you would have to commit civil disobedience again? Are you certain enough in what you did that you would have to react to an equally outrageous military escalation, say a year from now, by getting arrested again?

WARD: The danger there is whether or not one is able to recapture the thought and feelings that motivated you to do something a few weeks ago, let alone a year ago. I can certainly imagine now situations in which I might have to do something extra-legal or extra-ordinary to register my protest and to try to reach those in power. The sense that there is a grave and imminent danger that cannot be reversed or affected by writing a letter, to use that as a shorthand for going through other established processes. . . .

STUDENT: Can you try to reconstruct the thoughts and arguments that passed through your mind as you came to the decision to commit civil disobedience?

WARD: To recall it as best I can, I should go back to the night before I spoke in Johnson Chapel, when for a while I seriously tried to write a letter, as several students had suggested. And I kept asking myself whether I seriously believed in what I was doing.

STUDENT: Do you mean whether you believed in the political efficacy of such a letter?

WARD: Yes. And I asked myself, further, whether I was just writing this to appease a couple of students. And I realized deep down in my guts that a letter was not going to make very much difference. And I'm not sure that I feel the act of civil disobedience at Westover field is going to make very much difference either. But I guess the sheer proximity of Westover and the urgency of the cause made the act of civil disobedience personally necessary. More abstractly, I guess I chose civil disobedience because it was morally as well as politically the wisest choice. I meant to speak louder than words. I meant the action to be a symbolic and tutelary word—that is, educational—to remind people that civil implies "civilized," and to recall anyone who would listen to a standard of civilized behavior I fear has been lost. I admit that the state has a right to my life, but I do not admit that the state has a right to my mind and conscience. I know the fear of moral anarchy lies that way and I feel the fear myself. The assent of the individual to the law of the state is of course fundamental to the existence of any society, and so on the exercise of civil disobedience I would be pragmatic. Only when one judges a wrong to be pressing and immediate and insensitive to other solutions, can one choose civil disobedience on the grounds of conscience.

The college was only two years old when Ralph Waldo Emerson stopped at Amherst in August 1823. It might be a stretch to say that Emerson, himself only 20, was the first professional writer to visit the campus. But he was already writing his observations into a journal. "The infant college," he reported, "is an infant Hercules. Never was so much striving, outstretching, and advancing in a literary cause as is exhibited here. . . . [The students] write, speak, and study in a sort of fury, which, I think, promises a harvest of attainments." A partial echo of that is heard in this essay, a portrait of the college drawn more than 150 years later by the English writer Julian Symons. Symons was at Amherst as visiting writer in 1975–76. "I think anybody must come away impressed by a sort of fervor, a sense of dedication to scholarly ideals in the faculty," he wrote. The foremost crime novelist of his day, Symons was also prominent in literary circles as a gifted biographer, critic, social historian, essayist, editor, and poet. His former student Chris Bogan '76 remembers that although Symons "walked with literary giants and counted them as his friends . . . he treated me as if my writing and ideas counted just the same as theirs. His criticism never had barbs. His words of encouragement . . . still fortify me three decades later." This article was first published January 29, 1977, in the *Times* of London. Symons died in 1994 at the age of 82.

AN ENGLISHMAN AT AMHERST

By Julian Symons

WHEN, ONE EVENING after dinner in London, Bill Pritchard—that is, Professor William H. Pritchard, chairman of the English Department at Amherst College in Massachusetts, and a fellow admirer of Wyndham Lewis—asked casually whether I would like to go out for a year as a visiting writer, I said with a casualness equal to Bill's own that it sounded a splendid idea. . . .

Eighteen months later I found myself at Amherst. I had been undeterred by the fact that I had never taught, and indeed was unacquainted with academic life. I shivered a little, it is true, at the frequent volleys of memoranda Bill sent across the Atlantic before I arrived, memoranda addressed to his colleagues after meetings. I quote from one of them, about the course in freshman English. We were, it seemed, to begin with the *Norton Anthology of Modern Poetry*, go on to collections of stories by Hawthorne and Flannery O'Connor, and then:

"Suppose we took a breath and picked up an Arnold essay or two, for the purpose of hearing a Sage speak largely about the large matters of Culture, Literature and Society. We don't need to clutch Matt to our bosoms. Just say, now here we are reading a Sage, and what is that like? I do think that 'On the Modern Element in Literature' would be provocative, and help give, at least tentatively, a context for the works to follow."

And what were they?

"Would Thucydides be attemptable? It would then look like this after the *Norton Anthology*, Hawthorne and O'Connor—Arnold, Thucydides (?), *Aeneid* (?all?), *Julius Caesar*, *Under Western Eyes*, *St. Joan*, Orwell's essays, and out by way of some contemporary poems or the new Doctorow."

Could it possibly be that we were meant to teach all of these books in a 14-week term? I disregarded this as a prospect too appalling to contemplate, but it proved to be the case. Thucydides and Doctorow disappeared, and we did only the first six books of the *Aeneid*, but there were replacements for the works omitted. When Bill's wife Marietta came round on the morning before my first class to offer a little reassurance, I felt in need of it. By this time, too, I had become uncomfortably aware that apart from one or two professors emeritus who rarely appeared, I was the oldest person on campus.

Somehow, however, what had seemed almost impossible was done. There were 18 freshmen in my English class, and they were by no means all easterners. A couple came from the West Coast, half a dozen from the South. Four came from private schools, the rest were state educated. They were without exception polite, pleasant, and eager to learn. The work of perhaps a third among them improved remarkably during the semester, and when they expressed general approval of me at the end of it, I felt momentarily like Mr. Chips.

Amherst is a small rich college. The financial problems of its early years, which culminated in 1844 when the unpopular President Humphrey resigned "before the institution was entirely ruined" as one historian puts it, belong to another world. The college now has a stock portfolio worth over $32 million, and it owns a sizable part of the town. The students, all male when I was there although it has since become coeducational, numbered about 1,300. The cost of tuition, room, and board is around $6,000 a year. The ratio of faculty to students is high, one to nine. Among colleges and universities in the East, only Harvard accepted a smaller percentage of applicants this year. Princeton, Dartmouth, and Yale are all a little easier to enter than Amherst.

The students might fairly be called a select group. Perhaps it is not surprising that one of the graffiti in the college lavatories says: "Amherst-social parasitism-training-ground of social uselessness," and that another says, "I like Amherst, the rich boys' playground," an observation to which a wit has added: "I like rich boys." Yet to a visiting Englishman the suggestion that Amherst gives an easy life to a leisured class does not seem persuasive. Distinctions by accent are much harder to make in the United States than in England, and in any case 60 percent of the students have reached the college through public education, and 30 percent receive financial support in the form of scholarships and loans. The freshmen from private schools like Choate and Andover were in general more self-assured, but they were not necessarily better informed than the rest.

In fact, a number of my freshmen in this select group were extremely ignorant. Only 3 out of the 18 were able to tell me what a sonnet was. In part this was because they were not at this stage specializing in English, but putting a toe in the water to see what it felt like, before deciding to major in economics, psychology, political science—or English. For some of them the discovery of English literature was more like a cold plunge than the dipped toe they intended. It would be safe to say that a third of them had never read a line of Matthew Arnold, and another third only knew one or two poems. The rest, on the other hand, had already encountered the Sage talking largely, and were quite prepared to talk largely about him themselves.

How did one deal with such a mixed collection? At our weekly departmental meetings the guidelines laid down—laid down with care, after fairly vivid argument—often seemed to be devised for those who could respond easily rather than those who, to change the watery image, found each successive book part of an increasingly difficult obstacle course. They were designed, I thought, for an ideal student rather than the actual flawed article under our eyes. But perhaps this is inevitable, and perhaps it is a good thing always to aim at the top level of your class. The system finds its justification in the transformation of these raw freshmen into fourth-year seniors with reactions almost invariably quick and sharp.

Some of my freshmen, however, found the course both indigestible and infuriating, and their very vocal indignation was not lessened by a final examination in which they were given free rein to write about Lenny Bruce. One of the brightest of them used the occasion for a moralistic attack, written with considerable verve, in the form of an open letter to the English Department:

"The examination is intellectually insulting, and representative of the callous, archaic, unthinking, irresponsible, disheveled way that members of the English Department have conducted themselves in relation to freshman English. . . . All the members of the department, those hip, free-thinking guys, those models of the open mind, have opened the way to the filth, decay and corruption of today's society. They do not have enough sense to recognize Bruce for what he was, a decrepit junkie, misdirected and potentially dangerous, the Richard Nixon of his time. They salute him, hail him, glorify him. . . .You, oh you members of this sterling academic community, are responsible for the hypodermic syringes and pornography on 42nd Street, for the collapse of our language, our writing and our art."

I was happy to read his prefatory note: "Mr. Symons, you are an outsider, and so not responsible," but it seemed a tribute to the free-thinking English Department that he should have been able to write his open letter without worrying about the result. Not that he had any need to worry. I gave him an A grade.

The Visiting Writer (the capital letters are the college's) is concerned also with Advanced Composition, which might elsewhere be called Creative Writing. There was a lot of competition for admission to this course, in which students wrote poems and short stories which were then discussed by the class and by me. One applicant told me that he had married a year or two earlier, out on the West Coast. "Then my wife was murdered in this really *bizarre* way, and I want to write about it, kind of documentary fiction, it's not a class I want really but personal guidance."

I turned him down with a shudder, but rashly accepted a student named Manzer, in spite of Bill Pritchard's head-shaking. "He's a troublemaker," Bill warned me, and he was right. Manzer, tall, thin, gingery, and inclined to twitch, produced very little work of his own, but criticized everybody else, often in wounding terms. He would wait until other people had finished, and then say "Just a few points," as though he rather than I was conducting the class. To circumvent this I tried to get him to speak first. "Any comments, Manzer?" He would shake his head, but at the end his hand would go up. "Just a few points . . ." I got rid of him at the end of the first semester. In a year's teaching I found two poets and one short-story writer who showed green hints of promise. An average sprouting perhaps, but it seemed to me thin.

Most of the poets were concerned only to express themselves, which they did in the most dismal dribbles of "free" verse. Only a few had ever tried to work within any poetic form. Pressed by me into writing sestinas and villanelles they resisted at first, but ended up enjoying it. A few, however, complained that it was hard work. It was very likely that they had joined in the expectation that advanced composition would be a gut course.

And what is a gut course? It is one in which you do practically no written work, and get a good grade at the end on the strength of a single paper. *You must have a gut*, said one ironical article in the *Amherst Student*. The classic gut of my year was a course called Human Sexuality, known colloquially as Holes and Poles, which was taken by nearly a quarter of the students. Why do you need a gut? Because in the other courses you are forced to work so hard. That, at least, is the theory. The practice varies considerably.

A student at Amherst, as at most American colleges and universities, takes four courses in each semester, 32 in his four years of education. To graduate as an English major he must have taken eight English courses in those four years. To work for honors he has to produce a thesis on an approved subject. I was advisor to two honors students. One of them was to write about George Orwell. The thesis of the other, Chris Bogan, was to be his own poems. And who would judge whether his poems deserved honors? Well, in the first instance, I would. Later on a number of my English Department colleagues would consider his work. This practice, revolutionary in English eyes, is common in the United States.

I was soon engaged in furious argument with the Orwell student, whose ideas were almost totally opposed to mine. The end of our discussions was that he abandoned the thesis, something about which I felt slightly guilty. Bogan was another matter. When he came into my office, I recognized him as one of four students who had, ever so gently, interrogated me earlier in the year when I had paid a flying visit to inspect and be inspected. Gentleness was, indeed, the key to his character. His voice was quiet, his manner nervous. He talked about his poems, and his doubts of their value, at length but hesitantly, in a way pleasantly different from what I had come to recognize as the bright student's characteristic eager aggression. He was fascinated by English literary life, and by modern English poets. Had I met Philip Larkin? What was he like? What about Roy Fuller? Did they write poems easily, or was it as difficult for them as for him? Did I know of a collection of poetic manuscripts that he could study which gave different versions of the same poem?

At long sessions we went through his work in detail. The first poems he brought me were near-Larkin, then they veered to almost-Frost, and in the end to something that seemed a genuine Bogan voice, a little naive and not grandly eloquent, but expressive and personal. Just before Christmas, when the first snow fell, he produced a short, slight poem that I liked:

> Kindness is not a thing you wear,
> That you put on and off with care
> Never to pull a thread or stretch
> It out of shape. Kindness doesn't stretch
> Or shrink or fade. There's never a need
> To put it in the wash. Indeed
> Kindness is not a thing at all.
> It's something like the first snowfall
> Of the season, the way the snow
> Is gentle in its overthrow
> Of the bare, half-frozen ground,
> The way it falls softly, without a sound.

Before the snow, during the long fall season after our arrival in August, Amherst seemed a lotusland. The changing colors of leaves and bushes, masses of dazzling reds, purples, and shades of brown, the undemanding pace of life, an eight-minute walk up College Hill past enormous birds and nearly tame squirrels to my office in Johnson Chapel or to the splendid Robert Frost Library instead of a half-hour journey to the London Library—it was easy to see this as something nobody but an incorrigible city dweller like myself would ever want to leave.

My wife and I stayed first for a few days at the Dickinson Homestead on Main Street, where Emily was born and where she lived for her last 30 years. Like much else in Amherst this formidable redbrick mansion, built in 1813, is owned by the college. Visitors are shown round on Tuesdays and Fridays, but there are few relics of Emily, although a child's chair and a kitchen clock in her bedroom-workroom were Dickinson family pieces. Later we moved to a typical white-painted clapboard house, and quickly tuned in to some of the basic facts of American small-town life.

In Amherst there is no individual butcher or greengrocer, and no public transport within the town. Everything has to be bought at the supermarket, and a car is a necessity. How else are you going to shop? And so a large car park is a necessity too. We discovered the excellence of American shoes, the horror of most American bread (there were 60 varieties in the town supermarket, almost all of them feeling and tasting like sponge rubber), the comparative cheapness of American liquor. We understood why all the houses have mosquito screens. We felt ourselves to be acclimatized.

Not, however, to the snow. The snow changed the landscape, making it romantically beautiful, and it also changed our feelings about Amherst as lotusland. Snow was there when we ate Christmas dinner with Bill and Marietta, snow had to be ploughed out of the drive after each storm, snow was a reminder that we were a long way from home. The students had gone, the campus was empty. Sitting in my study at the Frost Library while I worked on a book about Poe, I looked out on a suitably desolate scene, an endless white landscape under a sky of slate. All this continued for weeks. It seemed, symbolically at least, to end when students began drifting back ahead of time. In the library one day a largely bearded figure rose to greet me, smiling. It was Bogan, a formidable stranger in this disguise.

The spring semester began, bringing a course on the crime story to replace my freshman English, a mostly new section of Advanced Compositionists, a new editor for the *Amherst Student*, which I have already mentioned. The *Student* appeared twice weekly during term, a paper generally of 12 pages, edited, written, and wholly run by the students. The editor changed yearly, and had to do his eight courses a year, with no allowance made for his journalistic work. The paper contained news and opinion about the college, sections on sports and the arts, and its journalistic level was remarkably high. The money to run it was provided by the college, and no visible censorship was imposed. A single issue might contain an article on the "drug culture," a piece about the ethics of college investments, a study of the curriculum with suggestions for its improvement. The president and the faculty were generally referred to by their surnames, and sometimes attacked. President Ward wrote to rebut one attack, more in anger than in sorrow, but made no attempt to stop it. No paper like the *Student* could exist in Britain, and no other I saw in America was on such a high plane in writing and presentation.

The crime story course began with Poe and Collins and moved by way of Sherlock Holmes and Father Brown, Christie and Sayers, Hammett and Chandler, Le Carré and Deighton, to a book of my own and one by

Patricia Highsmith. It was a success, if one can judge by the enthusiasm of the students and the excellence of many papers. Students brought in to me crime memorabilia I had never seen, like a magazine section of a San Francisco newspaper devoted wholly to Hammett. Four of my freshman English students had followed me to this course, including the one so disgusted when asked to write about Lenny Bruce. His feelings, always fervent, fluctuated considerably. Now he was enchanted by Patricia Highsmith's criminal hero Tom Ripley, and wrote a fine essay about him.

March, April, May: examinations and considerations of theses. Students made an oral defense of their theses, under questioning by two or three members of the department, with the student's advisor serving as a kind of moderator. I acted as Bogan's advisor, and as questioner in relation to two other theses, one on Oscar Wilde and another on Auden, this last written by a blind student named Adrian Spratt. After the oral defense a recommendation was made that the student should graduate *cum laude, magna cum laude* or *summa cum laude*. If a thesis was rejected, the student received the degree Bachelor of Arts, *rite*. The fates of the students I was concerned with were interestingly varied. The Oscar Wilde thesis was agreed by everybody to be wholly inadequate, and the student graduated *rite*. Then came Bogan, now beardless again. Soon after questioning began it was apparent, to me if not to him, that the examiners liked his poems less than I did. He graduated *magna cum laude*, respectably enough I'd have thought, but he was disappointed.

And last, Adrian Spratt. His thesis was on the movement of Auden's early poems towards sincerity, and its quality seemed a remarkable tribute to the success of a flexible education. What begins for freshmen as something that seems to an outsider almost haphazard, with them being allowed and even encouraged to take in the same term courses in philosophy, classical civilization, Russian literature and twentieth-century European history (these were actually taken in a single semester by Spratt), has become canalized in the final year into an intensive course of study. How is a blind student to become fully aware of Auden? An immense amount of material not available in Braille was taped for him by willing helpers, so that he had a complete view not only of the poems but of the biographical background. He had "read," and used in his thesis, Isherwood's *Lions and Shadows*, Spender's *World Within World*, my

Thirties, John Fuller's *Guide to Auden*. His advisor, Richard Cody, spent hours talking to him, arguing, elaborating on difficult points, suggesting necessary footnotes. I spent an hour or two with him myself, and found him a true Auden scholar. At his oral examination, he was completely composed, knew exactly what he had put into the thesis and where it was to be found. He graduated *summa cum laude*.

Commencement, or as we would call it graduation, day. In gown and mortarboard, borrowed trappings of professordom, I sit outside the Frost Library listening to speeches, looking at the students as they file up to receive degrees. What thoughts stir after a year in American academe? It must reinforce that sense of openness, warmness, even naivete, in the American character. This is partly expressed through informality of dress (I could have spent the whole year at Amherst without a suit, quite unembarrassed) and of style. The president does not invite you to an informal luncheon in his garden, he asks you to a cookout in his backyard. But reinforced too is awareness of the bureaucratic and obscure language that creeps through American academies. You do not oppose something, you "move into an adversary relationship" towards it, you do not ask for support but say "we would be more than happy to have your input," you do not talk about sex but "discuss male-female relationships." I was not surprised when some students said that they could not understand the set of assignments. I often had trouble with them myself.

And what about Amherst, the Amherst experience, as students and faculty tend to call it? I think anybody must come away impressed by a sort of fervor, a sense of dedication to scholarly ideals in the faculty. More than a hint of self-conscious superiority goes with it, and that is often communicated to the students. Amherst men are arrogant, said two girls at nearby Smith College who attended one of my classes. Well, perhaps. "Amherst encourages idealistic ideas, and then encourages us to be skeptical about those ideas," Adrian Spratt said in a graduation speech. Perfectly true, but I liked better the comment of another graduating student made (where else?) in the *Amherst Student*. "When I got back into the world I realized that in a lot of ways this really is Camelot, and you just have to appreciate it for what it is." That seems just about right. Camelot, given stability and severity by quite a bit of New England high-mindedness. After a year, that seemed a good recipe for a liberal education.

Behind the programmatic certainties spelled out every year in the course catalog, there is a complicated faculty process that shapes them. For many years Hugh Hawkins, Anson D. Morse Professor of History and American Studies, participated in that process. He reports about it here with the understandings of a historian of American higher education and local insider—describing how a diligent, small-college faculty does its work in committees and faculty meetings. The account is slightly abbreviated from the original version, which appears in *General Education at Amherst* (1982). Hawkins tells of circumstances and opinions shaping the Introduction to Liberal Studies (ILS) courses that first-year students were required to take beginning in 1978. He is well suited to report on that subject, too, as a member of the committee that proposed the ILS program in 1977. Students at the time had nearly complete freedom in selecting courses outside their majors. (That free-elective system was almost the polar opposite of Amherst's famous required "core" curriculum, a regimen that lasted from 1946 to 1966.) In ILS, freshmen initially were required to take two special courses, one each semester. These were to be taught by three, four, or five members of the faculty, representing different disciplines, who collaborated to develop an interdisciplinary topic. As a curricular innovation, the ILS program was relatively modest. Here the faculty pares it back even more.

A NEW COURSE SURVIVES
AMID DIFFICULTIES

By Hugh Hawkins

Although the format of a chronicle may imply objectivity, the sophisticated reader knows that the predilections of the selector will give shape to the result. It seems best, then, to identify myself as both a member of the Amherst College committee that proposed the Introduction to Liberal Studies courses and thereafter an enthusiastic participant in one of them. Although favorably disposed toward ILS, I have consulted the written record of 1977 through 1982 in preference to my own recollection and have not hesitated to include opinions with which I disagreed and developments which I considered unfortunate. I have made virtually no effort to include two other parts of the Liberal Studies curriculum: the adjunct program and the modified advisory system.

1976–77

May 10, 1977

In the sixth of a series of meetings on the proposals of the Select Committee on the Curriculum, the Amherst College faculty passes by a vote of 66–29 the following motion: "That the faculty adopt two ILS courses, the adjunct program, an advisory pattern of distribution as described in the Alternate Proposal of the Select Committee, and the advisory system recommended in the Select Committee's report." Most of the debate at the meetings has centered on the requirement of

[243]

two Introduction to Liberal Studies courses for freshmen. The Select
Committee's original plan for three such courses to be required (see
Education at Amherst Reconsidered, pp. 46–52) has been modified in its
"Alternate Proposal . . ." There has been little discussion of the adjunct,
a self-designed program to be required of upperclassmen, uniting
four courses from various departments under a common theme or
question.

1977–78

SEPTEMBER 19, 1977

The Committee of Six (the executive committee of the faculty) shows
eagerness for a stronger Committee on Education Policy (CEP), one
that will urge departments to consider new courses more carefully.
"With the need for colleagues to teach in ILS courses, it will become
more important to be sure that a department has considered the relationship of individual courses to its total program."

OCTOBER 4, 1977

The CEP holds an open meeting for faculty members to discuss plans
and procedures for the ILS courses, which will be first offered next fall.
About 60 colleagues attend. Professor Norton Starr confesses that he is
the author of the recent want ad in the *Valley Advocate* "Personals"
which reads: "Straight WM41 seeks involvement as silent partner in
AC ILS. Discretion guaranteed. I take pride in my efforts. Send address
and interests to *Advocate* Box A-95." He has received no responses. The
meeting reveals, according to a later CEP account, "that, while there
existed a number of ideas for ILS courses, there was also uncertainty as
to how these ideas could be shared and how colleagues could be found
who would help to shape an idea into a feasible course."

OCTOBER 20, 1977

The CEP requests ideas for ILS courses and receives 17 by the end of
the month. These are circulated with the suggestion that those interested in an idea contact the proposer.

NOVEMBER 28, 1977

The chairman of the CEP, Professor Joel Gordon, asks the Committee
of Six for clarification "about the qualifications of people who wished

to teach in the ILS courses." Concluding that the courses should be "the responsibility of those who hold regular teaching appointments," the Committee of Six adds the hope that others, such as interested administrators, will be invited to discuss ideas for the courses and suggest perspectives.

DECEMBER 6, 1977

The CEP sends the faculty an "ILS Course Approval Form," which, as a way of indicating how the proposed course "fits the special character of the ILS program," includes quotations from the Select Committee's report and asks for answers to these queries: "What 'basic questions' is your course designed to emphasize? What 'great issues' will it broach? In what ways does this course differ significantly from other courses you teach? . . . How is your course designed so as to establish some 'point of view exterior to the disciplines themselves'? . . . In what format (what combination of lectures, discussion sections, laboratories, field trips, etc.) do you intend to teach this course, and how is that format related to objectives of the course?" Some colleagues express resentment at the CEP's procedure.

FEBRUARY 9, 1978

In response to a request from five faculty members asking that they be allowed to include the college's clinical psychologist in the ILS course that they are planning, the Committee of Six declares, "The ILS courses are the only required courses which have been voted by the faculty, and, therefore, they require both literally and symbolically a commitment to their teaching by those who have been trained and hired to teach." Consultation and lecturing by others should, however, be welcomed.

FEBRUARY 21, 1978

At a faculty meeting, the chairman of the CEP reports that his committee is "gratified by the range of ideas and disciplines represented in the proposals" for the ILS courses, but that more faculty participation is needed. Dean Prosser Gifford indicates that several departments have asked permission to borrow faculty from other institutions in the Five College consortium to teach regular departmental courses because of the impact of staffing ILS. Professor Gordon Levin challenges the decision to limit ILS staffs to those holding regular teaching appointments as "unnecessarily restrictive and guildlike" and urges reconsideration. (In a later exchange of letters with Professor Levin, the Committee of Six says that it is willing to consider requests for exception on a case-by-case basis.)

MARCH 12–14, 1978

A committee from the New England Association of Schools and Colleges visits Amherst as part of a reaccreditation review. In a document prepared for this visit, the CEP reports that as of December 15, 1977, about 30 colleagues were involved in planning ILS courses, whereas the Select Committee's ideal of a 15/1 student/faculty ratio would require 50. An informal committee of four had been created to consult faculty members individually. It became clear that "there were a number of faculty members who were well-disposed toward (but not necessarily enthusiastic about) the ILS program and who could envision themselves as participating in the program during the coming academic year, provided that departmental instructional commitments could be sorted out.... However ... virtually no department had considered the possibility that the presence of ILS courses would reduce enrollments in other introductory courses and thereby lighten teaching loads in those courses."

The CEP report concluded that "on the whole ... the faculty shared the informal committee's view that, since the faculty had taken this task upon itself, it had now the obligation to see that the ILS program was staffed for next year. It was generally agreed that the program had little chance of success if staffing came about solely because of pressure from the administration." With a higher student/faculty ratio than originally planned, the program seems viable for the coming year.

1978–79

SEPTEMBER 7, 1978

In answer to a query at the first faculty meeting of the year, Registrar Gerald Mager announces that in assigning freshmen to the various ILS courses, he was able to give 81 percent their first choice and 14 percent their second choice. (Over the first eight semesters of the program it proved possible on the average to give 74.9 percent their first choice, 91.1 percent their first or second choice, and 97.9 percent their first, second, or third choice. Students had six courses to choose among each semester except for fall 1979 [seven], spring 1981 [eight], and spring 1982 [seven].)

NOVEMBER 6, 1978

The report of the reaccreditation committee of the New England Association of Schools and Colleges includes these findings on the ILS program: "The attitudes of the Evaluation Committee toward this proposal ranged from benign approbation to skepticism to sharp disagreement with the whole concept. No one on the committee was overly confident about the ideological underpinnings of the proposal, but it was assumed that, given the quality of the faculty and student body, the courses could hardly fail to be successful. Skepticism toward the ILS proposal was generated, not only by the shakiness of the basic rationale, but also by a rather notable lack of enthusiasm on the part of the faculty and the student body toward the program. It was clear that the faculty believed that doing something was probably desirable, and while the purveyors of the original ILS concept were very enthusiastic about the plan, a very large number of faculty seemed merely to acquiesce in the program."

MARCH 6, 1979

Professor John Pemberton, chairman of the CEP, reports to the faculty on discussions of the ILS program during his committee's recent meeting with the Instruction Committee of the Board of Trustees: "We were pleased to be able to report the positive response of the faculty and that there will be an increase, next year, in the number of ILS courses and teachers."

MARCH 1979

The first *Scrutiny* (student critique of courses) to include reports on ILS courses appears. The editors compare the average of freshmen's responses to ILS with the average of their responses to all of their courses, finding that ILS ranked lower in every category except "Lab or Studio Value" and "Accessibility of Professor."

APRIL 9, 1979

In an informal poll of freshmen, the *Amherst Student* finds that two thirds feel that "ILS has been a valuable experience," while one fourth are dissatisfied with the curriculum as it now stands. Asked to make a comparison with introductory departmental courses, many freshmen said that they found ILS courses "more creative, with a freer range of expression, but not always focused enough." There was overwhelming complaint against the large size of the sections.

1979–80

JULY 1, 1979

Julian H. Gibbs succeeds John William Ward as president of Amherst College.

DECEMBER 10, 1979

A letter from Acting Dean of the Faculty Designate William Kennick urges colleagues to consider participation in the next year's ILS courses: "The ILS program is a serious educational burden which the faculty imposed on itself. Those who have already assumed their share of this burden by taking part in the program have by and large enjoyed it and found it intellectually invigorating. But no member of this faculty should think of the ILS program as someone else's business. We are all equally obligated to see to it that this program flourishes."

DECEMBER 18, 1979

In farewell remarks at his last Amherst faculty meeting, Dean Gifford asks that "in the pursuit of your particular interests you not lose sight of the rather fragile common interests which we share."

FEBRUARY 20, 1980

President Gibbs sends a letter asking all faculty members to consider taking part in an ILS course: "Most of you probably know that when, prior to assuming the presidency of the College, I served on the College's reaccreditation committee, I expressed reservations concerning the then-proposed ILS course. I hope no one will assume that I accordingly do not support a determined effort to make them a success. . . . I recognize that some non-tenured members of the faculty may feel that teaching for the first time and originating a research program are in themselves enough for an individual to attempt. Accordingly, I especially urge every tenured member of the faculty to consider participating in an ILS course."

FEBRUARY 25, 1980

The Committee of Six and the CEP meet jointly. CEP chairman John Cameron reports that lack of faculty volunteers for next year's ILS courses has created "a dangerous, but not hopeless, situation." The CEP urges some new mechanism for generating ILS courses. A separate committee or director could provide needed leadership and free the CEP for the possibly conflicting function of evaluating the program.

MARCH 17, 1980

Responding to the minutes of a meeting of the CEP with the Trustees' Instruction Committee, which indicate that a trustee has suggested making the teaching of ILS an obligation for all faculty members, one Committee of Six member objects strongly, calling the remark *"ultra vires* and lawless."

MAY 6, 1980

The difficulties in staffing the ILS courses for 1980–81 dominate remarks by CEP chairman Cameron at a faculty meeting. With only 18 members of the faculty teaching ILS courses in the fall, and assuming 400 students in the freshman class, the student/teacher ratio would be 22.2/1. In the belief that "allowing drift would demoralize both the faculty and the students involved," the CEP requests suggestions from the faculty to help the CEP frame a report on ILS.

The faculty agrees to the CEP's request that a special committee be appointed by the Committee of Six "charged with taking responsibility in the coming year for organizing and supervising the ILS program." (The committee is soon formed, with Donald Pitkin as chairman.)

1980–81

SEPETEMBER 18, 1980

An editorial in the *Amherst Student* calls ILS "the object of much student dissatisfaction."

JANUARY 13, 1981

An "Interim Report of the Committee on Education Policy on the ILS Program" is issued, based on responses to a request made the previous May for letters from those who had taught in the ILS program and on a questionnaire to all faculty members in October. In the 32 letters from those who had taught in ILS, "some were puzzled by what they took to be a lukewarm student response. Many noted that teaching an ILS course required more work than teaching one's own course, particularly because participation required one to become familiar with new materials and new perspectives. . . . Though arduous, it was exciting to do something different. And it was particularly gratifying, at least for most, to collaborate with colleagues with whom one might otherwise have little contact."

The CEP considered its most important findings to be "first, principled opposition among the faculty to the ILS program (approximately 30 percent) is considerably less than has been widely conjectured, and, second, far and away the most prevalent reason (about 50 percent) cited for non-participation or for discontinued participation was the competing claim of departmental responsibilities." Among those who had not taught and did not intend to teach ILS, many expressed the view "that their best contribution to students and to the mission of the college comes in teaching the courses they have been specially trained to teach." Foreseeing persistent shortages of ILS staff, the CEP proposes to set out numerical guidelines indicating how much faculty time each department should make available to ILS.

FEBRUARY 9, 1981

In the wake of the CEP's report, the *Amherst Student* publishes an editorial entitled "Cure ILS, Don't Kill It." Declaring that "ILS is becoming terribly specialized, and many of the courses offered could hardly be called interdisciplinary," the editors call for fewer courses and broader topics, citing the course Light as a good example. They also call for more faculty in the courses and smaller sections.

FEBRUARY 10, 1981

A faculty meeting which the *Amherst Student* predicted would bring vigorous debate on the ILS program turns out differently. Chairman of the CEP Jan Dizard summarizes the committee's interim report and announces that since the report was adopted, two faculty members on the CEP have shifted to the view that the ILS courses should no longer be offered after the current academic year. Professor Geoffrey Woglom, one of these members, then speaks, saying that while he supports the goals of the program, he is discouraged by the disparity among the courses and by the faculty's negative response to a plan being offered by Professors Armour Craig and Joel Gordon to unite the courses through a series of shared questions for frequent essays.

Professor Pitkin then speaks on behalf of the special committee to encourage ILS offerings for 1981–82. He declares that the situation is better than last year at this time, with the program "nearly viable" for first semester, and "highly viable" for second semester. Professor Rose Olver, dean of freshmen, reports that she has received complaints from students about the specific courses to which they have been assigned, but not about the program as a whole. A call for further debate is met by silence, and President Gibbs says he assumes that this means that the program will continue next year. Toward the end of the meeting, Professor Walter Nicholson asks whether departments are to be given quotas for participation in ILS, as suggested in the CEP's report. Professor Dizard responds that no such device seems necessary for the immediate future, and that in any case it would be advisory, not mandatory.

FEBRUARY 12, 1981

"Diagnosing the Ills of ILS (Without Killing the Patient): A Special Report" by junior Brad Justus appears as a double-page spread in the *Amherst Student*. Besides offering a history of the program, he reports on a poll of students. Among those adding comments to his questionnaire, the most frequently cited objections to ILS courses were "the limitation on curricular choice and the unevenness experienced from one course to the next." The following numerical results of his poll are published:

ILS SURVEY—GENERAL RESULTS

In general, do you feel that the concept of ILS—to introduce students to alternative methods of reasoning through interdisciplinary study—is
　　a good idea, in theory as well as practice: 85
　　a good idea, but only in theory: 259
　　a bad idea: 47

Do you feel that ILS is a
　　valuable experience and an educational necessity at Amherst: 58
　　useful experience, but not necessary to one's education: 173
　　waste of faculty and student time: 160 . . .

Do you feel that the experience of ILS has aided you in other courses you have taken?
　　yes: 167
　　no: 225 . . .

Responses were solicited from the entire classes of 1982, 1983, and 1984 from February 10 to 12, 1981.

MAY 5, 1981

The faculty holds a "preliminary discussion" of the CEP's second report of the year on the freshman program: "ILS: Proposed Clarifications and Revisions." The report declares that the ILS program as constituted suffers from a split between two conceptions: one emphasizing process, exploration, and critical-mindedness; the other, interdisciplinary study and distribution among subject areas. These two, plus a third goal of "intellectual initiative, independence and self-development," could, the committee argues, be furthered by having the ILS courses of each semester united under a common theme and headed by a "Convenor," a faculty member who would nurture course proposals, solicit participants, and encourage some coordinated assignments and other common experiences. The theme for the first semester would be "Liberal Arts and Self-Discovery," for the second, "Liberal Education and Social Responsibility." Faculty response to the proposal is chilly. . . .

1981–82

NOVEMBER 13, 1981

Having dropped the idea of a common theme for each semester's ILS courses, the CEP sends to the faculty a document entitled "Draft Proposal: CEP Report to the Faculty on the ILS and Adjunct Programs." The committee has conducted interviews with 40 seniors and 20 juniors, randomly selected. "Contrary to the received wisdom of the *Student* and the snack bar, we found widespread student support for the idea of an ILS *program*. We also heard, however, a range of negative comments about the ILS *courses*." Most of the students interviewed had judged only one of their two ILS courses good or excellent. Though valuing their opportunity to be in an all-freshman class and to receive special attention from teachers, many criticized the courses for uncertainty over educational goals. "It is tempting to conclude that the faculty's difficulty in generating enough ILS courses and the students' perception that not enough are successful are but two sides of the same problem."

The CEP recommends the reduction of the requirement to one ILS course. The principal benefits of the change would be to make the program "more likely to be staffed only by genuinely interested faculty members," to allow smaller sections, and to free faculty to teach neglected departmental courses and new junior-year colloquia.

Elective junior-year colloquia are proposed as a way to continue an interdisciplinary approach beyond the freshman year. They would offer certain advantages over ILS, especially the likelihood that juniors would have "a degree of intellectual urgency and individually motivated curiosity that could hardly be expected of freshmen" as well as "the intellectual skills and sheer body of knowledge which allow the often highly sophisticated and elusive connections among disciplines to emerge."

DECEMBER 1, 1981

Chairman of the CEP James Denton introduces debate on the CEP's "Draft Proposal" at a faculty meeting, saying that his committee views its recommendations as part of an evolutionary curricular process. Professor Dale Peterson praises the new plan, seeing promise in the proposed junior colloquia. Recalling the Kenan Colloquia of the 1971–76 period, Professor Gordon Levin calls them among the college's finest courses and urges the faculty to free energies for such upper-level undertakings. Professor Austin Sarat presses the CEP on what it meant by calling ILS courses a "success," since it had not used that term in its questions for student interviews. Professor Woglom notes that the report had not been as positive as Professor Sarat implies. While students interviewed had been "surprisingly enthusiastic . . . a significant number said at least one of those courses really didn't work at all."

Professor Allen Kropf suggests that the basis of examination should be not student opinion but the educational reasons behind the courses. He calls for comment from members of the Select Committee that originally proposed ILS. Responding, Professor Lawrence Babb says that the college needs courses to introduce students to the institution's principal activity: the process of intelligent men and women reading books, talking together, and considering ideas. On the whole he believes the ILS courses have achieved this goal. Professor Willem de Vries expresses the view that Professor Babb has described what all Amherst courses are supposed to be doing.

President Gibbs reports that in recently rereading the Select Committee's report, he was struck by the enthusiasm expressed there for the recommended program and found that "the arguments are as cogent now as they were." Professor Hugh Aitken notes a keener appreciation now of the costs of ILS courses; no other courses have made such drafts on his time as the ILS course he is currently teaching. In response to a suggestion by Dean of Students James Bishop that ILS may have improved teaching at the college generally and especially by junior faculty, Professor Barbara Ansbacher testifies that she believes she has indeed received such help. Professor John Halsted finds it important to introduce students to "the character of liberal studies before we have totally jaded them in our disciplinary ways."

Two members of the Long Range Planning Committee, which was appointed by President Gibbs in the fall of 1980, answer a question about the relevance of its work to this discussion. Dean of the Faculty Catherine Bateson says it is not a curriculum committee, but it does see a need for maintaining a vigorous curriculum "that imparts skills as well as introduces students to ideas in the freshman year." Professor Joel Gordon says there is divergence of opinion on the committee, but its members agree that the freshman year is especially important. He warns that the faculty should be "careful about giving up what we are now doing before we have something to put in its place."

After an admonition from Professor Robert Townsend that a vote for continuing the requirement of two ILS courses should indicate willingness to teach such courses, the faculty takes a straw vote by written ballot. The results: for requiring two ILS courses—30; for requiring one—57; for requiring none—16; abstaining—4.

DECEMBER 15, 1981

In a second meeting the faculty continues its wide-ranging debate on the CEP's report. Among remarks made are the following: that the ILS courses should be dropped entirely if the requirement is not to remain at two, that the needs of college fund-raising played a coercive role in the original adoption of the ILS curriculum, that there have not been enough "high quality" ILS courses to justify requiring two, that the institutional reward system has offered inadequate motivation to take on the burdens of ILS teaching, and that some resistance to ILS teaching has rested on a principled sense that it was not the best way to teach. After voting down substitute motions to continue with the requirement of two ILS courses (49–67–4) and to drop the ILS courses entirely (36–66), the faculty adopts the change to one required ILS course, to be taken in the fall semester.

MAY 20, 1982

The Long Range Planning Committee submits its report. Its curricular proposals include a recommendation that a Freshman General Studies course be required in each of three categories: Nature and Numbers, Ethics and Social Life, and Style. The committee characterizes its proposal as "one that would allow up to one half of the freshman class to be taught in any single course and all freshmen to have at least one of their courses shared with a larger proportion of their class; that would de-emphasize (although not exclude) interdisciplinary teaching; and that would require that those who wish to teach freshmen submit their ideas to a rigorous process of scrutiny and judgment."

It may be wise now in conclusion to say explicitly how I interpret this five-year history of a particular educational venture. I see the ILS record as mingling success and failure. The program succeeded in that, despite voices predicting and wishing its early demise, it continued in its original form for four years and at that point was deemed worthy of continuation in abbreviated form. One source of this success was Amherst's tradition of collaborative interdisciplinary courses. The program drew on an already developed body of skill and interest.

Some faculty members had favored the program from the time it was proposed. Others who had argued against the program in the faculty debates of 1977 became stalwart supporters. Still others, though somewhat skeptical, were determined that ILS be given a fair trial. Thus, since roughly 30 percent of the faculty were disinclined to participate, there has been a strong tendency for faculty in the program to teach in it repeatedly. Of the 85 individuals who taught in ILS during the first four years, 3 did so four times; 17, three times; and 31, twice.

The survival of the program owes something also to faculty resistance to giving up even a modest curricular structure if nothing is agreed on to take its place. In a similar situation in 1971, the faculty had simply abolished most requirements and entered an "interim" period with the free-elective system restrained only by the major. Many did not want to repeat that experience.

The ILS program suffered from handicaps that led to repeated crises in staffing, followed by the decision in 1982 to cut its offerings by half. One such handicap was the power of departments. Since the voting out of the core curriculum in 1964, departments have increasingly become the center of faculty loyalties at Amherst College. In many ways this has been a benefit, attracting gifted scholars to the faculty who found that college teaching did not divorce them from their specialties and allowing students to test their preparation in a chosen field by means of advanced work. But the strengthening of departments has also created a set of vested interests that hamper efforts to revive general education by means other than distribution requirements. With faculty size frozen at 150 at the time of the decision to admit women as degree candidates and to enlarge the student body, many faculty members found themselves torn between the new ILS program and departmental needs for staffing introductory and advanced courses.

Among students, ILS courses received a modicum of praise in polls and formal interviews but were usually denigrated in casual conversation. Student dissatisfactions at Amherst varied, but, as a shared experience, ILS was a particularly tempting butt of criticism. It suffered from the lightning-rod effect. The proposers of the ILS program had hoped to establish a greater sense of community among students. Ironically, what students often shared were complaints about ILS.

Supervision of the program was inadequate from the beginning. This was caused partly by the Amherst faculty's traditional resistance to administrative controls, partly by an optimistic sense that the faculty would show its pedagogical initiative by creating ILS courses more or less spontaneously. In seeking sources of dissatisfaction with the Problems of Inquiry courses (required introductions to divisions, offered from 1966 to 1972), some had pointed to these courses' "superchairmen," who were named by the president. But ILS, with neither program nor course chairmen, suffered from the consequent diffusion of responsibility.

In retrospect, the work of the Pitkin Committee in 1980–81 seems crucial to the survival of the program. Yet in a final letter to the faculty, the committee referred to its own inadequacy as a mechanism for leadership of ILS. As for leadership from the administration, though President Ward and Dean Gifford were careful to let the faculty take the lead in designing and staffing the program, they were clearly in support. To have them resign during its first year was damaging. It took time for President Gibbs and Dean Bateson to convince faculty members that they found ILS a good thing.

Time has been generally on the side of the ILS courses. Teachers have been able to improve the courses as they learn what does and does not work. Those who want to repeat ILS courses they have enjoyed represent a vested interest in the program which to some extent counteracts the vested interest in departmental courses. The CEP interviews of 1981 found that students tended to raise their opinion of ILS when they could place the experience in the context of their later education.

Even its strongest supporters have never thought of the ILS program as a permanent curriculum, but it already seems clear after a half decade of development that ILS has invigorated Amherst's tradition of curricular reflection and innovation.

Used indiscriminately, "legendary" can be an overstuffed word that causes mild embarrassment or even derision. But among all the familiar, sometimes famous people in these pages, the word has most accurately and often been used to describe the late James Ostendarp. Some individuals—Emily Dickinson, Niels Bohr—are so famous that the adjective is superfluous. Others—Alexander Meiklejohn, Frederick Law Olmsted—are perhaps not endearing enough to be the stuff of out-and-out legends. But Ostendarp, Amherst's football coach from 1959 to 1991, had all the right ingredients: great success in his career, devoted followers, and a host of stories about the things he said and did naturally, every day, without show. Certainly it helped that Ostendarp—always known as "the Darp"—was a winning football coach: 169 wins, 91 losses, and 5 ties over 33 seasons. It helped that his players revered him: Al Deaett '62, a high school teacher and football coach in New Jersey, remembers Ostendarp as "a father figure. You wanted to win for him, because you just loved the man." It helped that there were all the stories—like the Darp taking football recruits to tour the college's art museum, or interrupting practice so his players could admire the sunset. No wonder the *Wall Street Journal* reporter Eugene Carlson, assigned in 1985 to write this preview of the Amherst–Williams centennial football game, found that Ostendarp was the best part of the story. Amherst and the Darp later won the game, 35 to 20.

THE WORLD ACCORDING TO DARP

By Eugene Carlson

THE 100TH FOOTBALL game between small-college archrivals
Amherst and Williams next month doesn't exactly sound like the stuff
nationally televised games of the week are made of. And, as it turns out,
it won't be. A cable-TV network, ESPN, wanted to televise the big game
at Williams College's Weston Field in Williamstown, Massachusetts, and
just about everybody agrees it would have been a great idea. Everybody
except Amherst College coach Jim Ostendarp, who blocked the idea.

A college football coach who doesn't want his team on national TV?
Holy Brent Musburger! "We're in education, we aren't in the entertainment business," says Mr. Ostendarp, who has won two-thirds of his
games in his 27 years as Amherst's coach. "We don't have the stadiums,
the crowds, the bands, the cheerleaders, or the teams to play on television," Coach Ostendarp says. "We're No. 1 in the country in small academics. To put us on TV and say, 'This is Amherst,' well, it just doesn't
measure up." Besides, he worries about the advertising that might run
during time-outs. "I'm against having Budweiser paying for it when we
don't allow drinking on campus," he says.

ESPN was thrown for a loss. "We weren't going to be able to sell much
advertising," says William Grimes, president of the sports network. "This
game was going to get small ratings. It didn't matter. We felt we had the

opportunity to show football in the tradition of small, great academic schools. Besides, we'd engender some goodwill with the alumni, who are customers, or potential customers, of ours." Coach Ostendarp's boycott cost both schools some income from TV rights, but the negotiations didn't reach the point where the amount was discussed.

Amherst President Peter Pouncey backs Coach Ostendarp, widely known as "the Darp." "I don't see it as a mortal sin to appear on a television screen," Mr. Pouncey says. "But I certainly wouldn't have crowded him on his decision. We spend half our time pointing to the Darp as a model of what a coach ought to be, a coach with his arm around an athlete's shoulder saying, 'Do you like Beethoven?'"

Mr. Ostendarp, who twice before has vetoed feelers for network coverage, concedes that his decision will make some people angry, but he notes cheerily, "I've got tenure. I'm a full professor." Robert Odell, the Williams coach, says he is "disappointed it fell through. I think it was a great opportunity for our young men to play on TV and for people to see the kind of football we play."

But even though Amherst won 15 straight games before being upset here this weekend by Tufts University of Medford, Massachusetts, Coach Ostendarp contends that TV viewers accustomed to watching the Brobdingnagians of the Big Ten would be turned off by the Lilliputians of the Little Three—the rivalry of Amherst, Williams, and Wesleyan University of Middletown, Connecticut. Viewers also wouldn't understand the lack of huge crowds and well-drilled marching bands, he suggests. Williams has a band with about 20 players, including one fellow who plays and pushes a bass violin on wheels. Their uniforms are white windbreakers and an assortment of outlandish hats. They do a few formations, play a few tunes, and poke fun at their school in the irreverent tradition of this Ivy League region. Amherst has no band, although the band from nearby Belchertown High School played at games in past years. Amherst has one cheerleader, who dresses in colonial garb.

The games at both schools are often halted to shoo away neighborhood dogs. The crowds at the games would barely fill the snack bars at a Big Ten stadium. At Amherst's tiny Pratt Field (capacity 6,000) there isn't even a public address system, by order of the head coach. And he doesn't like to put up with one at away games, either. One time during a game at

Bates College in Maine, when Mr. Ostendarp finally tired of hearing a
student announcer breathlessly providing every detail of the game over
the public address system, the coach achieved silence by ripping out the
wires of the stadium loudspeakers.

Little Three football resembles the game played with the enthusiasm
and sometimes considerable skill at hundreds of small colleges on fall
weekends. At the recent homecoming game at Amherst, about 2,000 fans
braved a daylong drizzle to watch the Lord Jeffs shut out Wesleyan 26–0.
(The nickname comes from the school's namesake, Lord Jeffery Amherst,
who led British troops in the French and Indian Wars.*)

Coach Ostendarp, ignoring the rain, paced the sideline in his traditional game garb, a three-piece blue serge suit, narrow striped tie, and a
brown fedora. Meanwhile, hundreds of fans, including a few former ball-
players, ignored the game altogether, clustering around station-wagon
tailgates and under makeshift tents behind the grandstand to eat, drink,
and tell stories about college life and about "the Darp." There is, for
example, Coach Ostendarp's Saturday morning, home-game ritual of
sweeping the autumn leaves from the sidewalk in front of his house, a
half block from the football field. On the day of one crucial game, the
coach, lost in his thoughts, swept on down the sidewalk. Kickoff time
neared and the coach hadn't appeared. He was eventually located still
sweeping, a couple of blocks from home. In their emphasis on scholarship, Amherst and Williams disdain recruiting [sic] and athletic scholarships. Coach Ostendarp holds practices just three days a week, and if a
class interferes with practice, the player is expected to skip that day's
workout.

Williams's school nickname, the Ephmen, is from Ephraim Williams,
a colonial soldier whose bequest founded the school. The mascot, however, is a purple cow. This may relate to the location of the college in the
so-called Purple Valley of western Massachusetts, but no one seems to
know for sure. "The oddness of our mascot says something about our
attitude toward athletics," says James Kolesar, the school's public information officer. "People play hard, but it's never too serious."

Nobody is taking the November 9 Amherst–Williams game lightly,

*Actually, the college was named for the town. It is the town that was named for Lord Jeffery.

however. "Football has a low-key feel to it until we get to the Amherst game," Mr. Kolesar says. "Then it gets intense." Over the years, Williams has won 52 games, Amherst 43, and there have been four ties. But Amherst has won the last four games. Williams is 2–3–1 this year; its followers say the team has a good defense but not much offense.

At Williams's Weston Field, temporary bleachers will be installed to handle an expected overflow crowd of 10,000 people, compared to the usual turnout of 3,000 or so. And though national TV has been rejected, the game will be televised in 29 cities via satellite over closed-circuit hookups arranged by Amherst and Williams graduates for the schools' alumni. "That's great," Coach Ostendarp says, because "they know what it's all about."

Not everyone agrees. Philip Lundquist, director of corporate finance for the accounting firm Deloitte Haskins & Sells and president of the Williams Alumni Association, says: "My regret is that 34 million households won't have a chance to watch Williams trounce Amherst and that this will be restricted to the fans at the closed-circuit television sites and the stadium."

This daguerreotype, made in the 1840s, is the only documented photograph of Emily Dickinson. She was 16. The image was given to the college's Archives and Special Collections in 1956.

The bronze nude statue of the river goddess Sabrina, a gift to the college, was placed on a pedestal near the Octagon in 1857 but soon became prey to generations of pranksters.

Joseph Hardy Neesima 1870, the first Japanese to graduate from a Western college, founded the Doshisha University in Kyoto. He was popular with his classmates, one even calling him the "ideal of a saint."

Alexander Meiklejohn near the end of his 12-year presidency told a trustee "that if the Board would give him autocratic power at the college for ten years, he would make it a good college."

Charles H. Houston '15 was a brilliant civil rights lawyer and law school dean whose legal strategies led to landmark Supreme Court rulings for desegregation— including *Brown v. Board of Education* in 1954.

This photograph of Robert Frost was taken in 1916, the year he agreed to teach at Amherst. He put students "on the operating table" and took ideas "out of them as a prestidigitator takes rabbits and pigeons . . . out of your pocket trousers legs and even mouth."

Photos Courtesy of Amherst College Archives and Special Collections.

Today, with coeducation, slightly more than half of Amherst's students, slightly more than a third of the faculty, and a third of the trustees are women. More than half the administrative positions at the college are filled by women. For many years one of those administrators was Terry Allen, who wrote this short historical survey. She was associate secretary for public affairs—a nonspecific title for a job with many specific responsibilities. With others in the Public Affairs Office she handled news media relations; wrote, edited, and produced news releases and college publications; and worked on the annual commencement and other public events. But she devoted her greatest energy and enthusiasm to her job as associate editor of *Amherst* magazine. Allen was, in effect, its managing editor. She pressed for steady improvements in the magazine's content and design. Most of all, she believed that a publication representing an intellectual enterprise should have intellectual content, and to that end she wrote many faculty profiles, book reviews, and pieces on literature and the arts. Two years before leaving the college to become a freelance editor and writer, Allen marked the 20th anniversary of coeducation with this review of women's changing roles through the college's history.

A HISTORY OF AMHERST WOMEN

⌒

By Terry Y. Allen

THE SHORT VERSION of the history of women at Amherst College is quickly told. Women were scarcely in evidence on the campus for roughly the first 150 years of the college's history. The daughter of a faculty member became a cataloger in the library in 1877. The first woman faculty member was hired in 1962. As for women students, they officially arrived, as transfer students, in 1975, after much deliberation, consultation, and fanfare. But, in fact, women have been here all along— since the earliest days of the college and even before that, when the college was only a dream.

In the familiar formulation that has come down to us, New England Congregationalists dreamed of a college to educate "indigent young men of piety" for the ministry. The new college was founded to prepare men— sons, brothers, and nephews—to go forth from Amherst and enlighten the earth. The historical record is crystal-clear on this point: women helped pay for the new institution, and very generously, within their limited means. Dozens of women from villages and towns in Massachusetts, Connecticut, and New York made pledges in their own names to the 1818–19 Charity Fund. Three years later, women gave to the $30,000 Subscription Fund. Some, like Mary Norton of Weymouth, Massachusetts, pledged $1 a year for five years. Others, like Lucinda and Thankful

Dickinson of Amherst, pledged $100 apiece. One can only wonder what these gifts cost their givers in deferred comfort and forgone necessities.

Of course women contributed more than a few precious dollars at their disposal. We know from Professor William Tyler's *History of Amherst College, 1821 to 1871* that the raising of the new college was a communal, even epochal endeavor, and was remembered that way by the many local residents who participated in it. Tyler tells us that South College, the first campus building (which served as a dormitory, library, laboratory, and recitation building), was raised in 1820–21 by a workforce of volunteer laborers, some of whom camped at the site. Materials and provisions for the workers were donated as well, he writes, with the womenfolk "ministering to the men that laid the foundations and erected the first building." At the very least, women must have visited the construction site with food and water, bedding and clean clothes for their men. It is possible that some female relations camped out as well—and even lent their labor to the great enterprise.

What we know for certain is that later, after the institution had opened, some of these same faithful women joined in good works initiated by women of higher social rank. "Faculty matrons," Tyler calls them: Mrs. Humphrey, Mrs. Hitchcock, Mrs. Fiske, "and other noble women who were not only helpmeets of the officers, but mothers to the students, especially students in indigent circumstances, and foster-mothers of the Institution." The Sewing Society, for instance, was composed of the female relations of presidents, faculty, and workingmen, and met regularly for sewing, knitting, mending, and otherwise salvaging worn garments for poor students who were far from home. From Tyler's homage to Mrs. Humphrey, wife of Amherst's second president, we glimpse the high standard of virtue and self-sacrifice expected of those early women. She was, Tyler writes, "a model housekeeper [who] with a large family to support on a small salary must have been often severely tasked to make both ends meet. But her ministries to the poor and the sick, the dying and the dead, were unceasing. At the same time, she was every inch a queen in every sphere, domestic, social, secular, or religious, in which she moved. The Martha and Mary of the Gospels"—the tireless servant and the eager disciple—"were harmoniously united in her."

Telling the story of a later first lady, the artist Orra White Hitchcock,

Tyler reports approvingly that she opened the president's house to student "levees," Monday evening prayer meetings, and countless overnight guests of the college. "To her, also, with the hearty cooperation of the other ladies, the College chapel owed its first renovation, early in Dr. Hitchcock's presidency."

Before their marriage, both Orra White and Edward Hitchcock taught at Amherst Academy, which was in many ways the precursor to the college. From its beginnings in 1814 the forward-looking academy offered education to girls as well as to boys. Thus, unlike most rural towns of the era, Amherst was populated by young women who had been schooled in a rigorous curriculum that included the sciences. "Indeed," Tyler writes, the academy's "ladies' department was in advance of the same department in the other institutions, as might be shown by a simple comparison of the studies pursued and text-books in use by the young ladies." He then enumerates impressive texts in chemistry, rhetoric, logic, history, moral philosophy, mathematics, natural philosophy, astronomy, Latin, and French.

At least one scholar of nineteenth-century Amherst believes it highly likely that academy-educated daughters and sisters attended lectures at the new college. Says David Porter, professor of English emeritus at the University of Massachusetts, "Amherst was never a closed institution; it was always open from its beginning." The bond between the institutions was only strengthened when the new college began to supply a steady stream of teachers for the academy.

Porter's special area of expertise is the poet Emily Dickinson, who as a student at the academy and later at Mount Holyoke Female Seminary demonstrated a flair for the natural sciences. Whether or not her scientific curiosity moved her to attend lectures at Amherst College, her life was very much shaped by the college. She was the granddaughter of Samuel Fowler Dickinson, without whom it is doubtful there would be an Amherst College. She was also daughter and sister to two of the college's early treasurers, Edward and Austin Dickinson, who were as visionary, conscientious, and indefatigable as any president in their championship of the institution. They took all their meals at home and entertained their guests at home as well.

Thus the Homestead, where Emily and her sister Lavinia Dickinson

spent their adult lives, was the scene of signal events in the college's life—
such as celebrations at commencement time and receptions for important
visitors. The Evergreens, next door, Austin's home after his marriage,
succeeded the Homestead as a center of the town's—and by extension,
the college's—social life [see "Magnetic Visitors," page 31]. Though the
two women never met, it was a faculty wife who eventually undertook
the monumental task of deciphering the handwritten poems found in
Emily's trunk after her death and shepherding them through publication. High-spirited and intent on making her mark, Mabel Loomis Todd
bore no resemblance to the pious, self-sacrificial "faculty matrons" of an
earlier era so admired by Tyler. As told by her biographer Polly Longsworth, in *Austin and Mabel* (1984), Mabel came to Amherst as a newly-
wed in 1991 with her husband, David Peck Todd, who was an 1875
alumnus and the college's first astronomer. She frequently accompanied
him on his professional travels to destinations around the world. Their
exotic experiences observing astronomical events provided material for
Mabel's career as travel writer, lecturer, and professional collaborator. In
1894, the Todds' *Total Eclipses of the Sun* was published, and in that same
year Mabel earned a handsome fee ($140) for an article about the Har-
vard Observatory that appeared in the magazine *Century*.

Mabel lectured mostly to women's clubs and church groups. However,
in June 1892, four years after the poet's death, she gave a memorable lecture at the college, attended by 110 people and introduced by President
Gates, on the subject of Emily Dickinson. Mabel often sang, played the
piano, and acted in theatrical events in the town. She starred in at least
one play on campus—*The Fair Barbarian*, performed in November 1883.
A tireless organizer, Mabel Todd was chairman of the executive committee that created the college's Faculty Club, where she eventually directed
a play. She was also elected first chairman of the organizing committee
for the establishment of an Amherst Woman's Club, which her daughter,
Millicent Todd Bingham, later remembered as "an experimental project
in those days."

Though her fame derives from her work on Emily Dickinson's poems
and letters, Mabel Loomis Todd has become a minor celebrity in her own
right for another reason. She kept unusually frank personal diaries that
reveal much about her own sexual attitudes and about her long-term

adulterous affair with Austin Dickinson. The historian Peter Gay has devoted a chapter to Mabel in *Education of the Senses* (1984), a volume in his multivolume study *The Bourgeois Experience: Victoria to Freud.*

For over a half century, one of the college's earliest and most brilliant graduates, Ebenezer Snell, taught mathematics and natural philosophy at Amherst. Professor Snell was father to five daughters who sometimes socialized with the college's students. Sabra, the youngest, was courted by Christopher Pennell of the Class of 1863. His surviving letters to her mention a college cricket match, where they first met, and a significant walk alone in the College Grove on a Fourth of July. Alas for the sweethearts, Pennell enlisted in the army after the attack on Fort Sumter, rose to the rank of lieutenant, and died in combat before they could marry.

Sabra, who was to live on to the age of 87, remained unmarried. When their father died in 1876, she and her sister Mary took over his "weather record"—which entailed logging in meteorological observations three times a day with instruments Snell had devised. An obituary notice in the *Amherst Record* tells us that Sabra, a graduate of Mount Holyoke Female Seminary, was a cataloger in the Amherst College Library from 1877 to 1917; moreover, she taught mathematics and English literature in the Stearnses' private school in Amherst. A posthumous tribute in the same newspaper praises "her long and useful life as librarian, teacher, and worker in good causes," adding that "in her Christian character she embodied the best type of the New England Puritan."

In 1871, a year when Emily Dickinson was attending her dying mother and young Sabra Snell was mourning her lost love, the Amherst alumni seriously considered the question of coeducation. The discussion did not occur in a vacuum. Amherst's Theodore P. Greene '43, emeritus professor of history and American studies, has noted that in the wake of the Civil War there was widespread national controversy over the higher education of women—specifically, over the options of coeducation and single-sex women's colleges. [See also "The Coeducation Debate of 1871," by Christopher Bohjalian, page 79.] It would be another century before Amherst's "woman" question was resolved with the admission of the first regular female students. But women first took instruction at Amherst in 1877, when Dr. Lambert Sauveur (not an Amherst faculty member) began his summer College of Languages. In its heyday, the six-week immersion program, which lasted more than a quarter century, drew an average of 200 students for the study of French, German, Italian, Spanish, and Greek. Women are well represented in surviving registration lists and photos of assembled students.

The Amherst College Archives and Special Collections contains only the sparest evidence of women's presence on the campus at the turn of the century. There are, however, bundles of neatly printed programs attesting to prom dances sponsored by the presidents' wives and special entertainments for faculty and administrators, courtesy of the Ladies of Amherst. One such endeavor was "Love's Labor Lost: A Farce for All Concerned after (very long after) Wm Shakespeare," given on St. Valentine's Night 1908 at the Tyler Place. Seven of the eight players were women, and the orchestra was directed by two women. The Ladies of Amherst, consisting of the presidents' wives and wives of faculty members, continued for decades. Besides hosting musicales and literary evenings, the Ladies performed charitable works as, a century before, had the Faculty Matrons. Near the end of World War I, for example, the Ladies supplied Christmas toys for needy local children and layettes for infants in war-torn France.

Young women thespians from Smith and Mount Holyoke were warmly welcomed onto the campus near the end of World War I by a newly reinvigorated Masquers student theater group. "A Year with the Masquers" by E. A. Richards in the *Amherst Graduates Quarterly* reports that, beginning in 1918, cooperation with the dramatic clubs of the women's colleges proved "so satisfactory that these arrangements are likely to be continued. . . . The only circumstance which some may regard as a drawback to the participation of college girls is the fact that they are not allowed to make trips." Richards seemed genuinely relieved that women had arrived on the College Hall stage: "Audiences have enough to allow for in amateur work without the additional strain of seeing men in female roles. It is heroism for a man to try it, but the effect is oftener like martyrdom."

Another woman who ventured briefly into the limelight was Madeleine Utter, wife of Professor Robert Utter of the English Department. Madeleine was instructor of French *ad interim* in 1918–19. Her name does not appear in the catalog for that year—or for any year after. Surviving faculty lists show that at least three women taught Amherst students during the Second World War. Maud Alice Marshall was visiting associate professor of chemistry in 1943–44, and Elinor Van Dorn Smith was visiting assistant professor of biology in the summer session of 1942. A little more is known about the third, Dr. Dorothy Wrinch, who was a visiting professor of biology in 1941–42. British-educated like Maud Marshall, Wrinch was Carlisle Fellow of Somerville College, Oxford. Her field was molecular biology, especially the investigation of protein structure. Some of Wrinch's published findings on the subject appear in articles and abstracts in the possession of Amherst College Archives. A brief news article in the *Springfield Union* (November 1941) reports on her lecture to a Smith College Assembly on "The New Synthesis in Science." The article identifies Wrinch as an "eminent scientist who is visiting professor at Smith, Mount Holyoke, and Amherst Colleges." Except for some teaching assistants, women disappeared from the Amherst faculty roster after the war years.

In June 1921 the college celebrated its centennial in high style. Prominent guests at the celebration included the French Ambassador to the United States; Jeffery John Archer Amherst, Viscount Holmesdale; Baron Naibu Kanda '79; and the Speaker of the U.S. House of Representatives, Frederick H. Gillett '74. The great entertainment at the event was a pageant re-creating the college's hundred-year history. Several photographs of the pageant feature Mrs. George Frisbee Whicher, wife of the English professor, dressed in Roman garb and a crown of laurel enacting her role as Alma Mater.

One of the college's first women administrators of professional rank was Gladys Kimball. Hired as secretary to the dean and the registrar in the summer of 1914, shortly after her graduation from Simmons College, she rose within the administration to become *recorder*—significantly, not college *registrar,* as the men who preceded and succeeded her were called. At the time of her retirement after 42 years of service, she told the *Amherst Journal Record* that when she arrived women were a novelty on the campus: only three other women worked in the college offices and the library (Sabra Snell may have been one, and Lydia A. Farnsworth, an assistant to the registrar, another). If a woman walked across campus, Kimball recalled, "The boys in the dormitories threw open their windows and shouted 'Fire!'"

Between 1944 and 1962, several women, none of them, of course, Amherst graduates, earned the Master of Arts degree from the college. Three earned their M.A.s in 1948, two in 1955. Their undergraduate degrees came from Massachusetts State/University of Massachusetts, Goucher, George Washington, Queens, University of Maine—and one from the Sorbonne.

"Four Colleges and an Idea," which appeared in the July 1958 issue of the Amherst alumni quarterly, makes the case for what was to become, in time, the Five College consortium. A section of that article, "Exchange of Students," provides abundant evidence that women were at Amherst in the mid-1950s:

> During each of the last three semesters fifty or sixty students from one of the four institutions [Hampshire did not yet exist] were taking courses at one of the other three. Amherst undergraduates went to Smith for courses in fine arts, music, education, and Russian, and to Smith and the University of Massachusetts for courses in sociology. Students from the other colleges came to Amherst for work in political science, economics, and dramatic arts. Meanwhile, Amherst and the university shared an instructor in Russian while Amherst and Smith shared instructors in fine arts and astronomy.
>
> During the past year psychology honors students from Smith and Amherst cooperated in a significant research project involving differences in male and female reactions to certain stimuli of form and color.
>
> A 1957 graduate of Smith reported that the two advanced physics courses she took at Amherst in 1956–57 were invaluable preparation for her graduate work. Despite the time taken by travel, she would do it again, she said.

The four colleges also collaborated in a joint astronomy club, biological conferences, and geology lectures. Throughout the 1950s, '60s, and early '70s, women on the Four College (later Five College) exchange would continue to take courses at Amherst.

Beginning with academic year 1975–76, the college admitted women as candidates for the B.A. degree—83 in number, all of them transfer students in their sophomore, junior, and senior years. In the following year, freshman women were admitted. But for women at Amherst, the modern era had already dawned, however faintly, in 1962, when Rose Olver, a new Ph.D. from Harvard, was appointed to Amherst's Psychology Department. The appointment itself and her progress from a temporary to a tenured position were greeted with alarm in some, though not all, quarters of the college. Now Faculty Marshal and the college's L. Stanton Williams '41 Professor of Psychology and Women's and Gender Studies, Olver prefers to downplay the professional difficulties and slights she encountered when she was Amherst's lone woman faculty member. In her view the course of women's progress at Amherst has been "torturous" over three decades. Still, she has observed a heartening "shift in the nature and magnitude of women's presence" at the college.

After Olver's appointment, the ranks of women faculty grew slowly but surely. In 1966 a woman was hired for the anthropology faculty, followed in the next year by a woman in classics, then by a woman in philosophy . . . and the trickle continued. Professor Jane Taubman recalls that in 1973–74, the first year of her part-time appointment in the new Russian Department, Amherst's eight faculty women could easily fit around a table. Three years later, in 1976–77, "the table wasn't big enough" for the 17 women who constituted nearly 13 percent of the regular Amherst faculty. By 1997, 47 women made up 30 percent of the faculty, and steadily, as older faculty members retired, the numbers of women faculty were increasing.

To Lisa Raskin, Amherst's dean of the faculty and a professor of psychology and neuroscience, these numbers represent an important shift in the college's identity. Raskin arrived at Amherst in 1979 from Princeton, shortly after four women faculty had announced at a public forum their decisions, for various reasons, not to stand for tenure. At the college in those days, Raskin recalls, "The atmosphere was one of unhappiness for women faculty. They felt out of place, unnoticed, unimportant, unattended to—as if we really weren't supposed to be here."

The late '70s and early '80s were difficult years for many women students as well. In the view of some observers, that may have been because the college did not expect the presence of women to make much difference to campus life. In the four-year consultative process that culminated in the admission of women to Amherst, a visiting committee of faculty, charged with surveying other colleges that had gone coed, reported that the addition of women would not threaten the college's traditions and fundamental identity. Thus reassured, the college made few preparations—in procedures, attitudes, or staffing—for the introduction of a new population to the campus. Many early women students felt acutely the lack of female role models and mentors. The generally male, intellectually confrontational style in the classroom was intimidating to some women students. For their part, the few overburdened women faculty were often called upon to provide an extra measure of guidance and nurturance for women students.

Many eloquent and disturbing student complaints were raised in a video called "A Question of Place: Women at Amherst College," prepared by Rebecca Hantin '85E and other women students, for the 10th anniversary of coeducation. On camera many spoke of losing confidence in the competitive environment. Others spoke of painful, hidden problems such as self-hatred, eating disorders, and sexual harassment by faculty and fellow students. Some minority and gay women testified to feeling marginal. One African-American woman who had regained her bearings only after moving off campus asserted that "Amherst College is not a healthy place for some of its students." A decade after "A Question of Place" was screened on campus, many of these and related concerns have been addressed. Probably most important, women are no longer a minority. In the 1996–97 academic year, they are for the first time on the verge of numerical parity with male students.

From his vantage point as dean of students, Ben Lieber has concluded that while still imperfect, "the climate is considerably better for women inside and outside the classroom than it was a decade ago." The abolition of fraternities, the fine-tuning of the disciplinary process, the growth in the numbers of women faculty, greater ethnic diversity of the campus— in Lieber's estimation, these factors have made a more comfortable climate for many women students.

In her 18 years at Amherst, Lisa Raskin feels she too has witnessed a gradual evolution in a traditionally male academic culture. But as a new faculty member, Raskin recalls, she made a commitment "to get with the program, to do whatever it took" to succeed at Amherst. Among other adjustments, she adopted a somewhat "tougher teaching style." In Raskin's view, her own success demonstrates in part Amherst's willingness to incorporate women into its culture. She continues: "I'm not considered one of the young radical voices anymore. I was part of the nucleus of women who have become integrated into the culture. I'm an Old Boy now!" Raskin noted at the time that three officers of the college—the dean of faculty, the treasurer, and dean of admission—were women. In her daily work as dean of the faculty, Raskin found that "Gender was almost never an issue. For me it has virtually disappeared. I feel that we now have a completely coeducational school."

When she gave this extraordinary talk in 1984, Eve Kosofsky Sedgwick, associate professor of English, may have ruffled some "old boy" feathers. But she was applauded by others who agreed that Amherst, after nine years of coeducation, needed to do much more to make women full and equal participants in the life of the college. To dramatize her message Sedgwick invoked the college's notorious icon, Sabrina. For nearly 125 years the hapless nude statue, given to the college by Massachusetts Lieutenant Governor Joel Hayden in 1857, had been the victim of burlesque student pranks and class rivalries. Sedgwick also said in the talk, sponsored by the college's orientation committee, that the Amherst catalog listed only 10 courses on the subjects of women and gender. Things have changed. Student interest in the anachronistic Sabrina has declined. A new department of Women's and Gender Studies was established in 1988. By 2006 it sponsored 35 courses and, by one count, the catalog included 49 others at least touching on issues of gender. Although setbacks occur, the campus also has become more "livable" for gays, as Sedgwick hoped. She left Amherst in 1989 after only five years, moving on to distinguished professorships first at Duke University and now at the Graduate Center of the City University of New York. In the meantime, the wishful thought Sedgwick voiced at Amherst may be coming true: Sabrina doesn't live here anymore.

SABRINA DOESN'T LIVE
HERE ANYMORE

By Eve Kosofsky Sedgwick

I wanted to start by saying a little about the story of the first woman at Amherst. When she arrived here in 1857, she was different from the other students. Not only was she female, but she weighed 350 pounds, she was bronze in color, and she had no clothes. A historian of Sabrina writes:

> For a while she occupied a place of honor upon a terrace between old North College and the Octagon. She remained here for several years and enjoyed comparative peace and quiet. The first prank which was played upon her occurred a few years later when a youth arrayed the goddess in divers garments stolen from a nearby girls' school. Needless to say, the student was dealt with by the faculty and to this day, Sabrina's fair cheek bears remembrance of the student's ill-timed vengeance. From this time on, Sabrina was the butt of the undergraduate body. She was whitewashed, indecorously decorated, and often anticipated her future career by frequent changes of color. Many were the humiliations Sabrina suffered at the hands of various blades. After a while the faculty, weary of the students' rude treatment of the gift to the college of such a distinguished man—the lieutenant governor who had donated her—decided to put an end to the affair. Then too, her appearance was becoming increasingly unattractive. Accordingly, the

college janitor was given the task of removing and doing away with the statue. [You probably know the end of the story from Oedipus.] This faithful servant of the college could not withstand the mute appeal of the goddess for mercy, and accordingly hid her away from the prying eyes of the students in his barn, where she remained hidden for two years as the tradition of the hidden goddess took root.

The history of abuses to Sabrina has been told in many articles. What I'd like you to imagine is Sabrina's point of view on what was happening to her during these years. What I think she mostly felt was confused. To begin with: she is told that she's a goddess, but she's compulsively degraded, humiliated, and treated like property. People pretend to feel awe for her, but they treat her as the most familiar of familiar objects. She is told that she is especially sanctified and spiritual, but she is totally identified with her body—both because it is a nude body and because it is a female body. She can't move, but other people's actions toward her are attributed to things that she mysteriously "does." In one newspaper article, for instance: "Sabrina eventually *lures* some susceptible Amherst student to slice her off at the base and stick her in a truck" (italics added). Another confusing thing: Sabrina doesn't know her real name. She's never sure if she is Sabrina or The Sabrina. Are there other Sabrinas? Is Sabrina a proper noun or a common noun? Is Sabrina a proper lady or a common property? Is Sabrina a goddess or a whore?

Then again, Sabrina is supposed to be important and powerful, but she is a completely passive object of violence and mutilation. Any time anybody is angry at anybody, they take it out on Sabrina. And I go back to that sentence from the historian, "Needless to say the student [who committed an indignity to Sabrina in the first place] was dealt with by the faculty and to this day *Sabrina's* fair cheek bears the marks of the student's ill-timed vengeance" (italics added). Faculty angry at student, student angry at faculty, student takes it out on *Sabrina*, which has been the problem in the first place. Plus, Sabrina keeps getting thrown down wells, buried in chicken guano, having her arms and her toes carelessly amputated—and everybody is giving her a hard time because she doesn't have a sense of humor! It's confusing.

How do I know that Sabrina is confused? I asked Sabrina. I asked her if she wasn't angry at the treatment that she had received. And you know what she said? She said, "I'm not angry, I'm just *confused.*" But her teeth were clenched so tightly together that it was difficult to hear her.

Why wasn't Sabrina angry? When men get angry, they beat up on Sabrina. Sabrina's immobilized; she can't beat up on anybody. If she got angry she couldn't take it out on anyone else, so she'd fall to pieces. She said, "I'd fall to pieces. *They wouldn't take me seriously anymore.*" For a final word from Sabrina, I asked her if she had any advice for undergraduate women. She said, "Don't let anyone put you up on a pedestal."

I think in a lot of ways women students today are grandchildren of this first alumna. Not that we're very close with granny, but every couple of years, the guys truss her up and dangle her from a helicopter and fly her across a field just so that we can get a sense of where we're coming from. Women students today have some of the same problems that Sabrina has and some different ones. But that basic structure of conflicting expectations—of a double bind—I think remains very much the same.

To start with, I think women students at a place like Amherst—recently coeducated, where you have only recently been admitted to the rights and privileges of access to a dominant culture—on the one hand feel eager to fit in, grateful to be here, wanting to buy in as much as possible. At the same time, there are other forces that pull us into a position of opposition toward that culture. On the other hand, the tug toward adopting an oppositional stance isn't all that immediate yet.

To begin with, as undergraduate women you're not experiencing many of the very important forms of gender oppression yet. The college environment really is more egalitarian than a lot of environments. And it's *especially* more egalitarian toward students than it is toward staff and faculty. Part of the reason that you as students are less discriminated against than women faculty and staff is that you are economically the equal of men students—you're paying the same tuition dollar that men students are. When you get to the workplace, and your economic value doesn't come from how much you're paying but from how much you're paid, you'll find that your economic value, compared with that of men, plummets.

Again, most of you women haven't faced an unwanted pregnancy. Most of you haven't had a child, either wanted or unwanted. Most of you haven't faced the difficulty of child-rearing in a society that devalues child-rearing. You haven't had much time to test out your hopes about romance and about work, so it's still easy to imagine that finding the "right" mate, finding the "right" job, adopting the "right" attitude will let you avoid pitfalls that you see or hear about other women falling into.

Another important point is that you're still young in a society where men's status and entitlement increase with age and women's status and entitlement decrease with age. When you go to the gynecologist and he calls you by your first name, you're used to it: everybody calls you by your first name because you're young. You haven't yet had the experience of having a gynecologist who's *younger* than you are call you by your first name. It will come. Generally speaking, your relative inexperience with discrimination probably makes it harder for you to imagine what it will be like, and a little harder to recognize it when you do come across it.

Then again, a lot of people, even people older than you are (although relatively fewer women and relatively fewer people of color) still believe that there is such a thing as reverse discrimination going on. They still believe that it's going to be easier for you and not harder for you to get that well-paying, visible, prestigious job because you're a woman. Part of the reason this happens is that women are so rare in prestigious jobs that we're very visible, so every time a woman gets a job, every time a person of color gets a job, "that person got that job *because* she was a woman, he was black, she was Hispanic" etc., whereas all the many times that a white man gets a job, nobody even notices that another white man has gotten a job. In study after study, this reverse discrimination that's such a large part of America's sense of what happens on the job market can't be found; it *isn't there*. The same *old* discriminations are going on and on.

All this puts you in a tricky position if you're an undergraduate woman. On the one hand, if you're trusting and interested in buying into this culture, you know at some level that you're making yourself vulnerable to some serious betrayals and disappointments. On the other hand, if you don't want that to happen and you're wary and trying to protect yourself intellectually and emotionally for coming across some heavy weather, a lot of these discriminations haven't arrived yet in your lives, and so you feel paranoid. You aren't quite sure what you're being so wary about, and other people look at you and say, "Why so mistrustful?" And again, if you're a woman and you're a feminist, or becoming a feminist, there's always that sword hanging over your head of being called a lesbian. But a lot of the most concrete discriminations aren't raining down on you yet.

At the same time, Elizabeth Tidball (George Washington University) did a study a few years ago that showed that by external measurements, like *Who's Who* or graduate degrees or professional degrees, that life achievements of women from quite mediocre women's colleges were higher than the life achievements of women from even *very* good coeducational colleges. Something's already going wrong for women at places like Amherst. Tidball thinks that maybe, if she did the study again, some of these numbers would be getting closer, but she's not so sure. But it's not very easy to figure out what's going wrong.

I think, though, we can point to some of the double binds that you're already running into, and I hope you'll recognize some of these. One is a double bind that all women share of whatever age. It's easiest to describe this one by going to another experiment. The experimenter sends out three sets of questionnaires to three different sets of psychotherapists. The first questionnaire says, "Give me a list of adjectives that describe a healthy adult person." Second set: "Give me a list of adjectives for a healthy adult man." Third set: "Give me a list of adjectives for a healthy adult woman." The healthy adult person and healthy adult man turn out to be very similar. For the healthy adult woman, though, there emerges a completely different set of adjectives! That means as long as you're acting like a woman you're not acting like a person, as long as you're acting like a person you're not acting like a woman. You're always going to be doing something wrong.

This experiment may be hard to believe, but I ran across something that made it easier for me to believe: a description of a test of psychological femininity that was administered in the '50s. According to this test, the things that would show you to be psychologically feminine were the following: "1. acceptance of traditional roles and hobbies and acceptance of clean white collar work [and of course that association of clean white collars with women is very suggestive—no ring around the collar for these white-collar workers], 2. social sensitivity, 3. timidity in both social and physical situations, 4. compassion and sympathy, 5. lack of interest in the abstract, political, and social world, 6. lack of braggadocio and hyperbole, 7. pettiness and irritability, 8. niceness and acquiescence." If you want to be that, you can be that, but it obviously means that you aren't a person. If you want to be a person, you can be a person, but it obviously means you aren't being that woman.

Those of you who are women students are probably running into this already in a conflict between being "tough-minded" in that Amherst combative, abrasive, really-on-top-of-things style, as you expect yourself to be, your professors expect you to be, your friends expect you to be, and being nurturing, as you expect yourself to be, your boyfriends, your girlfriends expect you to be. It's hard to fit these two together. Some people can do it, but it takes a particular kind of balancing act, and it's not one that should be demanded of everybody.

This is something that gets highlighted in the recent ad hoc committee's report on the conditions of women faculty at Amherst; it's something women faculty feel, too. To quote a couple of paragraphs from the report: "A senior female faculty member commented, 'There is a sense here at Amherst that bright people are abrasive and less bright people are nice.'" Recognize that? "Another woman felt that intellectual toughness was often assumed to be inextricably linked to personal toughness. Yet a female assistant professor noted that women are not simply expected to assimilate stereotypical male behavior." Here comes that double bind again. For here are "two conflicting demands on women—to be silent and decorous and to perform." Then, in another part of the report, a discussion of advising: "Some women faculty report that if and when they try to resist student pressure to play a maternal supportive role, they encounter deep resentment and harsh criticism from the students. At the same time, students sometimes equate supportiveness with a lack of intellectual rigor." So that there's a demand for the supportiveness and at the same time a contempt for the people who provide it, as if "They're just doing my emotional housekeeping for me."

There are more double binds students can run into. Be sexual, don't be sexual. Be sexual—dress up; look as if you're on the sexual market or else you're a man hater, you're being unpleasant, you're not making yourself agreeable. On the other hand, don't be *too* sexual because then you're asking for it, you're not intellectually serious. And of course these two categories have always overlapped. You're always wrong, one way or the other.

Again, for students who come from cultural backgrounds that aren't the exact WASP background that we find here, there's going to be a whole other layer of double binds. If you're coming from another culture of one sort or another, that culture in itself is going to have its own demands, often conflicting demands, on you as a gendered person. So if you're still figuring out what it means to be a Jewish woman (and I speak from my own experience), and what the demands on a Jewish woman are for being, say, nurturant, warm, *but not possessive*, then to have to take up that position in relation to a WASP culture that has a whole different set of conflicting expectations of you as a Jewish woman means that you're facing conflicting expectations. It's going to be tough, because every issue of ethnic identity, racial identity, cultural identity, also gets played out as an issue of gender identity. I don't come here just as a Jew, I come here as a Jewish woman.

Another problem is tokenism. There's a whole group of double binds around tokenism. You're going to run into this much more when you graduate, because every woman and person of color here is among other things being educated to be a terrific token. You're going to be in demand to be the only person of your kind on that board of directors. Demands are going to be made of you that will essentially ask you to deny who you are. And it takes a lot of maturity to deal with that—a lot more maturity than anybody could expect you to have at this point. You'll feel this even at the undergraduate level. For instance, you may be a woman who hangs out with guys, and guys say to you things like "I like you because when I'm with you I don't feel like you're a woman." That means that either you can have the friends you have or you can be a woman, but you're always doing it one way *or* the other. Be a woman, but be our kind of woman. But being our kind of woman means *not* being "like" a woman.

There are other speculations on why coed schools tend sometimes to suppress women's development. There is a reluctance by women, relatively speaking, to speak in mixed groups. There's pressure on women to underachieve: that famous fear of success that Martina Horner writes about. At the same time, there's a fear of failure. And when you get a fear of success it can be in the riptide of the fear of failure. There are some very debilitating possibilities. Say you're one of the five women in that particular major or one of the three women in that math class: there's pressure on you to represent your gender. And it's a very frightening thing to fail at something. It's not just you failing, but women failing.

Also there's a tendency for women to underestimate not only their own potential but their own achievements. Studies show that when a woman and a man get the same SAT scores in math, in the medium range, the man will say, "Great, I can be a math major," and the woman will say, "Gee, I really don't think this is good enough. You really have to be awfully good to be a math major." That same B– means different things to men and women.

There's another interesting hypothesis that I don't think has been tested out. I heard Elizabeth Tidball speaking about this, and it was just starting to get researched. It was about the effects of long-term hetero-sexual relationships on men and women undergraduates. What she said she was starting to find was that, when men were involved as under-graduates in long-term sexual relationships, their self-image and self-esteem went way up. They felt great about themselves, their engagement with the community increased, their performance in their classes got bet-ter, they were right on top of things. When women got involved in the same relationships, just the opposite happened. Their self-esteem tended to go down, they withdrew from the college community, from engage-ment with classes; their grades went down. Something serious and detri-mental to women is happening within some of those bonds.

The lack of female role models for women at a coed college also is a problem. It doesn't mean just one role model, it means having 5 role models or 50. None of you women are going to be me when you grow up. You're not going to be Amherst Professors Rose Olver, Andrea Rushing, Rosalina de la Carrera. You're going to be somewhere in among us. One model isn't enough. One model in each department isn't enough. You need a whole smorgasbord.

There's the additional problem of the absence of women and gender perspective from the curriculum: this will surprise those of you who are freshmen and taking "Race and Sex" and English 11. There are 500 courses in the Amherst catalog; 10 of them have to do with women or gender, 490 of them do not. You're going to be running into the other 490 very soon.

One thing that women students have in common with Sabrina is her fear of anger, her fear of her own fury. I think this is related to a fear in women, a fear of starting to recognize the things that are going to be coming down on us: you know that once you start to see those things, you're going to get angry. But what you think is going to happen to you when you get angry is just what Sabrina thinks is going to happen to her. You're going to go to pieces. You feel immobilized, disempowered, as though when you get angry it's not going to do the same thing for you that happens when your professor gets angry and he slams the table and looks mightier and more in control than ever. Quite the opposite. You're going to burst into tears. You're not going to be able to talk anymore. You won't even be able to finish the sentence. Who would want to get angry? And worst of all, you're going to be shown to be a woman because after all it's women who lose control. It's women who burst into tears. You'll really just blow it.

I think the proportion of women who have thought, "I really can't go in and talk to that professor because I'm about to burst into tears" is probably equal to the proportion of women faculty who have thought, "I really can't go meet that class today because I'm sure I'll burst into tears." I sense a discrediting power of tears that is very, very strong. Men talk a lot about how men aren't allowed to cry, and it's true men aren't allowed to cry. Women *do* cry, but it's always seen as a terrible liability. We've solved this problem of anger that we aren't allowed to feel by self-accusation, by turning anger against ourselves, by making up some other story about why our fists are clenched. "I'm not angry, just confused." "I'm cold." We've solved this problem of anger by turning against ourselves with all the kinds of self-destructive behavior that are increasing among young women—smoking, alcohol abuse, anorexia, oblivious sexuality, and by having self-destructive feelings of worthlessness and depression.

Don't men have conflicting demands too? Of course. The majority of men who aren't WASP men have that whole set of conflicting sets of conflicting demands that we discussed in the case of women. And then there's a whole litany of other conflicting demands that I'm sure you men know better than I do. Be sensitive, but be macho. Be feminists. You can't be a feminist, you're a man. Be well groomed and well behaved, but don't be effeminate. Bond closely with other men. But don't bond *too* closely with other men. Or if you do bond very closely with other men, find some female figure to route it through, like Sabrina. The greatest sentence in that one article about Sabrina is something like, "Sabrina served as an instrument for class bonding." And you have to understand "class" in the broadest possible sense!

It's tough for men; it's tough structurally in a lot of the same ways that it's tough for women. Double binds are similar in shape. On the other hand, for men, the pathway from Amherst College to positions of real power in the world is relatively clear and unobstructed. If you don't ask too many questions and if you manage to get out of here with exactly the right mixture of self-knowledge and self-ignorance, the rewards for filing straight through this defile of double binds are power, love, money.

Even good, nice, loving, sympathetic men who are supportive to women benefit from the oppression of women. They benefit from violent, threatening, and misogynist men, in the same way that men who aren't physically threatening benefit from rapists. What you probably *feel* most strongly, if you're one of these supportive men, is the loss that you suffer because other men are violent against women. You feel that women don't trust you as you wish they would, and as you feel you deserve to be trusted. You feel a loss in the possibilities of intimacy that you think you deserve. Those are real damages. But what you aren't feeling is how high your market level rises as a nonviolent, supportive, and sympathetic man: how much in demand you are, how rare you are, and how valued you are for these traits that really ought to be able to be taken for granted from *all* men.

Men do face these double binds, and all men lose something in navigating through them. Some men lose a great deal. But the general entitlement of men at the cost of women is so pervasive and so hard to pin down that men need to look seriously to see where and how they're moving ahead on the basis of the oppression of women. They can't do this just by introspection. If you just look inside yourself and say "Am I sexist?" you're not going to see the structural things in the society that let you profit from the oppression of women. Just the way that if, as an Amherst College student, you simply look inside yourself and say "Am I a racist?" you're not going to realize how, for instance, a lot of the money that's supporting your education comes from investments in racist society. You have to look analytically around you.

I've had a lot of people say to me, "When I look at a woman I don't see a woman. I see a person. How could I be a sexist?" But to say that is already denying and devaluing and making invisible the experience of that woman *as a woman*, which is a large part of her experience: her oppression as a woman, her acculturation as a woman, her resourcefulness in surviving as a woman, and her making of a female self for herself. And to blind yourself to that, in the name of gender-blindness, fairness, not being a sexist, I think is the wrong tack to take.

So, what can students do? Women, feel anger. Think about what to do with the anger. If you know it's anger, then you're in control. If you feel that anger and it's a moment in which you just can't afford to blow up, as long as you know it's anger, you can say to yourself, "All right, this is anger. I'm not going to blow up. I'll do it later." It's if you don't know it's anger that you're out of control. Think about things you can do with anger. Think about people you can share it with who will validate it, and let you make something interesting out of it. *Write it.* Also, women, learn how to weep without stopping talking. Just let the water come out of your eyes and keep talking. You know: you're a woman, you cry sometimes. It doesn't mean that you can't finish the sentence. And they always try to make themselves stop crying because the anger is so upsetting. You can cry and talk at the same time. And once you aren't busy trying to make yourself stop crying, then your voice will be able to come out. You can finish the sentence. You can finish the class, whether you're a student in the class or a teacher in front of the class. It'll get said. The women around you and the men around you will learn to listen to somebody talking who's crying at the same time.

The next thing that students can do is to work actively—and get faculty working actively, and get administration working actively—to create a nonhomophobic community on campus. You probably noticed when I was going through that list of double binds that some of them for women, and a very high proportion of them for men, were structured in the first place by the threat of homosexual labeling. If that threat stops being a threat, some of those double binds disappear, and so do some of the ugly self-ignorances that are enforced by those double binds. This isn't just an issue of making things nice for gay students, though it is very important to make a campus livable for gay students. It's important also for heterosexual students or for students who are probably heterosexual that the campus be livable for gay students. Otherwise, there's that whole potential for blackmailing you about your sympathy for women, your love for women, whatever, whether you're a man or a woman. That threat simply disappears if you're in an environment that's not homophobic. There's a wave of homophobia obviously sweeping the country, sweeping prestigious campuses in the Northeast now, which is very, very dangerous. I've been told that a few years ago there were 30 to 40 gay and lesbian students out on this campus, and this year there are fewer than half a dozen out. The proportion of gay and lesbian students who are out on this campus is a very good indicator of the level of general trust on the campus. And if that trust isn't there, women and men can't go about leading their affective and political lives safely, heterosexual *or* gay women and men. It's got to be a priority.

Next, all students need to be aware—or at least need opportunities to become aware—of gender structures in their lives, whether as oppressors or as oppressed—or, as in most of our cases, as both—just as all of us need to become aware of class and economic and racial technological structures that are shaping our lives. What you as students can do is make this faculty aware of your felt curricular needs in all your courses, even the ones where they seem least likely to be met. Keep asking the questions that you are learning to ask in those freshmen courses on gender. In your upperclass courses, those questions are going to be fresh and important and break open new territory in the coverage of the courses.

Again, though, don't recycle your double binds on the faculty. Don't demand emotional nurturance from women faculty, and then devalue them for giving it to you. Value the emotional nurturance you get from all of your professors highly, and value it *as part of* their intellectual worth, not *as opposed to* their intellectual worth. When you are dealing with men faculty, don't either devalue the nurturance you get from them or deprive them of the opportunity to give you nurturance. Don't go to men faculty for brain stuff and women faculty for heart stuff. The women faculty have brains, and a lot of the men faculty have hearts.

Don't let your interest in ending gender oppression stop at the meta-

phorical gates of the college. If you want to have choices in the family structures that you form, if you want to have a choice of a nuclear family or
extended family or a couple of one sort or another, you should be interested
in the wholesale regulation of families under systems like apartheid. If you
want reproductive freedom, you should be speaking out for all women—
whether it's for their access to safe, legal abortion, or for their freedom from
sterilization abuse. If you want to have choices about child-rearing and day
care, you'd better be working for economic and cultural recognition for
child-care workers. If you want to be free from the terrorism of rape, you
need to oppose *all* of the political and terroristic uses of rape: for instance,
its use as torture in authoritarian societies. And in general if you want other
people to reflect on how their entitlement can be a tacit part of your oppression, you need to be ready to do the same thing.

The final thing you can do is value your own community. If you're a
woman, one of the things that means is the community of women around
you, and if you're a man, one of the things it means is the community of
like-minded men around you. One way to start that is through a process
of consciousness-raising groups.

I'm going to conclude in the most obvious way, by asking you the three
questions that Rabbi Hillel would ask you now if *he* were standing up
here:

If you are not for yourself, who will be for you?

If you are only for yourself, what are you?

And if not now, when?

At the conference reported here, a scientific gathering at Marsh House in 1990, one participant said he could not get stirred up about historical questions. He and his colleagues had just heard a captivating lecture on historic disagreements between the twentieth-century physicists Niels Bohr and Albert Einstein. It was odd that one would not be stirred by such history. Curiosity about the past brings many rewards—among them, often, the discovery of surprising connections and continuities. In relation to this conference, for instance, consider that Bohr himself had appeared many years earlier to speak in College Hall, not far from the site of the 1990 gathering. Bohr was at Amherst in October 1923 as the college's first Simpson Lecturer, giving talks on atomic physics. But history has its discontinuities, too. Ted Greene's opening essay in this collection describes the confidence of the founders in 1821 that they knew the answers—the ultimate truth. As Greene put it, "They presumed that they could and should convert all the other races and religions of the world to New England Congregationalism." This closing selection describes a far different time more than a century later: a moment when some of the world instead came to Amherst—not to preach the answers of religion but, more modestly, to talk about basic, unanswered questions of science.

JOHN BELL AND HIS FRIENDS
AT AMHERST

⌒‿⌒

WHEN THE WEEK dawned fair over the hills above Amherst on Sunday, June 10, 1990, Professors George Greenstein and Arthur Zajonc welcomed the promise of brilliant weather. Later that day, 26 of their colleagues were gathering from the local Five College faculties, other U.S. institutions, and even Europe for a lively six-day conference that the two men had organized months earlier. The visitors were lodged and the sessions held at Marsh House (formerly Phi Gam), a Greek Revival temple that overlooks the town center.

The attraction for the group was a chance to talk about fundamental mysteries of the universe, to join other investigators in the field of theoretical and experimental physics—a few philosophers and mathematicians, too—for a "Workshop on the Foundations of Quantum Mechanics." Quantum mechanics is a theory that accounts for experimental measurements on subatomic particles. It defies explanation in terms of classical physics; to most of us, it almost defies explanation at all. But its predictions in science and engineering have been stunningly successful; it accounts for the development of computer chips, lasers, and other modern-day wonders.

The chief wonder to scientists Greenstein and Zajonc and those they invited to Amherst, however, was not the applications but the quantum theory itself. The classical view in physics involves presumed certainties, for example, whereas quantum mechanics deals only in probabilities. Although subatomic particles behave in a classical fashion, like localized objects, when experimenters observe them, at other times they behave in a bizarre, nonlocalized manner, like waves. Scientists have been unable to come up with one description that can account for both kinds of behavior. Thanks in part to a man named John Bell, these discrepancies were high on the agenda at Amherst.

Toward the end of the conference Herb Bernstein from Hampshire College said the contradictions between quantum mechanics and classical physics reminded him of the story about a rabbi who was asked to resolve a boundary dispute between two neighbors. The rabbi and his attendant met with one of them, and the rabbi listened intently while the man pleaded his case. The argument was elegant and persuasive, and when the man finished speaking the rabbi said to him, "You're right." Then the rabbi and his aide went to the other man, whose argument was just as compelling. After hearing it, the rabbi immediately said to him, "You're right."

As soon as they were alone, the rabbi's attendant protested. "You told the first man *he* was right, and now you're telling this man *he* is right. But they can't *both* be right!"

The rabbi looked at him thoughtfully for a moment and then said quietly, "You're right."

In quantum mechanics, what depictions are "right"? The conference schedule prepared by Zajonc and Greenstein allowed time for presentations and discussions on several key issues, including "experimental loopholes," "the quantum measurement problem," and "the transition from micro-world to macro-world." Equations and diagrams were enlarged on overhead projectors, and conferees asked each other for definitions of terms, or fuller explanations of methodology. (From the back of the room one afternoon, physicist Larry Hunter of Amherst quickly scanned a screen filled with equations and suggested gently: "Eighth line down— shouldn't that be minus instead of plus?" He was right.) But the workshop was not theories and equations nonstop. There was ample time for fellowship and humor. They kidded a speaker whose talk ran longer than others. "Your theory doesn't reduce your own wave packet," someone told him.

The meetings were freewheeling; even the lecture sessions were sociable, more like roundtable discussions than formal talks. Greenstein and Zajonc had designed it that way. "For scientists the best part of conferences is not when talks are going on, but when everybody's standing around in the hallway and yakking," said Greenstein. "We wanted to formalize that and make it a week of chatting."

On Tuesday morning Greenstein invited the entire group to a picnic supper at his house. When he handed out directions on how to get there, one out-of-town visitor, city-bred measurement theorist Daniel Greenberger of CCNY, asked rhetorically, "How can you go '3.5 miles from downtown Amherst'? Is downtown Amherst less than a tenth of a mile?" Many of the scientists were accomplished musicians, so the evening at the Greensteins' turned into a jam session. Another night, seven of them suspended abstract talk of eigenvectors and probability amplitudes and shot pool at the Campus Center. And President Pouncey, the workshop's sponsor, hosted a dinner for everyone at the Merrill Dining Commons—for which a few of the unprepared visitors borrowed ties.

At Marsh House all the sessions were informal. Abner Shimony of Boston University gave a virtuoso lecture on the second day, analyzing the historic points of disagreement between the two giants of twentieth-century physics, Albert Einstein and Niels Bohr. Shimony, an ebullient speaker, talked excitedly about nuances he found in what the two scientists had written 50 and 60 years ago. There were lively exchanges: would Einstein, for instance, ever have been willing to give up the concept of "locality," the classical-physics requirement that causes and their immediate effects occur at the same place? One mystery in quantum physics is that subatomic particles sometimes exhibit "nonlocality": a cause at one place appears to produce immediate effects at another.

During a coffee break that followed this discussion, Kurt Gottfried of Cornell said he could not get stirred up about historical questions. He thought it "odd" that people still worried about what Einstein and Bohr would have said. "Anyway," Gottfried said, "Bohr just whispered. He was extremely insistent on what he had to say, and since you couldn't hear it, that made it even worse."

Another conferee had worked closely with Bohr those many years ago, however, and in private conversation he spoke of him reverentially.

This was the Viennese-born Victor Weisskopf of MIT, once director general of CERN, the European nuclear research center in Geneva, and a man in his 80s. Weisskopf recalled the heady challenge of assisting Bohr in Copenhagen in the 1930s. He said the great Nobel laureate formulated his ideas and even wrote his papers by thinking out loud in a seminar with a small group of scientists and choosing an assistant to write down what he said. The person he chose to do this was known as the "victim." "I was the guy for less than half a year," Weisskopf said, "because Leon Rosenfeld was his preferred victim." From time to time Bohr's victims would have to interrupt him and say, "I don't understand that; say it differently," Weisskopf related. Also, "Bohr didn't write clearly. He loved extremely long sentences, and his thinking interfered with his expression." In editing the draft of a paper, a victim would suggest that Bohr divide a sentence into two or even three sentences. "But usually what happened," said Weisskopf, "was that he then made the sentence even longer." Weisskopf sighed. "I loved him dearly, you know. He was an intellectual father figure for me. I would talk with him about love, about death, about everything."

If the historical presences of Bohr and Einstein were felt at the workshop, another renowned scientist was there in person. This was John Bell—a quiet, intense Irishman, world famous in science as the author of Bell's Theorem, who had come to the Amherst meeting all the way from Geneva. Bell's Theorem, developed in the 1960s, is believed to demonstrate conclusively that no "local hidden variable" theory based on classical physics can account for the predictions that are demonstrated in quantum mechanics. Tests of the theorem seem to confirm the mysterious disparity, the "inequality," between those two descriptions of nature. In his highly readable book *Quantum Physics: Illusion or Reality?*, Alastair Rae calls Bell's Theorem the mainspring of most of the theoretical and experimental research in quantum mechanics that has been done for the past 20 years.

The group at Marsh House treated Bell with deference and affection. He was one of the reasons they were there. The third day, opening a discussion of "effects of the environment on simple quantum systems," David Mermin of Cornell said that "depending on who you are, you will regard what I am about to say as trivial, wrong, well known, or crazy." Mermin then launched into something called "C-star algebra" with the jest, half serious, that no one really understands what C-star algebra is. "And John," he said, "is the one who's going to point out where it goes wrong."

Bell smiled from his end of the table. "I'm watching."

Slight, sandy-haired, a little disheveled, Bell was unprepossessing until he joined a discussion. Then listeners were struck by his extraordinary clarity and precision, his instinct for the heart of the question. Zajonc called it his "radical honesty." Bell spoke in a gently musical voice, mixed with notes of imminent exasperation and infinite patience. He especially liked metaphors—the stronger the better. He once said of the scientist who seems undisturbed by the discrepancies between quantum and classical physics—the theorist who is willing to have it both ways—that it was "like a snake trying to swallow itself by the tail. It can be done up to a point," he said, "but it becomes embarrassing for the spectators even before it becomes uncomfortable for the snake."

Bell's work has confirmed those discrepancies, but it was clear at the Amherst meeting that they troubled him still. It became a point of difference, early and dramatically, between Bell and Gottfried. "It's an empirical fact," Gottfried said, "that in the micro-world it is only statistical probabilities that are reproducible." Quantum mechanics' lack of total precision and certainty did not concern Gottfried. "The astonishing thing about the theory is not its failing but its success," he declared.

Bell, on the other hand, said he wanted to know "the kinematics." "I don't know what the kinematics of your world is," he told Gottfried. "We have to be able to describe what *can* happen before we can describe what *will* happen, and quantum mechanics is an enormously sophisticated avoidance of this question." As philosophy professor Jonathan Vogel of Amherst remarked, it was like "having probabilities but nothing that they are probabilities *of*."

"I think John Bell goes too far as a purist," Weisskopf said later. "Physics is never completely exact. It is not mathematics. There are little dark points that may be cleared up as time goes on. But the good thing about John is he always puts question marks where other people wouldn't. He also has a good sense of humor—a strong way of expressing his opinions."

To Bell the informal, give-and-take conference that Zajonc and Greenstein created was a winning formula. "This is probably the best session on quantum mechanics that I've been to," he said. "The number of people is quite small, and the discussions are intense. Physics can progress very well without discussing these deep problems; but they ought to be discussed." Friends from the Amherst workshop were shocked and saddened four months later, when Bell died in Geneva of a cerebral hemorrhage. He was 62.

When the workshop drew to a close on Friday, June 15, Bell was asked to make some concluding remarks. He was clear and concise as always, but meditative too. The point he wanted to make in his disagreement with Gottfried, he said, was that it is good to return to unresolved issues "and attempt reformulation *without* approximation." His concern in quantum mechanics was that "the nonlocality problem has not been digested"— though he thought efforts at a new synthesis being made by one of the conference participants, Philip Pearle of Hamilton College, were promising.

Bell granted that the early pyramids had been built "by people who did not know Euclidean geometry. It would never have been done," he acknowledged, "if they had waited until people got it into good logical shape." But it was important, Bell said, to keep trying to get quantum physics into better logical order. He likened it to the problem of someone losing a key along a dark street at night: the key could be anywhere, but the only place where the person could see well enough to look for it is under the streetlight. Bell said he suspected that, in quantum mechanics, "most experiments are being done in the area where we did not lose the key." The best advice he could give his colleagues, he said, was to "go on looking under the lamppost. If I had a better program, I would tell you."—DCW

Issues of *Amherst* magazine where selections
in this book appeared earlier:

"Wood Fires and Mud," Fall 1991; "Antislavery Activity" (originally
"Crimes of Impropriety"), Summer 1998; "Magnetic Visitors," Spring 1981;
"Looking at Emily Dickinson," Winter 2006; "Brave Among the Bravest,"
Summer 1999; "Yankee Samurai" (originally "Neesima, Doshisha and
Amherst"), Winter 1976; "The Coeducation Debate of 1871" (originally
"No Women—Said the Menfolk—Need Apply"), Spring 1984; "The
Olmsteds at Amherst," Fall 1981; "The Story in the Meiklejohn Files,"
Part I, Fall 1982; Part II, Spring 1983; "Coolidge Reconsidered" (originally
"New Praise for an Amherst Man"), Fall 1998; "A Good Day for Stuffy
McInnis" (originally "Forty Days Ago in June"), Spring 1988; "Unfraternal
Conduct," Fall 2000; "Reacquainted with the Night," Winter 2002; "The
Long and Happy Reign of Maude Miner," Spring 1991; "With Respect to
John Moore," Spring 1996; "Reflections of a Black Son," Fall 1977; "An
Englishman at Amherst," Summer 1977; "A Short History of Women at
Amherst" (originally "175 (Plus) Years of Amherst Women"), Winter
1997; "Sabrina Doesn't Live Here Anymore," Spring 1985; "John Bell and
His Friends at Amherst," Winter 1990.

INDEX

Abolitionists, 24, 26–29, 51

Adams, Henry, 194, 211

Administrators, 202; women as, 273

Admissions requirements, original, 3–5

Advanced Composition, 236–37

Africans: *Amistad* prisoners, 23, 26–28; missionaries and, 26–29

Afro-Americans. *See* Blacks; Slavery

Afro-American Society, Amherst, 218

Agard, Walter Raymond, 123–24, 129, 134

Aitken, Hugh, 253

Allen, Terry, 266

Allis, Frederick S., 94, 103

Alpha Delta Phi, 17, 19

American Board of Commissioners for Foreign Missions, 65, 68, 71

Amherst, Jeffery John Archer, 273

Amherst, Lord Jeffery, 136, 261

Amherst, town of: blacks in, 24–25; Symons's view of amenities in, 238–39

Amherst Academy, 269

Amherst Afro-American Society, 218

Amherst Christian Association, 77

Amherst House at Doshisha University, 76–77

Amherst magazine, 266

"Amherst Milestones," 114–15

Amherst Student, 239, 241; on coeducation, 86–87; on ILS, 249–51; on Phi Kappa Psi, 183–84; on Ward's civil disobedience, 225–31

"Amherst System," 80

"Amherst Tomorrow," 174

Amherst Women's Club, 270

Amistad prisoners, 23, 26–28

Andrew, John A., 52

Anger, women and, 287, 289

"Annals of the Evergreens, The" (Dickinson), 30

Ansbacher, Barbara, 254

Antislavery movement, 24, 26–29, 51

Antislavery Society (Amherst), 22–24

Antivenenean Society, 19, 79

Appleton Cabinet, 20, 93

Arons, Arnold, 192

Art Nouveau, 91

Athletics: baseball, 162–71; football, 258–62; in 1840s, 17–18

Babb, Lawrence, 253

Bacon, Helen, 209

Bacon, Theodore, 203

Bailey, Gillian Barr, 48

Bailey, William R., 47–49

Baird, Theodore, 203–4, 219; *English at Amherst,* 186; freshman English and, 186–95; influence of, 192; reading lists of, 194

Baker, Fran, 165

Baker, Ray Stannard, 103

Bandeen, James, 178, 185

Barber, C. L., 192, 209

Barnes, Harry G., 175–76, 178

Barrett Hall, 88, 95

Barry, Jack, 164–65, 167–71

Barton, Bruce, 103

Baseball, 162–71

Bateson, Catherine, 254, 256

Bath houses, 13

Beautification scheme (1903), 92

Beebe, Ralph A., 181

Beecher, Henry Ward, 5, 16, 37, 37n, 61; coeducation and, 80, 83–85

Bell, John, 294, 296–98

Bell's Theorem, 296

Benton, Thomas Hart, 32–34, 32n

Berg Collection (New York Public Library), 48

Bergin, John, 168

Bernhard, Mary Elizabeth, 46–47

Bernstein, Herb, 294

Bingham, Millicent Todd, 46–47, 270

Birnbaum, Norman, 219

Birth of a Nation, The (film), 138

Bishop, James, 253

Bishop, Jonathan, 192

Bixby, Harold M., 122

Bixler, J. Seelye, 103

Blacks: in Amherst, 24–25; fraternities and, 173–85; graduates, Jones as first of, 22; Houston and racial equality for, 154–61; language and, 216–17; Porter's reflections and, 213–23; as visitors to Amherst, 204–5. *See also* Africans; Afro-Americans; Slavery

Blaisdell, Nesbitt, 176, 181

Bluford, Lucy, 159

Bluford v. Canada, 159

Boating, 79

Bogan, Chris, 232, 237–40

Bohjalian, Christopher, 78

Bohr, Niels, 292, 295–96

Booraem, Hendrik, 136, 140

Boston Globe, 183

Bowen, Ezra, 166, 169–71

Bowles, Samuel, 37, 41, 80, 84, 87

Bragdon, Paul E., 184

Broderick, James H., 194–95

Brower, Reuben, 192

Brown, John, 24

Brown v. Board of Education, 154

Bruce, Lenny, as writing topic, 235–36

Buildings: early, 7; Olmsteds and, 88–95; in 1840s, 11–15; at Semicentennial, 79. *See also* by individual names

Bullard, Otis A., 45

Bullock, Alexander H., 5, 39–40, 85

Burnett, Charles T., 115

Burnett, Frances Hodgson, 41–42, 41n

Burnett, Lionel, 42

Burns, Ward, 178–82, 184–85

Burnside, Ambrose, 57–58, 62

Butler, John F., 192

Calvert, George, 181

Cameron, John, 192, 248–49

Campus: Olmsteds and, 88–99, 98; original, 6–7; in 1840s, 10–21; Symons's view of, 238–39

Carlson, Eugene, 258

Carter, Robert L., 154

Centennial, 114–15, 273

Chapel: Row, Old, 98; in 1840s, 14, 17. *See also* Johnson Chapel

Charity Fund, 4, 267

Charles Pratt Dormitory, 91

Churchill, George Bosworth, 144–45; Meiklejohn and, 118–19, 122–27

Cinque, 26–28

Civil disobedience of John William Ward, 224–31; effect of, 229, 231; public versus private role and, 228–30

Civil War, 50–63; Frazar Stearns in, 57–63; Massachusetts regiments in, 52–53, 55–59

Clark, Alden, 75

Clark, David, "A Plea for a Miserable World," 7–9

Clark, William S., 52, 55, 58–60

Class abuse, 18, 87

Classics 97, 207

Class suppers, 81

Clausen, W. V., 192

Coeducation, 5–6, 78, 266, 271, 274–77; 1871 debate on, 78–87; difficulties for women in, 278–91; lack of preparation for, 275–76

Cole, Charles W., 174, 185

Coles, William, 192

College Chapel, 17. *See also* Johnson Chapel

College Church, 64, 98. *See also* Stearns Church

College Hall, 11–12, 32, 292

College of Languages, 272

College Row, 93, 98

College Street, 98

Collins, Eddie, 165

Collins, Russell J., 183

Colloquium 36, 207–9

Commager, Evan, 197–98, 200

Commager, Henry Steele, 197–99, 219–20

Commager, Steele, 197

Commager house, 197–98

Commencements: of Horace Porter, 222–23; in 1840s, 15–16; Symons's view of, 241; visitors at, 37–39

Committee of Six, 244–45, 248–49

Committee on Education Policy (CEP), 244–46, 248–49; Interim Report of, 249–50; proposed changes of, 252–54

Community: sense of, 9; valuing of, 291

Composition, freshman. *See* English 1–2

Congregationalism, 8, 75

Converse Hall, 220

Converse Library, 95

Convivialism, 19, 81

Cook, Mercer, III, 173

Coolidge, Calvin, 108, 112, 114, 128, 136; race relations and, 138–39; reconsidered, 137–41

Coolidge, Calvin, Jr., 139

Coolidge, Grace, 139

Coolidge, John, 137

Craig, G. Armour, 192, 250

Crawford, George, 158

Cronin, Joe, 165

Cunnane, Joe, 171

Curious Footprints (Pick and Ward), 10

Curriculum: early, 7–8; gender and, 278, 286; junior-year colloquia in, 252–53; post–World War II, 209; Select Committee on, 243–45, 253. *See also* Advanced Composition; Classics 97; Colloquium 36; Freshman English; Introduction to Liberal Studies (ILS)

Curtis, George W., 34, 39

Daguerreotype, of Emily Dickinson, 46–47, 263

Dalton, Harry, 170

Dances, 272

D'Arienzo, Daria, 44
Darp, The. *See* Ostendarp, James
Deaett, Al, 258
DeMott, Benjamin, 192, 219
Dennison, Ami, 59
Denton, James, 253
Departments, power of, 255–56
De Vries, Willem, 253
Dickinson, Austin, 30, 45, 53–54, 91,
    269–71
Dickinson, Edward, 51, 54, 62, 269
Dickinson, Emily, 30, 32, 35, 263, 269–
    70; Civil War and, 53–54, 57, 61–62;
    treasures related to, 44–49
Dickinson, Francis H., 53
Dickinson, Lavinia, 38–39, 38n, 45, 45n,
    47, 270
Dickinson, Lucinda and Thankful, 267–68
Dickinson, Mason A., 106
Dickinson, Moses, 19
Dickinson, Samuel Fowler, 269
Dickinson, Susan, 54; "The Annals of
    the Evergreens," 30
Dickinson Homestead, 238, 270
Discrimination, 4–5, 281–82
Dizard, Jan, 250–51
Doane, Robert, 178
Dodge, William E., 66
Domingue, Gregory, 219
Dormitory residences, in 1840s, 12–13
Doshisha University, 64, 66, 72–73, 75;
    Amherst and, 75–77
Double binds: homophobia and, 289–90;
    imposing on faculty, 290; men and,
    287–88; for women, 283–85
Doughty, Howard W., 120–21, 134
Drinking, 18–19, 79
DuBois, W. E. B., 215
"Ducking," 19–20

Ebina Danjo, 75
Eckley, Paul, 165

Einstein, Albert, 292, 295
Elliot, Bob, 209
Ellison, Ralph, 221; *Invisible Man,* 215
Emerson, Benjamin K., 117, 121
Emerson, Ralph Waldo, 34–36, 232
English 1–2, 186–95; assignments for,
    189–93; Baird's influence and, 192;
    criticism of, 192–93; origins of, 193–
    95; team-teaching of, 186–89
English at Amherst (Baird), 186
Entertainment: in early 1900s, 114–15,
    272–73; in 1840s, 15–16
Epstein, Joseph, 208
Erskine, John, 143
Esty, Edward T., 113, 124, 129
Esty, John C., 204
Esty, Robert P., 120
Evangelizing, 68; as college purpose, 4,
    8–9, 79–80
Evergreens, The, 30, 270
Exhibitions, in 1840s, 17

Faculty: ILS and, 243–57;
    interdisciplinary courses and, 255;
    matrons, 268; under Meiklejohn,
    116–24; size frozen, 256; -student
    ratio, 234; women as, 272–73, 275–77,
    284. *See also* individual faculty names
Faculty Club, 270
Fair Employment Practices Committee
    (FEPC), 160
Farnsworth, Lydia, 273
Fayerweather Hall, 91–92
Felzenberg, Alvin, 138
Fenn, Elipha, 52
Ferry, Mrs., 19
Financial status of Amherst, 234
Fires, wood, 13–16
First Church. *See* College Hall
Fiske, Mrs., 268
Fitch, Albert Parker, 120, 134
Fitch, Clyde, xi

Five College Consortium, 274
Football, 258–62
Foote, Kate, 41–42
Ford, Emily (née Fowler), 48
Forte, Jack, 164, 169–71
Foster, John G., 58–59
Founding of Amherst, 3–9
Fourteenth Amendment, racial equality and, 155
Fowler, Emily (Ford), 48
Fowler, William Chauncey, 48
Frankfurter, Felix, 134–35, 156
Fraternities, 79, 87, 172–85, 276; Jewish students and, 175; post–World War II, 174–75; "unfraternal conduct" and, 175–85. See also individual fraternities
Frazier, Miss, 85
Freshman English, 186–95, 233–36
Frost, Robert, 142–53, 192, 265; at Commager house, 196–201; imagination and, 151; Meiklejohn and, 119, 143–46, 150–52; moral personality of, 149–50; teaching of, 148–53; "The Road Not Taken," 146–48
Frost (Pritchard), 142
Fuller, George, 59
Fundraising: early, 4, 9; women and, 267–68

Gaines, Lloyd Lionel, 159
Garman, Charles, xii, 136
Garrison, William Lloyd, 25
Gates, Merrill, 91–92
Gay, Peter, 271
Gay students, 278, 289–90
Gender: curriculum and, 278, 286; oppression, 281–82, 288–91; structures, 290. See also Women; Women at Amherst
Genovese, Bill, 170–71

Genung, John F., 117
Geraghty, Jay, 184
Gerety, Tom, 207
Gibbs, Julian H., 100, 248, 251, 253–54, 256
Gibbs, Thomas W., 173, 175–85
Gibson, Walker, 186
Gifford, Prosser, 245, 248, 256
Gilbert, Robert E., 139
Gillett, Arthur L., 41, 113
Gillett, Edward B., 39–40, 39n
Gillett, Frederick H., 273
Gillman, Richard, and Michael Paul Novak, Poets, Poetics, and Politics, 199
Goggans, Rick, 209
Gold, Dave, 170
Gordon, Joel, 244–45, 250, 254
Gorgas, Harry S., 177, 179
Gottfried, Kurt, 295, 297–98
Greenberger, Daniel, 295
Greene, Frederick, 177–79, 181–82, 185
Greene, Frederick S., 120
Greene, John M., 80–81, 83–84
Greene, Theodore P., xiii, 2, 221, 271, 292
Greene, Theodore Phinney, 42
Greenstein, George, 293–95
Griffin, Solomon Bulkley, 41
Grimes, William, 259–60
Grosvenor, Edwin A., 117
Gut courses, 237
Guttmann, Allen, 212, 221

Hall, John Whitney, 64
Halsted, John, 254
Hamill, Hugh M., 176
Hamilton, Howard L., 182–84
Hamilton, Walton H., 134
Hammond, Lew, 170–71
Hampshire College, 274
Hantin, Rebecca, 276
Harding, Warren G., 108, 139
Hardy, Alpheus, 68–69
Harris, George, 92, 102

Harris, Jim, 19
Harvard's Society of Fellows, 209
Haskell, Nelson C., 106
Hawkins, Hugh, 242
Hayden, Joel, 278
Haynes, Ulric, Jr., 205
Hazing, 19–20
Heath, William, 192
Heating, wood, 13–16
Hendricks, John, 209
Henshaw, Marshall, 17
Hewlett, Horace W., 184
Hitchcock, Edward, Jr. ("Doc"), 10, 44, 79
Hitchcock, Edward, Sr., 10, 20–21
Hitchcock, Orra White (Mrs. Edward), 82, 268–69
Holy Cross Crusaders, 164, 167–71
Homophobia, 289–90
Honors theses, 237, 240–41
Hopkins, Arthur J., 120–21
Horner, Martina, 285
House Management Committee, 175
Houston, Charles Hamilton, 154–61, 265; background of, 156–57; separate but equal doctrine and, 158–59
Houston, Mary, 156
Houston, William, 156
Howard Law School, Charles Hamilton Houston and, 157, 159
Howe, Julia Ward, 36–37
Hubbard, Henry, 57–58
Huggins, Robert, 178, 185
Hughes, Langston, 223
Humanities I–II, 209
Humphrey, Heman, 15, 22, 24, 26, 86, 234
Humphrey, Heman, Mrs., 268
Humphries, Rolfe, 197–201
Hunter, Larry, 294
Huntington, Frederic Dan, 36–37, 36n
Hurd v. Hodge, 160

Hurricane of 1938, 205

Introduction to Liberal Studies (ILS), 242–57; proposed changes to, 252–54; skepticism toward, 247; student critiques of, 247, 249–52, 256; success and failure of, 255–57; supervision of, 256
Invisible Man (Ellison), 215

Jagannathan, Kannan, xii–xiii
James, Arthur Curtiss, 119
Japan, 66–67, 72–74, 77
Jewish students, 175
Johnson, George, 219
Johnson Chapel, 52, 64, 136, 221, 224; Olmsteds and, 88, 90, 93–94
Jones, Edward, 5, 22
Jordan, Jack, 169–70
Jordan, Lloyd, 165
Joy, Pete, 197
Junior-year colloquia, 252–53
Justus, Brad, 251

Kanda, Naibu, 273
Kateb, George, 207, 219–20
Kato Hiroyuki, 74
Kaw-Mendi (Africa), 28–29
Keep, Austin Baxter, 47
Keep, Wallace, 47
Kelsey, C. E., 120
Kennedy, Gail, 181
Kennedy, John F., 205
Kennick, William, 248
Kidder, H. W., 108
Kimball, Arthur L., 92
Kimball, Gladys, 273
King, Stanley, 95–96, 113, 124–25, 128–31
Kolesar, James, 261–62
Kornblith, Gary, 219

Korzybski, Alfred, 191, 193–94
Kropf, Allen, 253
Ku Klux Klan, 138–39, 212

Ladd, Henry, 149–50
Ladies of Amherst, 272
Lancaster, John, 48, 162
Lane, Henry W., 106–7
Latham, Earl, 219
Lattimore, Richard, 209
Laws, college, 18–19
Lecturers, visiting: Frederic Dan
    Huntington, 36–37; Ralph Waldo
    Emerson, 34–36; Thomas Hart
    Benton, 32–34, 32n; Wendell Phillips,
    34–35, 34n
Le Duc, Thomas, 80
Letters of Emily Dickinson (Todd), 47
Levin, Gordon, 245–46, 253
Lewis, William Henry, 138
Libraries, 95, 222, 239; in 1840s, 16–17
Lidd, Miss, 85
Lieber, Ben, 276
Lindley, Ernest K., 184
Lippmann, Walter, 130, 135
Liquor, 18–19, 79
Literary societies, 16–17, 79, 87
Lonczak, Ed, 171
Long Range Planning Committee, 254–55
Longsworth, Polly, 50, 270
Loomis, Frederic B., 121–22, 127
Lord, Otis Phillips, 38, 38n
Lord Jeffs (nickname), 261
"Lost Arts, The" (Phillips), 34–35, 34n
Love and Friendship (Lurie), 193
Lovett, Edward, 158
Luddy, Fred, 203
Lumley, Albert E., 181
Lundquist, Philip, 262
Lurie, Alison, *Love and Friendship,* 193
Lyon, Mary, 18

Lyons, Louis, 130

Mack, Connie, 164–65
Mager, Gerald, 246
Maher, Maggie, 47
Mallon, George B., 123
Mann, Horace, 83
Manning, J. M., 19
March, Francis Andrew, 17
Marsh, Justin, 8
Marshall, Maud Alice, 273
Marshall, Thurgood, 154, 158
Marsh House, 293
Marx, Anthony, xiii
Marx, Leo, 219–20
Masquers student theater group, 272
Maynard, Edward, 52
McEvoy, Al, 168–69
McGrath, John W., 176
McInnis, John ("Stuffy"), 162–71
McManus, Parker, 59
McNeish, Dave, 166–71
McReynolds, James C., 159
Mead, William R., 92–95
Meiklejohn, Alexander, 75, 100–135, 264;
    Centennial speech of, 115; educational
    views of, 102–3, 115, 118–20, 145;
    faculty under, 116–24; financial
    affairs of, 103–14, 125–26; Frost and,
    143–46; inaugural address of, 102–3,
    145; investigations of, 124–31;
    presidency of, 102–3, 105–6; press
    and, 130, 134–35; resignation of, 101–
    2, 131–35; speech of, to alumni, 116–
    17, 133
Men, double binds and, 287–88
Mendians, 26–28
Mermin, David, 296
Merrill Dining Commons, 295
Merves, Ed, 209
Miner, Harry, 202, 205

Miner, Maude, 202–5
Ministry: as college purpose, 4, 79–80; of
    Joseph Neesima, 65–66, 71–74; of
    William Raymond, 26–29
Missionaries: in Africa, 26–29; in Japan,
    65–66, 68, 71–74; at Semicentennial,
    79–80
Missouri ex rel. Gaines v. Canada, 159
Moore, John, 197–98; teaching of, 206–
    11
Moore, Zephaniah Swift, 3, 5
Moot Hill, 7
Morgan, Charles, xii
Morgan, Vincent, xii
Morgan Hall, 50, 94
Morris Pratt Dormitory, 95
Morrow, Dwight, 101, 104–8, 110–11,
    115, 123, 135; committees and, 113,
    125, 128–29
Morse, Anson, 64
Motto, *Terras Irradient,* 9, 222
Mount Holyoke, 18, 78, 80–81, 269, 271–
    73
Moynahan, Julian, 192
Mud, in 1840s, 12
Murphy, Charlie, 167–71
Murray, Donald, 159

NAACP, Houston and, 157–59
Natural History Society, 16
Neesima, Joseph Hardy, 64–77, 264;
    Christianity and, 68–70; death and
    funeral of, 74; Japanese Diplomatic
    Mission and, 70–71; ministry of, 66,
    71–74; passage of to U.S., 67–68;
    pleas for funds by, 65–66; samurai
    class and, 66–67
Negro Alliance, 160
Neill, Heman Humphrey, 36
New Bern, N.C., battle of, 58–60, 62
New Republic, 134
Newton, Francis C., 175–77

New York American, 134
New Yorker, 184
New York Herald Tribune, 184
New York Times, 184
New York World, 135
Nichols, Stewart, 76–77
Nicholson, Harold, 105–6
Nicholson, Walter, 251
Nixon, Richard, 224, 226–27
North, William C., 46–47
North College, 12–13, 16, 19
Norton, Charles D., 94–95
Norton, John, 27
Norton, Mary, 267
Novak, Michael Paul, 199

Oberlin College, 80
Octagon, 11; Olmsted and, 88–90, 94–95
Odell, Robert, 260
Old Chapel Row, 98
Old North College, 13, 16, 19
Olds, George D., 104, 107
Olmsted, Frederick Law, 41, 41n;
    Amherst campus and, 88–93, 96–97,
    98, 99
Olmsted, Frederick Law, Jr., 90–96
Olmsted, John, 91–92, 95
Olsen, Tillie, 221
Olver, Rose, 250–51, 275
Ostendarp, James, 258–62

Packard, Laurence, xii
Page, John, 66
Paine, William, 85
Park, Edwards, 85–86
Parke, John G., 58–59
Parker, Peter, 66
Patton, Cornelius, 119
Pearle, Philip, 298
Pearson v. Murray, 158–59
Pemberton, John, 247
Pennell, Christopher, 271

Peterson, Dale, 253

Phelps, Amos, 27

Phi Alpha Psi, 184–85

Phi Beta Kappa, 114, 154

Phi Delta Sigma, 185

Phi Delta Theta, 185

Phi Kappa Psi, 173, 175–85

Phillips, Wendell, "The Lost Arts," 34–
35, 34n

Pick, Nancy and Frank Ward, *Curious
Footprints,* 10

Pierce, Henry Reuben, 60

Piety, and college purpose, 4, 79–80

Pitkin, Donald, 249–50

Pitkin Committee, 249

"Plea for a Miserable World, A" (Clark),
7

Plessy v. Ferguson, 154

Plimpton, Calvin H., 204

Plimpton, George A., 104–5, 108–12;
committees and, 113, 116, 121, 126–
29, 131–32

Plimpton Committee, 128, 131–32

Poets, Poetics, and Politics (Gillman and
Novak), 199

Porter, Bill, 169

Porter, C. Scott, 163, 205

Porter, David, 269

Porter, Horace, 212–23; background of,
212; black authors and, 215–16; black
consciousness of, 216–19;
commencement of, 222–23; first
experiences at Amherst, 213–15;
intellectual experience of, 219–22

Potter, William Appleton, 90

Pouncey, Peter, 260, 295

Powell, Sumner, 178

Pratt, Charles, 92, 104–5

Pratt, Ransom, 59

President's House, 11, 14–16, 44, 94

Press: Meiklejohn and, 130, 134–35; Phi
Kappa Psi and, 183–85

Pritchard, Marietta, 234

Pritchard, William H., 192, 233, 236;
Frost: A Literary Life Reconsidered,
142

Privies, 13

Protest at Westover Air Force Base, 224

Psi Upsilon Society, 17, 69

Purpose of Amherst: original, 4–5, 7–9;
at Semicentennial, 79–80

Quadrangle, 98; Olmsteds and, 90, 93, 95

Quaintance, Richard, 175, 178–79, 185

Quantum mechanics, workshop on, 293–
98

Race relations/equality: black writers
and, 215; Calvin Coolidge and, 138–
39; Charles Hamilton Houston and,
154–61

Rae, Alastair, 296

Rainey, Clarke, 167

Ransom, Leon, 158

Raskin, Lisa, 275–77

Raston, Thomas, 28–29

Raymond, Eliza (Mrs. William), 27–28

Raymond, William, 22; at Amherst, 23–
26; background of, 23; ministry of,
26–29

Recitation rooms, in 1840s, 14

Recreation: in 1840s, 17; at
Semicentennial, 79

Red Room (Converse Hall), 220

Religion: and college purpose, 4–5, 7–9,
79–80; Meiklejohn and, 119–20;
Society of Religious Inquiry, 16

Reno, Jesse L., 58–59

Reverse discrimination, 282

Revivals, 8, 79

Rhea, James, 52

Richards, E. A., 272

Richards, Jim, 19

Road map, as writing topic, 190–91

"Road Not Taken, The" (Frost), 146–48
Robbins, Edward, 52
Robert Frost Library, 222, 239
Romer, Alfred S., 177–81, 185
Rosendale, Ivar, 166–67, 170–71
Rounds, Arthur C., 124
Rounds Committee, 122, 124–28
Rubin, M. Wallace, 175
Rugg, Arthur P., 113
Rugg Committee, 113–14, 124–28

Sabrina statue, 115, 263, 278–81
Sale, Roger, 192
Salmon, E. Dwight, 163, 168
Salvation, sense of, 9
Samurai issue, 65–67
Sanderson, Frederick M., 55, 60
Sarat, Austin, 253
Sauveur, Lambert, 271
Scatchard, George, 121
Scheer, Peter E., 224
Schmeidel, Stacey, xiii
Sedgwick, Eve Kosofsky, 278
Seelye, Julius, 80, 90–91
Seelye, L. Clark, 5–6, 80–84, 86
Select Committee on the Curriculum,
    243–45, 253
Semicentennial, 79–80; coeducation
    debate and, 80–87
Sewing Society, 268
Sexism, 289
Shellenback, Dick, 169–70
Shelley v. Kraemer, 160
Shepard, Charles W., 6
Shimony, Abner, 295
Sibley, Donald, 178
Sidey, Hugh, 140
Simpson, John W., 104–5, 110, 121
Slavery: Amistad prisoners and, 23, 26–
    28; in Stearns's correspondence, 56–
    57; Whigs and, 51–52
Smith, Al, 140

Smith, Harry deForest, 122, 125, 127
Smith, Luther Ely, 120
Smith, Richard Norton, 140
Smith, Sophia, 80, 83
Smith College, 6, 78, 80–84, 272–74
Snell, Ebenezer, 79, 271
Snell, Mary, 271
Snell, Sabra, 271, 273
Snively, Susan, 196
Sobel, Robert, 140
Social Darwinism, 74
Social life: in 1840s, 18–20; at
    Semicentennial, 79, 81; at turn of
    century, 272. See also Fraternities
Society of Religious Inquiry, 16
South College, 7, 268
South Hadley, 18–20
Sperry, Willard L., 133
Spratt, Adrian, 240–41
Springfield Republican, 130
Starr, Norton, 244
Stearns, Frank W., 117
Stearns, Frazar: in Civil War, 50, 52, 56–
    60; death and funeral of, 60–63; early
    life of, 55–56
Stearns, William A., 52, 54–57, 60, 85,
    89–90
Stearns, William F., 55–56, 89
Stearns Church/Steeple, 50, 90
Steele, James, 28
Steele v. Louisville & Nashville Railroad
    Co., 160
Stern, Sheldon M., 138
Stewart, Walter W., 122, 128, 134
Stone, Harlan Fiske, 101, 111, 129–30,
    134
Storrs, Charles, 59
Storrs, Richard Salter, 37, 37n
Stoves, wood, 13–14
Stowe, Harriet Beecher, 42–43; Uncle
    Tom's Cabin, 5, 43, 43n
Strout, Richard, 140

Student Army Training Corps, 123
Students: behavior of, 18–20, 87; early lifestyles of, 7; Englishman's view of, 234–35; original principles of selection of, 3–5; ratio to faculty, 234. *See also* Gay students; Women at Amherst
Swan, Alice, 47
Sweatt, George A., 180–81
Symons, Julian, 232–41; Advanced Composition and, 236–37; crime story course of, 239–40; freshman English and, 233–36

Tappan, Lewis, 26–28
Tappan, Samuel, 24
Tate, Winston R., 179
Taubman, Jane, 275
Taylor, William R., 192
Teaching: Baird, freshman English and, 187–95; of John Moore, 206–11; of Robert Frost, 148–53
Teichgraeber, Richard F., III, 206
Temple, Charles, 46
Terras Irradient, 9, 222
Theater at Amherst, 272
Theses. *See* Honors theses
Thinking: Frost's view of, 151; Meiklejohn on, 118
Thomas, Edward, 148
Thompson, Frederic L., 122, 127
Tidball, Elizabeth, 283, 286
Tobacco, 19, 79
Todd, David Peck, 117, 270
Todd, Mabel Loomis, 46, 270; *The Letters of Emily Dickinson,* 47
Tokenism, 285
Torrance, Dwight Jonathan, 20
Townsend, Robert, 254
Trilling, Lionel, 201
Tyler, John M., 53, 60, 117
Tyler, Mason, 53

Tyler, William Seymour, 52–53, 80–84, 268–69

Uncle Tom's Cabin (Stowe), 5
Unionists, 51
Union Missionary Society, 28–29
Unitarianism, 9, 73–74
University of Massachusetts, 274
Untermeyer, Louis, 144, 151
Urinals, 13–14
Utter, Madeleine, 272
Utter, Robert, 272

Van De Graaff, Merrill, 197–98, 200–201
Van Dorn Smith, Elinor, 273
Vassar, 80
Vaux, Calvert, 41, 41n, 89
Vietnam War, 218, 224, 226–28
Visitors, magnetic, 31–43, 196–201
Vocation, sense of, 9
Vogel, Jonathan, 297
Von Schmidt, Helen, xiii
"Vulgar Arithmetic," xii
Vusi, Sixtue, 219

Walker, John, 181–82
Walker, Williston, 121–22
Walker Hall, 93
"Walking to Sleep" (Wilbur), 196–97
Walkways: Olmsteds and, 91; in 1840s, 12
Ward, Barbara, 224
Ward, Calvin, 219
Ward, Frank, and Nancy Pick, *Curious Footprints: Professor Hitchcock's Dinosaur Tracks and Other Natural History Treasures at Amherst College,* 10
Ward, John William, 219, 221, 239, 248, 256; civil disobedience of, 224–31; public versus private role of, 228–30
Ward, Robert, 218
War memorials, 50
Wasserstein, Wendy, 209

Webster, Noah, 7, 9, 48

Weisskopf, Victor, 295, 297

Westover Air Force Base protest, 224

Whicher, George F., 143–44

Whicher, George F., Mrs., 114–15, 273

Whicher, Harriet, 197

White, Orra White (Mrs. Edward
    Hitchcock), 82

Wilbur, Richard, 209; "Walking to
    Sleep," 196–97

Wilcox, Walter, 120

Williams, "Dab," 179

Williams, Ephraim, 261

Williams, Wilburn, 219

Williams College, 258–62

Williston Hall, 11, 93

Wills, David, xiii

Wilson, Eugene S. ("Bill"), xi, 163, 173,
    181, 212

Wilson, Woodrow, 138

Woglom, Geoffrey, 250, 253

Women: anger and, 287, 289; in college
    in 1870s, 80; double binds and, 283–
    85; fear of success and failure of, 285–
    86; heterosexual relationships and,
    286; oppression of, 281–82, 288–91;
    tears and, 287, 289; tokenism and,
    285; underestimation of achievements
    by, 286; view of, in coeducation
    debate, 81–84

Women and Gender Studies, 278

Women at Amherst, 5–6, 266–77; as
    administrators, 273; as B.A.
    candidates, 274–77; difficulties of,
    275–76, 278–91; in early years, 267–
    69; entertainment, theater and, 272;
    as faculty, 272–73, 275–77, 284; lack
    of female role models for, 286; as
    Master of Arts students, 274; as
    nonenrolled students, 269–72. See
    also Coeducation

Woodbridge, Frederick, 112–13

Wood fires, 13–16

Woods Cabinet, 11, 19–20, 80

Woodson, Carter G., 215

Workshop on the Foundations of
    Quantum Mechanics, 293–98

World War I, 122–23; women faculty
    during, 272

World War II: curriculum, post, 209;
    fraternities and, 174–75; veterans of,
    163–64; women faculty during, 273

Wrinch, Dorothy, 273

Writing: order of actions in, 190. See also
    English 1–2

Young, Stark, 143–45

Zajonc, Arthur, 293–95, 297

Ziegler, Benjamin, 163, 219

Zinn, John B., 120–21